T0511311

Lecture Notes in Computer Science   9726

Commenced Publication in 1973
Founding and Former Series Editors:
Gerhard Goos, Juris Hartmanis, and Jan van Leeuwen

Editorial Board

David Hutchison
  Lancaster University, Lancaster, UK
Takeo Kanade
  Carnegie Mellon University, Pittsburgh, PA, USA
Josef Kittler
  University of Surrey, Guildford, UK
Jon M. Kleinberg
  Cornell University, Ithaca, NY, USA
Friedemann Mattern
  ETH Zurich, Zürich, Switzerland
John C. Mitchell
  Stanford University, Stanford, CA, USA
Moni Naor
  Weizmann Institute of Science, Rehovot, Israel
C. Pandu Rangan
  Indian Institute of Technology, Madras, India
Bernhard Steffen
  TU Dortmund University, Dortmund, Germany
Demetri Terzopoulos
  University of California, Los Angeles, CA, USA
Doug Tygar
  University of California, Berkeley, CA, USA
Gerhard Weikum
  Max Planck Institute for Informatics, Saarbrücken, Germany

More information about this series at http://www.springer.com/series/7407

Martyn Amos · Anne Condon (Eds.)

Unconventional Computation and Natural Computation

15th International Conference, UCNC 2016
Manchester, UK, July 11–15, 2016
Proceedings

 Springer

Editors
Martyn Amos
Manchester Metropolitan University
Manchester
UK

Anne Condon
University of British Columbia
Vancouver, BC
Canada

ISSN 0302-9743   ISSN 1611-3349   (electronic)
Lecture Notes in Computer Science
ISBN 978-3-319-41311-2   ISBN 978-3-319-41312-9   (eBook)
DOI 10.1007/978-3-319-41312-9

Library of Congress Control Number: 2016942527

LNCS Sublibrary: SL1 – Theoretical Computer Science and General Issues

© Springer International Publishing Switzerland 2016
This work is subject to copyright. All rights are reserved by the Publisher, whether the whole or part of the material is concerned, specifically the rights of translation, reprinting, reuse of illustrations, recitation, broadcasting, reproduction on microfilms or in any other physical way, and transmission or information storage and retrieval, electronic adaptation, computer software, or by similar or dissimilar methodology now known or hereafter developed.
The use of general descriptive names, registered names, trademarks, service marks, etc. in this publication does not imply, even in the absence of a specific statement, that such names are exempt from the relevant protective laws and regulations and therefore free for general use.
The publisher, the authors and the editors are safe to assume that the advice and information in this book are believed to be true and accurate at the date of publication. Neither the publisher nor the authors or the editors give a warranty, express or implied, with respect to the material contained herein or for any errors or omissions that may have been made.

Printed on acid-free paper

This Springer imprint is published by Springer Nature
The registered company is Springer International Publishing AG Switzerland

Preface

This volume contains papers presented at the 15th Unconventional Computation and Natural Computation Conference (UCNC 2016), which was held in Manchester, UK, during July 11–15, 2016.

As a field of research, *unconventional computation* augments classical modes of computation (i.e., the Turing and von Neumann models), by offering new conceptual frameworks, abstractions, substrates, and applications. Intersecting with this field is the study of *natural computation*, which draws inspiration from the physical world to develop new forms of computing. Taken together, these two deeply related fields offer the possibility of entirely new forms of computational devices and applications, as well as providing a space in which to rethink the entire notion of "computation" and "computability."

Topics that are generally considered to be within scope of the conference include (but are not limited to):

- Molecular, cellular, quantum, optical, and chaos computing
- Cellular automata
- Neural and evolutionary computation
- Artificial immune systems
- Ant algorithms and swarm intelligence
- Amorphous computing
- Membrane computing
- Computational systems biology and computational neuroscience
- Synthetic biology

The first UCNC was held in Auckland, New Zealand, in 1998, organized by the Centre for Discrete Mathematics and Theoretical Computer Science, University of Auckland, and the Santa Fe Institute. Since then, it has been held in Brussels, Belgium (2000), Kobe, Japan (2002), Seville, Spain (2005), York, UK (2006), Kingston, Canada (2007), Vienna, Austria (2008), Ponta Delgada, Portugal (2009), Tokyo, Japan (2010), Turku, Finland (2011), Orléans, France (2012), Milan, Italy (2013), London, Ontario, Canada (2014), and Auckland, New Zealand (2015, the first time the conference has returned to a site).

The 15th iteration of UCNC was organized and hosted by the Informatics Research Centre of Manchester Metropolitan University, UK. The conference received 30 full-paper submissions, of which we accepted 15 for oral presentation. We were also pleased to host six distinguished speakers:

Invited Lectures:

- Bob Coecke (University of Oxford, UK): "In Pictures: From Quantum Foundations to Natural Language Processing"
- Steve Furber (University of Manchester, UK): "The SpiNNaker Project"

– Friedrich Simmel (Technische Universität München, Germany): "Chemical Communication Between Cell-Sized Reaction Compartments"

Tutorials

– Masami Hagiya (University of Tokyo, Japan): "Gellular Automata"
– Rebecca Schulman (Johns Hopkins University, USA): "Self-Assembling Adaptive Structures with DNA"
– Jon Timmis (University of York, UK): "Many Hands Make Light Work: A Case Study in Swarm Robotics"

Fundamental to the spirit of UCNC are the satellite workshops, which allow participants to focus on specific areas of interest. We were delighted to host two such sessions:

– Membrane Computing (organized by Marian Gheorghe and Savas Konur)
– Physics and Computation (organized by Alastair Abbott and Dominic Horsman)

We thank the authors and invited speakers for contributing to the meeting, and the workshop organizers for enriching the event. We thank the Program Committee and the additional reviewers for their exemplary work in assessing the submissions, and the Organizing Committee for their efforts on behalf of the meeting. We also thank the Dean of Science and Engineering and the Informatics Research Centre for sponsoring the event, the LNCS team at Springer (Alfred Hofmann and Anna Kramer) for supporting the continued publication of the UCNC proceedings, and the EasyChair project for providing essential infrastructure.

July 2016   Martyn Amos
                                                                             Anne Condon

Organization

Steering Committee

Thomas Bäck	Leiden University, The Netherlands
Cristian S. Calude	University of Auckland, New Zealand; Founding Chair
Lov K. Grover	Bell Labs, USA
Natasha Jonoska	University of South Florida, USA; Co-chair
Jarkko Kari	University of Turku, Finland; Co-chair
Lila Kari	University of Western Ontario, Canada
Seth Lloyd	Massachusetts Institute of Technology, USA
Giancarlo Mauri	Università degli Studi di Milano-Bicocca, Italy
Gheorghe Paun	Institute of Mathematics of the Romanian Academy, Romania
Grzegorz Rozenberg	Leiden University, The Netherlands; Emeritus Chair
Arto Salomaa	University of Turku, Finland
Tommaso Toffoli	Boston University, USA
Carme Torras	Institute of Robotics and Industrial Informatics, Spain
Jan van Leeuwen	Utrecht University, The Netherlands

Program Committee

Andy Adamatzky	University of the West of England, UK
Martyn Amos	Manchester Metropolitan University, UK; Co-chair
Peter Banda	University of Luxembourg
Kobi Benenson	ETH Zurich, Switzerland
Cristian Calude	University of Auckland, New Zealand
Anne Condon	University of British Columbia, Canada; Co-chair
Mark Daley	University of Western Ontario, Canada
Giuditta Franco	University of Verona, Italy
Àngel Goñi Moreno	National Centre for Biotechnology, Spain
Natasha Jonoska	University of South Florida, USA
Jarkko Kari	University of Turku, Finland
Lila Kari	University of Western Ontario, Canada
Viv Kendon	Durham University, UK
Niall Murphy	University of Cambridge, UK
Turlough Neary	University of Zurich/ETH Zurich, Switzerland
Pekka Orponen	Aalto University, Finland
Jennifer Padilla	Boise State University, USA
Matthew Patitz	University of Arkansas, USA
Susan Stepney	University of York, UK
Scott Summers	University of Wisconsin Oshkosh, USA

Organizing Committee

Martyn Amos   Manchester Metropolitan University, UK; Co-chair
James Charnock   Manchester Metropolitan University, UK
Matthew Crossley   Manchester Metropolitan University, UK
Rene Doursat   Manchester Metropolitan University, UK; Co-chair
Emma Norling   Manchester Metropolitan University, UK

Additional Reviewers

Robert Brijder   Max Garzon   Ethan Jackson
Alexander Carruth   Daniela Genova   Sandi Klavzar
Cameron Chalk   Mehrsa Golestaneh   Kalpana Mahalingam
Ho-Lin Chen   Jacob Hendricks   Daniel Richards
Matthew Cook   Mika Hirvensalo   Trent Rogers
Matthew Crossley   James Hughes

Abstracts of Invited Talks

In Pictures: from Quantum Foundations to Natural Language Processing

Bob Coecke

Department of Computer Science, University of Oxford, UK
coecke@cs.ox.ac.uk

Abstract. This talk requires no background in physics, nor in linguistics, nor in fancy math! Earlier work on an entirely diagrammatic formulation of quantum theory, which is soon to appear in the form of a textbook [1], has somewhat surprisingly guided us towards an answer for the following question [2]: how do we produce the meaning of a sentence given that we understand the meaning of its words? This work has practical applications in the area of natural language processing, and the resulting tools have meanwhile outperformed existing methods.

References

1. Coecke, B., Kissinger, A.: Picturing Quantum Processes. A First Course on Quantum Theory and Diagrammatic Reasoning. Cambridge University Press (2016, to appear)
2. Coecke, B., Sadrzadeh, M., Clark, S.: Mathematical foundations for a compositional distributional model of meaning. arXiv:1003.4394 (2010)

The SpiNNaker Project

Steve Furber

School of Computer Science, The University of Manchester,
Manchester M13 9PL, UK
steve.furber@manchester.ac.uk

Abstract. Just two years after the world's first stored program computer ran its first program at Manchester in 1948, Alan Turing published his seminal paper on "Computing Machinery and Intelligence". The paper opens with the words: 'I propose to consider the question, "Can machines think?"'. Turing then goes on to explore this question through what he calls "The Imitation Game", but which subsequent generations simply call "The Turing Test". Despite spectacular progress in the performance and efficiency of machines since Turing's time, we have yet to see any convincing demonstration of a machine that can pass his test. This would have surprised Turing - he believed that all that would be required was more memory. Although cognitive systems are beginning to display impressive environmental awareness, they do not come close to the sort of "thinking" that Turing had in mind. My take on the problems with true artificial intelligence is that we still really haven't worked out what natural intelligence is. Until we do, all discussion of machine intelligence and the "singularity" are specious. Based on this view, we need to return to the source of natural intelligence, the human brain.

The SpiNNaker project has been 18 years in conception and 10 years in construction, but is now ready to contribute to the growing global community (exemplified by the EU Human Brain Project) that is aiming to deploy the vast computing resources now available to us to accelerate our understanding of the brain, with the ultimate goal of understanding the information processing principles at work in natural intelligence. SpiNNaker is a massively-parallel computer system, ultimately to incorporate a million ARM processor cores (the largest machine to date has 500,000 cores) with an innovative lightweight packet-switched communications fabric capable of supporting typical biological connectivity patterns in biological real time.

Gellular Automata

Masami Hagiya

University of Tokyo, Japan
hagiya@is.s.u-tokyo.ac.jp

Abstract. Computational models derived from the research efforts to implement cellular automata by gel materials are presented. The models are given the name "gellular automata" using the adjective "gellular" which resembles "cellular". The efforts have been made in the research project "Molecular Robotics". In addition to computational models and their theoretical investigations, implementation techniques and possible applications of gellular automata are also touched upon.

Two kinds of gellular automata models have been investigated. One is diffusion-based and implemented by capsules made of gel shells containing water solutions. The problems caused by relying only on free molecular diffusion for cellular communication are discussed together with some approaches to solve the problems. The efforts to actually implement this kind of model using the alginic acid gel are also presented.

The other kind of model is based on gel walls (or valves) that can be opened or closed by molecules in solutions separated by the gel walls. In relation to this kind of model, DNA-based gels have been examined for implementing gel walls. Theoretical contributions in this line of research include the proof of computational universality and the implementation of block cellular automata with the Margolus neighborhood.

Possible applications of gellular automata include soft materials that form patterns possibly under stimuli from the environment, e.g., artificial organs.

Some efforts in the research project to go beyond models of cellular automata are also touched upon, i.e., efforts to realize swarm intelligence by molecular robots.

Self-Assembling Adaptive Structures with DNA

Rebecca Schulman

Chemical and Biomolecular Engineering and Computer Science,
Johns Hopkins University, USA
rschulm3@jhu.edu

Abstract. How could we program the self-assembly of a something as complex as an animal or a human being? From a strictly organizational point of view, self-assembly of such a structure would require organization across scales ranging from the angstrom scale to the meter scale. At the smallest size scales, it is possible to directly encode structure using a molecular sequence or set of sequences such that each unit of the structure is encoded by a specific molecular unit. But at larger size scales new mechanisms for organization are required. One general emerging principle of organization at these scales is that molecules encode a self-assembly process in which the final structure is functional but its shape can vary from one incarnation to the next. I'll describe how we might phrase such a problem of "adaptive" or "self-adjusting" self-assembly as a computational question and how we might implement such processes using molecules such as DNA.

As a case study of adaptive materials, we will consider networks formed from one-dimensional structures and junctions. Such networks exist across all size scales: networks of wires and devices form circuits, beams and joints form buildings. In biological systems, networks of axons, dendrites and neuronal cell bodies make up the brain and filaments such as actin and organizing proteins make up the cytoskeleton. I'll describe how we can consider how local programmable rules could be used to form such complex structures and how we could program many of these rules using interactions between DNA molecules.

Many Hands Make Light Work: A Case Study in Swarm Robotics

Jon Timmis

Department of Electronics, University of York, UK
jon.timmis@york.ac.uk

Abstract. There is increasing research in the area of swarm robotics, that is using many robots working together to solve problems, inspired (typically) by social insects. In this tutorial we will explore the area of swarm robotics, but also the wider area of collective robotics and how to develop collaborative distributed systems. We will also examine the use of evolutionary algorithms in swarm robotics to evolve both the controller and morphology of the robot at the same time, creating embodied artificial intelligence. We will end the tutorial on challenges for the area. This tutorial assumes no knowledge of swarm robotics.

Chemical Communication Between Cell-Sized Reaction Compartments

Friedrich Simmel

TU München – Physics Department E14, 85748 Garching, Germany

Abstract. The exchange of signals between information-processing agents is an important requirement for the coordination of their actions and may be utilized for the implementation of various "amorphous" computing schemes [1]. In biology, chemical interactions between cells are utilized, e.g., in differentiation and pattern formation, sensing and signaling. One of the most studied processes in bacteria is the "quorum sensing" phenomenon, in which bacteria exchange small diffusible genetic inducers and thus mutually influence their gene expression [2]. In this talk, we will discuss various implementations of synthetic chemical communication schemes between artificial cell-sized compartments, between bacteria, and also between bacteria and cell-free compartments [3–5]. In particular, we will discuss the production and detection of quorum sensing signals within emulsion droplets containing either genetically engineered bacteria or bacterial cell extract, and their utilization for simple computation and pattern formation processes.

References

1. Abelson, H., Allen, D., Coore, D., Hanson, C., Homsy, G., Knight, T.F., Nagpal, R., Rauch, E., Sussman, G.J., Weiss, R., Homsy, G.: Amorphous computing. Commun. ACM **43**, 74–82 (2000)
2. Waters, C.M., Bassler, B.L.: Quorum sensing: cell-to-cell communication in bacteria. Annu. Rev. Cell. Dev. Biol. **21**, 319–346 (2005)
3. Weitz, M., Mückl, A., Kapsner, K., Berg, R., Meyer, A., Simmel, F.C.: Communication and computation by bacteria compartmentalized within microemulsion droplets. J. Am. Chem. Soc. **136**, 72–75 (2014)
4. Ramalho, T., Meyer, A., Mückl, A., Kapsner, K., Gerland, U., Simmel, F.C.: Single cell analysis of a bacterial sender-receiver system. PLoS One **11**, e0145829 (2016)
5. Schwarz-Schilling, M., Aufinger, L., Mückl, A., Simmel, F.C.: Chemical communication between bacteria and cell-free gene expression systems within linear chains of emulsion droplets. Integr. Biol. **8**, 564–570 (2016)

Contents

Reachability Problems for Continuous Chemical Reaction Networks

Adam Case, Jack H. Lutz[✉], and D.M. Stull

Department of Computer Science, Iowa State University, Ames, IA 50011, USA
{adamcase,lutz,dstull}@iastate.edu

Abstract. Chemical reaction networks (CRNs) model the behavior of molecules in a well-mixed solution. The emerging field of molecular programming uses CRNs not only as a descriptive tool, but as a programming language for chemical computation. Recently, Chen, Doty and Soloveichik introduced rate-independent continuous CRNs (CCRNs) to study the chemical computation of continuous functions. A fundamental question for any CRN model is *reachability*, the question whether a given target state is reachable from a given start state via a sequence of reactions (a *path*) in the network. In this paper, we investigate CCRN-REACH, the reachability problem for rate-independent continuous chemical reaction networks. Our main theorem is that, for CCRNs, deciding reachability–and constructing a path if there is one–is computable in polynomial time. This contrasts sharply with the known exponential space hardness of the reachability problem for discrete CRNs. We also prove that the related problem Sub-CCRN-REACH, which asks about reachability in a CCRN using only a given number of its reactions, is NP-complete.

1 Introduction

Abstract chemical reaction networks (CRNs) model chemical interactions in a well-mixed solution. Informally, a CRN consists of a finite set of species of chemicals (usually written abstractly as capital letters A, B, etc.) and a finite set of reactions among these species. A simple example is the CRN consisting of species A, B and C, with one reaction $2A + B \xrightarrow{k} 2C$ (taking A to be the hydrogen molecule H_2, B to be the oxygen molecule O_2, and C to be the water molecule H_2O, this CRN models the formation of water molecules with kinetic rate constant k). CRNs have historically been used as a descriptive tool, allowing researchers to formally analyze the behavior of natural chemical systems. However, the field of molecular programming has recently brought CRNs to prominence as a programming language for chemical computation. Molecular programming, as the

This research was supported in part by National Science Foundation Grants 1247051 and 1545028. Part of the second author's work was carried out while participating in the 2015 Focus Semester on Computability and Randomness at Heidelberg University.

© Springer International Publishing Switzerland 2016
M. Amos and A. Condon (Eds.): UCNC 2016, LNCS 9726, pp. 1–10, 2016.
DOI: 10.1007/978-3-319-41312-9_1

name suggests, is devoted to engineering complex computational systems from molecules. Recent work in this area has come to view abstract CRNs as a programming language to engineer "chemical software" [9,19]. Exciting new developments have shown methods of compiling arbitrary chemical reaction networks into computation using DNA strands [2,4,20]. Thus the programmable power of chemical reaction networks is no longer simply of theoretical interest. To achieve the goal of engineering large scale, robust chemical computation, tools to analyze CRNs will be vital.

There are many ways to define the behavior of abstract CRNs, the two most prominent being mass action kinetics and stochastic chemical reaction networks. Mass action kinetics was the first model to be studied extensively. It is a continuous, deterministic model of chemical reaction networks. Mass action kinetics is used to study systems with sufficiently large numbers of molecules so that the amount of a given molecule can be represented as a real-valued concentration. The dynamics of reactions under mass action kinetics are governed by ordinary differential equations. However, the deterministic mass action model is not well suited if the number of molecules of the system is low. Stochastic CRNs are widely used to analyze those systems with a relatively low number of molecules [7,17]. The stochastic CRN model is discrete and non-deterministic. Unlike mass action, the amount of each species is represented as a non-negative integer, and the reactions of a system are modeled as Markov jump processes [8]. The stochastic model is closely related to many well-studied models of computation such as Vector Addition Machines [10], Petri Nets [6] and Population Protocols [1]. Recently, Chen, Doty and Soloveichik introduced rate-independent continuous CRNs (CCRNs). The CCRN model is continuous, dealing with real-valued concentrations of species, but, unlike the stochastic or mass action models, it is rate-free (reactions do not have any associated kinetic rate constant). Chen, Doty and Soloveichik used CCRNs to study which real valued functions $f : \mathbb{R}^k \to \mathbb{R}$ are computable by a chemical reaction network. By being a rate-free model, it allows for the study of the computational power of large chemical systems relying on stoichiometry alone (i.e., without depending on specific rates of the reactions). This is important, as rate constants are hard to experimentally determine and vary under external factors such as temperature.

A fundamental question that one can ask of a stochastic chemical reaction network is whether a particular state is reachable from a starting configuration; this is called the reachability problem. The reachability problem for stochastic CRNs is equivalent to an important problem in theoretical computer science, the Vector Addition System Reachability problem (VAS reachability) [5]. The VAS reachability problem was proven to be at least EXPSPACE-hard by Lipton in 1976 [15]. In 1981, building on the work of Sacerdote and Tenney [18], Mayr proved that the reachability problem is decidable [16]. Subsequently, Kosaraju [12] and Lambert [13] gave two additional proofs of the decidability of VAS Reachability. However, all proofs that the reachability problem is decidable were very difficult, until Lérôux [14] gave a greatly simplified proof. Unfortunately, we still do not even know whether this problem is primitive recursive.

In this paper, we investigate two variants of the reachability problem in the context of CCRNs. In Sect. 3, we analyze the complexity of the direct analog of the reachability problem for CCRNs, the continuous chemical reaction network reachability problem, CCRN-REACH. Informally, the CCRN-REACH problem is: given a CCRN C and states $\mathbf{c}$ and $\mathbf{d}$, output a path taking $\mathbf{c}$ to $\mathbf{d}$, if one exists, else state that there is no such path. To effectively compute CCRN-REACH, we will require the states to be over the rationals instead of over arbitrary reals. We show that, contrary to the difficulty of the VAS reachability problem, CCRN-REACH can be computed in polynomial time. In the process, we give new definitions and lemmas which we believe will be useful in further investigations of the continuous chemical reaction network model.

Reachability analysis is often used to determine safety and liveness properties of a distributed system. For example, one often wants to know whether an unsafe state is reachable. If so, then one might want to know whether this lack of safety is an inherently global part of the system or can be localized to a small part of the system. In this spirit we define the problem Sub-CCRN-REACH, which asks whether a path exists between two states using at most a given number of the reactions in the network. This problem naturally arises in CRNs with a high number of reactions. The Sub-CCRN-REACH problem is to determine whether a small subset of the available reactions is sufficient to reach a given state from some initial state. In contrast to the computational "ease" of CCRN-REACH, we show that Sub-CCRN-REACH is NP-complete.

2 Rate Independent Continuous CRNs

Throughout the remainder of this paper $\| \cdot \|$ is the max norm. In this section, we review the definitions and notations for continuous CRNs introduced in [3].

A *continuous chemical reaction network (CCRN)* is a pair $C = (\Lambda, R)$, where Λ is a finite set of *species* and R is a finite set of *reactions* over Λ. We typically denote species by capital letters, so that $\Lambda = \{A, B, \ldots\}$. A *reaction* over the set of species Λ is an element $\rho = (\mathbf{r}, \mathbf{p}) \in \mathbb{N}^\Lambda \times \mathbb{N}^\Lambda$, where $\mathbf{r}$ and $\mathbf{p}$ specify the stoichiometry of the reactants and products, respectively. We require the *net change* $\Delta\rho = \mathbf{p} - \mathbf{r}$ of a reaction $\rho = (\mathbf{r}, \mathbf{p})$ to be nonzero. We will usually write a reaction using the "reactants, right arrow, products" notation; for example, $\rho = A + B \to C$. (In this example $\mathbf{r} = (1, 1, 0)$ and $\mathbf{p} = (0, 0, 1)$.) A reaction $\rho = (\mathbf{r}, \mathbf{p})$ is *catalytic* if, for some species s, $\mathbf{r}(s) = \mathbf{p}(s) \neq 0$. (For example, $A + B \to A + C$ is catalytic.) In this case, we call the species s a *catalyst*. Each CCRN $C = (\Lambda, R)$ has an associated *reaction stoichiometry matrix* $\mathbf{M}$ specifying the net change of each species for every reaction. Formally, $\mathbf{M}$ is a $|\Lambda| \times |R|$ matrix over $\mathbb{Z}$ such that $\mathbf{M}(i, j)$ is the net change of the ith species for the jth reaction. Note that $\mathbf{M}$ does not fully specify a CCRN C, since, e.g., it does not identify catalytic reactions. A *state* of a CCRN $C = (\Lambda, R)$ is a vector $\mathbf{c} \in \mathbb{R}^\Lambda_{\geq 0}$ specifying the (non-negative) concentration of each species. The *support* of a state $\mathbf{c}$ is the set $supp(\mathbf{c}) = \{s \in \Lambda \mid \mathbf{c}(s) > 0\}$ of all species with non-zero concentrations at $\mathbf{c}$. The *support of a reaction* $\rho = (\mathbf{r}, \mathbf{p})$ is the set $supp(\rho) =$

$\{s \in \Lambda \mid \mathbf{r}(s) > 0\}$ of all reactants of ρ. A reaction $\rho = (\mathbf{r}, \mathbf{p}) \in R$ is *applicable* at a state $\mathbf{c}$ if $supp(\mathbf{r}) \subseteq supp(\mathbf{c})$ (i.e., if the concentration of each reactant is non-zero at $\mathbf{c}$). A *flux vector* of a CCRN $C = (\Lambda, R)$ is a vector $\mathbf{u} \in \mathbb{R}^R_{\geq 0}$. Intuitively, a flux vector is a vector of non-negative real numbers, each of which specifies the "amount" of the corresponding reaction that is to be performed. The *support of a flux vector* $\mathbf{u}$ is the set $supp(\mathbf{u}) = \{\rho \in R \mid \mathbf{u}(\rho) > 0\}$. A flux vector $\mathbf{u}$ is *applicable at a state* $\mathbf{c}$ if the following conditions hold:

1. Every $\rho \in supp(\mathbf{u})$ is applicable at $\mathbf{c}$.
2. $\mathbf{c}(s) + \sum\limits_{\rho \in R} \mathbf{u}(\rho)\Delta\rho(s) \geq 0$ for every $s \in \Lambda$.

If a flux vector $\mathbf{u}$ is applicable at state $\mathbf{c}$, we can *apply* $\mathbf{u}$ *to* $\mathbf{c}$, resulting in the state

$$\mathbf{c} * \mathbf{u} = \mathbf{c} + \sum_{\rho \in R} \mathbf{u}(\rho)\Delta\rho.$$

Equivalently, $\mathbf{c} * \mathbf{u} = \mathbf{c} + \mathbf{Mu}$. A *flux vector sequence*, $\mathbf{U} = (\mathbf{u}_1, ..., \mathbf{u}_k)$ is a tuple of flux vectors. We apply a flux vector sequence $\mathbf{U} = (\mathbf{u}_1, ..., \mathbf{u}_k)$ iteratively to a state $\mathbf{c}$,

$$\mathbf{c} * \mathbf{U} = (\mathbf{c} * (\mathbf{u}_1, \dots, \mathbf{u}_{k-1})) * \mathbf{u}_k.$$

A flux vector sequence $\mathbf{U} = (\mathbf{u}_1, ..., \mathbf{u}_k)$ is *applicable* at state $\mathbf{c}$ if $\mathbf{u}_i$ is applicable at $\mathbf{c} * (\mathbf{u}_1, \dots, \mathbf{u}_{i-1})$ for every $1 < i \leq k$. If $\mathbf{c}$ and $\mathbf{d}$ are any states, we say that $\mathbf{d}$ *is reachable from* $\mathbf{c}$, denoted $\mathbf{c} \rightarrow^* \mathbf{d}$, if there exists a flux vector sequence $\mathbf{U}$ applicable at $\mathbf{c}$ such that $\mathbf{c} * \mathbf{U} = \mathbf{d}$. We say that $\mathbf{d}$ is reachable from $\mathbf{c}$ *in k steps*, denoted $\mathbf{c} \rightarrow^k \mathbf{d}$, if there exists a flux vector sequence $\mathbf{U} = (u_1, \dots, u_k)$ applicable at $\mathbf{c}$ such that $\mathbf{c} * \mathbf{U} = \mathbf{d}$. A reaction $\rho \in R$ is *eventually applicable from* $\mathbf{c}$ if there exists a state $\mathbf{d}$ reachable from $\mathbf{c}$ so that ρ is applicable at $\mathbf{d}$. A reaction is *permanently inapplicable from* $\mathbf{c}$ if it is not eventually applicable from $\mathbf{c}$.

The following theorem, proven in [3], will be used in the proof of our first main theorem.

Theorem 0. *If* $\mathbf{c} \rightarrow^* \mathbf{d}$, *then* $\mathbf{c} \rightarrow^{m+1} \mathbf{d}$ *where* $m = |R|$ *is the number of reactions.*

3   The Reachability Problem for Continuous CRNs

Having defined the relevant concepts for continuous chemical reaction networks, we are now able to formally define our problem CCRN-REACH.

The Continuous CRN Reachability Problem. Given a continuous CRN $C = (\Lambda, R)$ and two states $\mathbf{c}, \mathbf{d} \in \mathbb{Q}^\Lambda$, output a flux vector sequence $\mathbf{U}$ such that $\mathbf{U}$ is applicable at $\mathbf{c}$ and $\mathbf{c} * \mathbf{U} = \mathbf{d}$, if one exists; output "not reachable" otherwise.

Note that this problem would be an easy matter of solving a system of linear equations if it were not for the requirement that the flux vector sequence must be applicable at **c**. We will prove that CCRN-REACH is computable in polynomial time. Intuitively, the dramatic difference in the computational difficulty between the VAS reachability problem (known to be at least EXPSPACE-hard) and CCRN-REACH is the additional flexibility given by the rational valued flux vectors. To compute CCRN-REACH, we show how to build a flux vector sequence leading from the starting state to a state of maximal support. This is only possible in the CCRN model of chemical reaction networks, which allows arbitrarily small additions via flux vectors. Once we are in such a maximal state we are able to get to the end state with the application of a single flux vector. To formalize this intuition, we will introduce several definitions and lemmas.

Fix a continuous CRN $C = (\Lambda, R)$.

Definition. Let **c** be a state, and $\epsilon > 0$. We say that a vector **u** is an ϵ-**max support flux vector of c** if **u** satisfies the following:

1. **u** is a flux vector that is applicable at **c**.
2. for every flux vector **v** applicable at **c**, $supp(\mathbf{c} * \mathbf{v}) \subseteq supp(\mathbf{c} * \mathbf{u})$.
3. $\|\mathbf{u}\| \leq \epsilon$.

That is, a vector is an ϵ-max support flux vector of a state **c** if it is applicable at **c** and maximally increases the support of **c** while giving at most ϵ flux to each reaction. We will show that ϵ-max support flux vectors exist for every state and $\epsilon > 0$.

Let $\epsilon > 0$. We now construct a specific ϵ-max support flux vector of **c**, which we will henceforth call the *principal ϵ-max support flux vector* of **c**. Define $App_{\mathbf{c}}$ to be the set of all applicable reactions at **c**. Let $\epsilon_{\mathbf{c}} = min\{\mathbf{c}(s) \,|\, s \in supp(\mathbf{c})\}$ (the lowest nonzero concentration of any species at state **c**), $\Gamma_{\mathbf{c}} = max\{1, |\Delta\rho(s)| : \rho \in App_{\mathbf{c}}$ and $s \in supp(\mathbf{c})\}$, and $\delta_{\mathbf{c},\epsilon} = \frac{1}{\Gamma_{\mathbf{c}}|R|}min\{\frac{\epsilon_{\mathbf{c}}}{2}, \epsilon\}$.

Definition. The **principal ϵ-max support flux vector of c** is the vector $\mathbf{u}_{\mathbf{c},\epsilon}$ defined by

$$\mathbf{u}_{\mathbf{c},\epsilon}(\rho) = \begin{cases} \delta_{\mathbf{c},\epsilon}, & \text{if } \rho \in App_{\mathbf{c}} \\ 0, & \text{otherwise} \end{cases}$$

for every $\rho \in R$.

The following lemma says that $\mathbf{u}_{\mathbf{c},\epsilon}$ is a well defined ϵ-max support flux vector of **c**.

Lemma 1. *Let* **c** *be a state, and* $\epsilon > 0$. *Then* $\mathbf{u}_{\mathbf{c},\epsilon}$ *is an ϵ-max support flux vector of* **c**.

When the context is clear, we will refer to $\mathbf{u}_{\mathbf{c},\epsilon}$ as the principal max support flux vector. The following observation can be easily seen from the definition of the principal ϵ-max support flux vector.

Observation 1. *The principal ϵ-max support flux vector of $\mathbf{c}$, $\mathbf{u}_{\mathbf{c},\epsilon}$, is computable in polynomial time in terms of $(C, \mathbf{c}, \epsilon)$.*

Since $\mathbf{u}_{\mathbf{c},\epsilon}$ is a flux vector applicable at $\mathbf{c}$, we are able to discuss the principal max support flux vector of the state $(\mathbf{c} * \mathbf{u}_{\mathbf{c},\epsilon})$. For convenience, we will use the following notation:

1. $\mathbf{u}_{\mathbf{c},\epsilon}^1 := \mathbf{u}_{\mathbf{c},\epsilon}$.
2. $\mathbf{u}_{\mathbf{c},\epsilon}^k :=$ the principal ϵ-max support flux vector of the state $\mathbf{c} * (\mathbf{u}_{\mathbf{c},\epsilon}^1, ..., \mathbf{u}_{\mathbf{c},\epsilon}^{k-1})$.

It is important to note that the vectors $\mathbf{u}_{\mathbf{c},\epsilon}^i$ are distinct, as the successive principal max support flux vectors are distinct. Our goal is to reach a state of maximum support. Therefore, the hope is that the set of applicable reactions grows with successive applications of the principal max support flux vectors.

Definition. Let $\epsilon > 0$, $m = |R| + 1$ and $\gamma = \frac{\epsilon}{m}$. The **principal ϵ-max support flux vector sequence of $\mathbf{c}$**, denoted $\mathbf{U}_{\mathbf{c},\epsilon}$, is defined to be the sequence

$$\mathbf{U}_{\mathbf{c},\epsilon} = (\mathbf{u}_{\mathbf{c},\gamma}^1, \ldots, \mathbf{u}_{\mathbf{c},\gamma}^m).$$

From Observation 1 it is clear that $\mathbf{U}_{\mathbf{c},\epsilon}$ is computable in polynomial time in terms of $(C, \mathbf{c}, \epsilon)$.

Observation 2. *For any state $\mathbf{c}$ and any $\epsilon > 0$, the principal ϵ-max support flux vector sequence of $\mathbf{c}$ is a flux vector sequence that is applicable at $\mathbf{c}$. Moreover,*

$$\| \sum_{i=1}^{m} \mathbf{u}_{\mathbf{c},\gamma}^i \| \le \epsilon.$$

Proof. This follows immediately from Lemma 1 and the choice of γ.   □

The choice of restricting the length of the flux vector $\mathbf{U}_{\mathbf{c},\epsilon}$ to $|R| + 1$ follows from Theorem 0.

Definition. Let $\mathbf{c}$ be a state and $\epsilon > 0$. We say that a state $\mathbf{m}$ is an **ϵ-max support state of $\mathbf{c}$** if, for every state $\mathbf{d}$ that is reachable from $\mathbf{c}$, $supp(\mathbf{d}) \subseteq supp(\mathbf{m})$.

We now define the **principal ϵ-max support state of $\mathbf{c}$** to be $\mathbf{m}_{\mathbf{c},\epsilon} := \mathbf{c} * \mathbf{U}_{\mathbf{c},\epsilon}$.

Lemma 2. *If $\mathbf{c}$ is a state and $\epsilon > 0$, then $\mathbf{m}_{\mathbf{c},\epsilon}$ is an ϵ-max support state of $\mathbf{c}$.*

Proof. Let $\mathbf{d}$ be a state reachable from $\mathbf{c}$. By Theorem 0, there exists a flux vector sequence of length $r = |R| + 1$ taking $\mathbf{c}$ to $\mathbf{d}$, i.e., $\mathbf{c} \rightarrow^r \mathbf{d}$. By induction and use of Lemma 1, we see that for every state $\mathbf{d}$ such that $\mathbf{c} \rightarrow^r \mathbf{d}$, $supp(\mathbf{d}) \subseteq supp(\mathbf{m}_{\mathbf{c},\epsilon})$.
      □

By Lemma 2, we see that for every $\epsilon, \epsilon' > 0$, $supp(\mathbf{m}_{\mathbf{c},\epsilon}) = supp(\mathbf{m}_{\mathbf{c},\epsilon'})$. Recall that a reaction ρ is eventually applicable from a state $\mathbf{c}$ if ρ is applicable at some state $\mathbf{d}$ that is reachable from $\mathbf{c}$. By Lemma 2, a reaction ρ is eventually applicable from a state $\mathbf{c}$ if and only if ρ is applicable at $\mathbf{m}_{\mathbf{c},\epsilon}$ for any $\epsilon > 0$. This allows us to compute all the permanently inapplicable reactions from $\mathbf{c}$, which will be vital in the algorithm computing CCRN-REACH.

Observation 3. *The set of all permanently inapplicable reactions from* **c** *is computable in polynomial time.*

Proof. By Observation 1 we compute the principal 1-max support state of **c**, $\mathbf{m}_{\mathbf{c},1}$, and eliminate all reactions not applicable at $\mathbf{m}_{\mathbf{c},1}$. □

An interesting property of CCRN's is that, if **d** is reachable from **c**, then there is a "universal" flux vector sequence taking **c** to **d**.

Definition. Let $\mathbf{c}, \mathbf{d} \in \mathbb{R}^A_{\geq 0}$ be two states of CCRN $C = (A, R)$. A reaction $\rho \in R$ is **helpful** for $(\mathbf{c}, \mathbf{d})$ if there exists a flux vector sequence $\mathbf{U} = (\mathbf{u}_1, \dots, \mathbf{u}_k)$ where $\mathbf{c} * \mathbf{U} = \mathbf{d}$ and $\mathbf{u}_i(\rho) > 0$ for some $i \leq k$. We denote the set of all helpful reactions by

$$H_{\mathbf{c},\mathbf{d}} = \{\rho \in R \,|\, \rho \text{ is helpful for } (\mathbf{c}, \mathbf{d})\}.$$

Theorem 4. *Let $C = (A, R)$ be a CCRN and $\mathbf{c}, \mathbf{d} \in \mathbb{R}^A_{\geq 0}$ be two states such that $\mathbf{c} \to^* \mathbf{d}$. Then there exists a flux vector sequence $\mathbf{U}$ taking* **c** *to* **d** *giving positive flux to every reaction $\rho \in H_{\mathbf{c},\mathbf{d}}$.*

Proof. Let $R' = H_{\mathbf{c},\mathbf{d}}$. Define a new CCRN $C' = (A, R')$. For every reaction $\rho \in H_{\mathbf{c},\mathbf{d}}$, let $\mathbf{U}_\rho$ be a flux vector sequence taking **c** to **d** that gives positive flux to ρ. Define the vector

$$\mathbf{t} = \frac{1}{|H_{\mathbf{c},\mathbf{d}}|} \sum_{\rho \in H_{\mathbf{c},\mathbf{d}}} \sum_{\mathbf{u} \in \mathbf{U}_\rho} \mathbf{u}.$$

Let $\epsilon = \frac{1}{2} min\{\mathbf{t}(\rho)\}_{\rho \in H_{\mathbf{c},\mathbf{d}}}$. Define

$$\mathbf{v} = \mathbf{t} - \sum_{\mathbf{u} \in \mathbf{U}_{\mathbf{c},\epsilon}} \mathbf{u},$$

where $\mathbf{U}_{\mathbf{c},\epsilon}$ is the principal ϵ-max support flux vector sequence of **c** in the new CCRN C'. By our definition of **t**,

$$\mathbf{c} * (\mathbf{U}_{\mathbf{c},\epsilon}, \mathbf{v}) = \mathbf{c} * (\mathbf{U}_{\mathbf{c},\epsilon}, \mathbf{t} - \mathbf{U}_{\mathbf{c},\epsilon})$$
$$= \mathbf{c} + \sum_{\rho \in R'} \mathbf{t}(\rho) \Delta \rho$$
$$= \mathbf{c} + \frac{1}{|H_{\mathbf{c},\mathbf{d}}|} \sum_{\rho \in H_{\mathbf{c},\mathbf{d}}} \sum_{\mathbf{u} \in \mathbf{U}_\rho} \mathbf{u}$$
$$= \mathbf{c} + \frac{1}{|H_{\mathbf{c},\mathbf{d}}|} \sum_{\rho \in H_{\mathbf{c},\mathbf{d}}} \mathbf{d} - \mathbf{c}$$
$$= \mathbf{d}.$$

It remains to prove that $(\mathbf{U}_{\mathbf{c},\epsilon}, \mathbf{v})$ is a flux vector sequence applicable at **c**. By Observation 2, $\mathbf{U}_{\mathbf{c},\epsilon}$ is applicable at **c**. By our choice of ϵ and Observation 2, $\mathbf{v}(\rho) > 0$ for every reaction $\rho \in R'$, and therefore **v** is a flux vector. By Lemma 2, $\mathbf{c} * \mathbf{U}_{\mathbf{c},\epsilon} = \mathbf{m}_{\mathbf{c},\epsilon}$ is a max support state. Hence, **v** is applicable at $\mathbf{c} * \mathbf{U}_{\mathbf{c},\epsilon}$. Therefore $(\mathbf{U}_{\mathbf{c},\epsilon}, \mathbf{v})$ is a flux vector sequence applicable at **c**, and the proof is complete. □

We are now ready to prove our first main theorem. Intuitively, the algorithm deciding CCRN-REACH constructs the "universal" flux vector sequence consisting of all reactions from $H_{\mathbf{c},\mathbf{d}}$.

Main Theorem 1. *CCRN-REACH is computable in polynomial time.*

Proof. Consider the algorithm below (Algorithm 1) deciding CCRN-REACH. From our previous observations, and the fact that linear programming (line 5 of the algorithm) can be done in polynomial time [11], it is clear that the algorithm runs in polynomial time in terms of the input. We now prove that $\mathbf{d}$ is reachable from $\mathbf{c}$ if and only if the algorithm outputs a flux vector sequence $\mathbf{U}$ applicable at $\mathbf{c}$ such that $\mathbf{c} * \mathbf{U} = \mathbf{d}$.

Algorithm 1. CCRN-REACH on input $C = (\Lambda, R)$, $\mathbf{c}$, $\mathbf{d}$

1: On input $C = (\Lambda, R)$, $\mathbf{c}$, $\mathbf{d}$
2: If $\mathbf{c} = \mathbf{d}$, halt and output the zero vector.
3: Eliminate from R all permanently inapplicable reactions from $\mathbf{c}$
4: **for** each reaction $\rho \in R$ **do**
5:     Compute a vector $F_\rho \in \mathbb{Q}_{\geq 0}^R$ such that $\mathbf{c} + \mathbf{M}F_\rho = \mathbf{d}$ and $F_\rho(\rho) > 0$, if one
       exists
6:     if no such vector exists, eliminate ρ from R, GOTO 1.
7: **end for**
8: if $R = \emptyset$, output "not reachable"
9: otherwise define vector $S \in \mathbb{Q}_{\geq 0}^R$ as follows
10: for each $\rho \in R$, set $S(\rho) = \frac{1}{|R|} \sum\limits_{i=1}^{|R|} F_i(\rho)$
11: Compute $\epsilon = \frac{min\{S(\rho)\}_{\rho \in R}}{2}$
12: Compute the principal max support flux vector sequence $\mathbf{U}_{\mathbf{c},\epsilon}$ of $\mathbf{c}$
13: Compute $\mathbf{v} = S - \sum_{\mathbf{u} \in \mathbf{U}_{\mathbf{c},\epsilon}} \mathbf{u}$
14: Output $(\mathbf{U}_{\mathbf{c},\epsilon}, \mathbf{v})$ (padded with 0s for eliminated reactions)

Assume that, on input $C = (\Lambda, R)$, $\mathbf{c}$ and $\mathbf{d}$, the algorithm outputs a sequence of vectors $\mathbf{U}$. Let R be the set of reactions left after exiting the loop (necessarily non-empty), and $m = |R|$. By the choice of ϵ and Observation 2, for each $\rho \in R$,

$$\sum_{i=1}^{m+1} \mathbf{u}_{\mathbf{c},\gamma}^i(\rho) < S(\rho),$$

where $\mathbf{U}_{\mathbf{c},\epsilon} = (\mathbf{u}_{\mathbf{c},\gamma}^1, \ldots, \mathbf{u}_{\mathbf{c},\gamma}^{m+1})$ (recall that $\gamma = \frac{\epsilon}{m+1}$). Therefore, the vector $\mathbf{v} = S - \sum_{\mathbf{u} \in \mathbf{U}_{\mathbf{c},\epsilon}} \mathbf{u}$ is a flux vector (in fact $\mathbf{v}$ is strictly positive). Hence the output $\mathbf{U} = (\mathbf{U}_{\mathbf{c},\epsilon}, \mathbf{v})$ is a flux vector sequence. By Observation 2, $\mathbf{U}_{\mathbf{c},\epsilon}$ is applicable at $\mathbf{c}$. Upon exiting the loop we are guaranteed that any reactions remaining in R must be eventually applicable from $\mathbf{c}$ using only the other remaining reactions. Let $\rho \in supp(\mathbf{v})$. Then $\rho \in R$, and so ρ must be eventually applicable from $\mathbf{c}$ using only reactions remaining in R. By Lemma 2, $\mathbf{c} * \mathbf{U}_{\mathbf{c},\epsilon} = \mathbf{m}_{\mathbf{c},\epsilon}$ is a max support state, therefore ρ is applicable at $\mathbf{c} * \mathbf{U}_{\mathbf{c},\epsilon}$. Since ρ was arbitrary, $\mathbf{v}$ is applicable at $\mathbf{c} * \mathbf{U}_{\mathbf{c},\epsilon}$, and so $(\mathbf{U}_{\mathbf{c},\epsilon}, \mathbf{v})$ is a flux vector sequence that is applicable at $\mathbf{c}$. Finally, we have

$$\mathbf{c} * (\mathbf{U}_{\mathbf{c},\epsilon}, \mathbf{v}) = \mathbf{c} + \mathbf{M}(\mathbf{U}_{\mathbf{c},\epsilon} + \mathbf{v})$$
$$= \mathbf{c} + \mathbf{M}S$$
$$= \mathbf{c} + \mathbf{M}\frac{1}{|R|}\sum_{i=1}^{|R|} F_i(\rho)$$
$$= \mathbf{c} + \frac{1}{|R|}\sum_{i=1}^{|R|} \mathbf{M}F_i(\rho)$$
$$= \mathbf{c} + \frac{1}{|R|}\sum_{i=1}^{|R|} \mathbf{d} - \mathbf{c}$$
$$= \mathbf{d},$$

where $\mathbf{M}$ is the stoichiometry matrix of $C = (\Lambda, R)$. Hence, if the algorithm outputs a vector sequence, then $\mathbf{d}$ is reachable from $\mathbf{c}$.

For the other direction, assume that $\mathbf{d}$ is reachable from $\mathbf{c}$. Then, by definition, there is a nonempty subset $R' \subseteq R$ such that, for all $\rho \in R'$,

1. ρ is eventually applicable from $\mathbf{c}$ using only reactions from R', and
2. there exists a vector F_ρ such that $\mathbf{M}F_\rho = \mathbf{d} - \mathbf{c}$ and $F_\rho(\rho) > 0$.

Hence, the algorithm will exit the loop with R nonempty and output a flux vector sequence $(\mathbf{U}_{\mathbf{c},\epsilon}, \mathbf{v})$. As we have just shown, $(\mathbf{U}_{\mathbf{c},\epsilon}, \mathbf{v})$ is applicable at $\mathbf{c}$ and $\mathbf{c} * (\mathbf{U}_{\mathbf{c},\epsilon}, \mathbf{v}) = \mathbf{d}$. $\qquad\square$

4   The Subset Reachability Problem

Define the decision problem Sub-CCRN-REACH as follows.

The Continuous CRN Subset Reachability Problem. Given a continuous CRN $C = (\Lambda, R)$, states $\mathbf{c}$, $\mathbf{d}$ and an integer k, accept if and only if there exists a path from $\mathbf{c}$ to $\mathbf{d}$ using only k reactions from R.

In contrast to the computational ease of CCRN-REACH, we give evidence that the related problem Sub-CCRN-REACH is quite difficult.

Main Theorem 2. *Sub-CCRN-REACH is NP-complete.*

Acknowledgments. We thank Tim McNicholl, Xiang Huang, Titus Klinge, and Jim Lathrop for useful discussions. We also thank two anonymous reviewers for detailed improvements to this paper.

References

1. Angluin, D., Aspnes, J., Diamadi, Z., Fischer, M.J., Peralta, R.: Computation in networks of passively mobile finite-state sensors. In: PODC 2004: Proceedings of the Twenty Third Annual ACM Symposium on Principles of Distributed Computing, pp. 290–299. ACM Press (2004)
2. Cardelli, L.: Strand algebras for DNA computing. Nat. Comput. **10**(1), 407–428 (2011)
3. Chen, H.-L., Doty, D., Soloveichik, D.: Rate-independent computation in continuous chemical reaction networks. In: ITCS 2014: Proceedings of the 5th Innovations in Theoretical Computer Science Conference, pp. 313–326 (2014)
4. Chen, Y.-J., Dalchau, N., Srinivas, N., Phillips, A., Cardelli, L., Soloveichik, D., Seelig, G.: Programmable chemical controllers made from DNA. Nat. Nanotechnol. **8**(10), 755–762 (2013)
5. Cook, M., Soloveichik, D., Winfree, E., Bruck, J.: Algorithmic bioprocesses. In: Condon, A., Harel, D., Kok, J.N., Salomaa, A., Winfree, E. (eds.) Programmability of Chemical Reaction Networks, pp. 543–584. Springer, Heidelberg (2009)
6. Esparza, J., Nielsen, M.: Decidability issues for petri nets - a survey. J. Inf. Process. Cybern. **3**, 143–160 (1994)
7. Elowitz, M.B., Levine, A.J., Siggia, E.D., Swain, P.S.: Stochastic gene expression in a single cell. Science **297**, 1183–1185 (2002)
8. Daniel, T.: Gillespie: exact stochastic simulation of coupled chemical reactions. J. Phys. Chem. **81**(25), 2340–2361 (1977)
9. Jiang, H., Riedel, M., Parhi, K.: Digital signal processing with molecular reactions. IEEE Des. Test Comput. **29**(3), 21–31 (2012)
10. Karp, R.M., Miller, R.E.: Parallel program schemata. J. Comput. Syst. Sci. **3**(4), 147–195 (1969)
11. Kleinberg, J.M., Tardos, É.: Algorithm Design. Addison-Wesley, Boston (2006)
12. Rao Kosaraju, S.: Decidability of reachability in vector addition systems (preliminary version), In: STOC 1982, pp. 267–281. ACM (1982)
13. Lambert, J.L.: A structure to decide reachability in petri nets. Theor. Comput. Sci. **99**(1), 79–104 (1992)
14. Leroux, J.: Vector addition reachability problem (a simpler solution). In: The Alan Turing Centenary Conference, vol. 10 of EPiC Series, pp. 214–228. EasyChair (2012)
15. Lipton, R.J.: The reachability problem requires exponential space, Technical report (1976)
16. Mayr, E.W.: An algorithm for the general petri net reachability problem. In: STOC 1981, pp. 238–246. ACM (1981)
17. McAdams, H.H., Arkin, A.P.: Stochastic mechanisms in gene expression. Proc. Natl. Acad. Sci. **94**, 814–819 (1997)
18. Sacerdote, G.S., Tenney, R.L.: The decidability of the reachability problem for vector addition systems (preliminary version), In: STOC 1977, pp. 61–76. ACM (1977)
19. Soloveichik, D., Cook, M., Winfree, E., Bruck, J.: Computation with finite stochastic chemical reaction networks. Nat. Comput. **7**(4), 615–633 (2008)
20. Soloveichik, D., Seelig, G., Winfree, E.: DNA as a universal substrate for chemical kinetics. Proc. Natl. Acad. Sci. **107**(12), 5393–5398 (2010)

An All-Optical Soliton FFT Computational Arrangement in the 3NLSE-Domain

Anastasios G. Bakaoukas[✉]

Computing and Immersive Technologies Department, University of Northampton,
St. Georges Avenue, Northampton NN2 6JB, UK
Anastasios.Bakaoukas@northampton.ac.uk

Abstract. In this paper an all–optical soliton method for calculating the FFT (Fast Fourier Transform) algorithm is presented. The method comes as an extension of the calculation methods (soliton gates) as they become possible in the Cubic Nonlinear Schrödinger Equation (3NLSE) domain, and provides a further proof of the computational abilities of the scheme. The method involves collisions entirely between first order solitons in optical fibers whose propagation evolution is described by the Cubic Nonlinear Schrödinger Equation. The main building block of the arrangement is the half–adder processor. Expanding around the half–adder processor, the "Butterfly" calculation process is demonstrated using first order solitons, leading eventually to the realisation of an equivalent to a full Radix–2 FFT calculation algorithm.

Keywords: Solitons · 3NLSE domain · All–optical FFT · Cubic Nonlinear Schrödinger Equation · Soliton collisions · Soliton computational schemes

1 Introduction

There is a number of studies in which the use of soliton optical pulses for the purposes of carrying out computations has been investigated [1, 2]. In this present paper only temporal solitons (involving a balance between Kerr type nonlinearities and dispersive effects in glass fibres) are concerned. At this early point the fact that the interactions between solitons of this type can be a relatively long–range phenomenon need to be emphasised, because the Kerr nonlinearity is a relatively weak effect. Temporal solitons in optical fibres where the nonlinearity is of the Kerr type, are well described by the 3NLS Equation which, for very short (fs) pulses, requires corrections to account for "Higher Order Dispersion", "Raman scattering" etc. If pulse widths are such that these higher order effects can be neglected, then solitons in optical fibres, are solutions of the integrable nonlinear Schrödinger equation and since collisions between fibre solitons are elastic they were not previously considered to be capable of useful computation [2].

In what follows in this introduction section, a brief description of the background theory is presented for the benefit of the reader. For a more extensive and

© Springer International Publishing Switzerland 2016
M. Amos and A. Condon (Eds.): UCNC 2016, LNCS 9726, pp. 11–24, 2016.
DOI: 10.1007/978-3-319-41312-9_2

thorough discussion the reader is referred to [3, 4] where the application of first order and second order solitons, following the Toffoli gates prototype as well as others, has been presented and verified regarding their computational abilities in terms of logic gates formations.

When higher order dispersive and nonlinear effects are neglected, short pulse propagation in nonlinear optical guides is described by the integrable Cubic Non-Linear Schrödinger (3NLSE) Equation. A positive value for "Dispersion" parameter describes the formation of bright optical solitons whilst a negative value leads to the formation of dark solitons. The 3NLS Equation in general, describes a modulated wave packet propagating through a nonlinear dispersive medium with a constant velocity. For certain initial pulse shapes (the "Reflectionless Potentials"), the 3NLSE is completely integrable and the evolution of the soliton can be found in closed form by means of the Inverse Scattering Transform (IST) [7]. Solitons arising out of a balance between dispersive and Kerr nonlinearity effects possess dominant characteristic features one of which is the elastic collisions between them. Solutions described by non–integrable nonlinear wave equations on the other hand are usually referred to as solitary waves and collisions between solitary waves are inelastic and more complex in character. A solution of the integrable 3NLSE applicable to pulse propagation in optical fibres is the hyperbolic secant where an arbitrary positive number representing the soliton order, the distance along the fibre, and time,

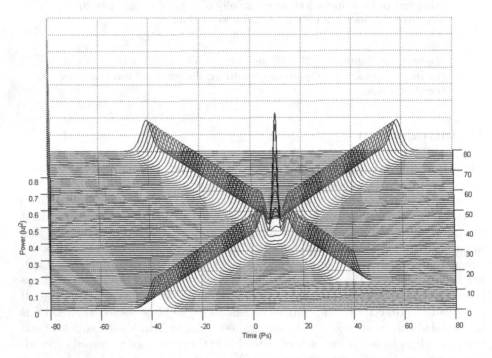

Fig. 1. A collision between two solitons. The second soliton is a "Time–Gated" input soliton.

all in normalised dimensionless units, are the main parameters forming the initial soliton propagation envelope. By coupling pulses in and out of a fibre at appropriate points (distance and time), useful computation could be possible based on collisions between solitons within the fibre.

The material presented in [3,4] shows that in situations where optical solitons are formed within optical fibres (simulations have been carried out using the Split–Step Fourier Technique (SSFT)), with appropriate practical arrangements, computationally universal systems based on collisions between first order solitons are possible using logical gates based on the "Controlled" type of gates originally proposed by Toffoli and Fredkin [5,6]. As an extension to what presented in the above mentioned papers, in this present paper, the numerical study of collisions between first order solitons is expanded leading towards an all–optical FFT (Fast Fourier Transform) calculation. The CN and CCN soliton gates continue to be the essential ingredient of the computational model.

In what follows in this paper, the encoding rules for the bit/s representation into our system (by admitting the existence of only two solitons, one with a phase value of π and one with a phase value of 0) follow exactly those outlined in [3,4] where the reader is referred for more details. This way there can only two types of collisions exist between solitons in our system: (a) two solitons

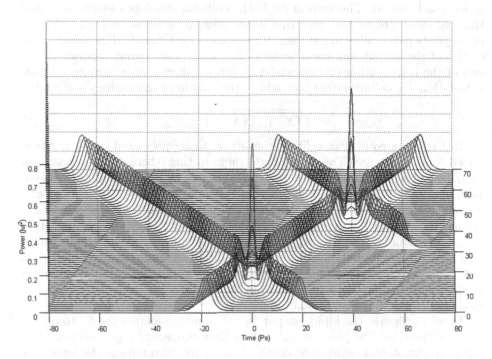

Fig. 2. Collision between three solitons in the cubic 3NLSE domain. The third of the solitons taking part in the collision is a "Time–Gated" soliton in phase with the initial two.

collide and are in phase (Figs. 1 and 2) or, (b) two solitons collide and are out of phase (Fig. 4). This way we can directly use the solitons themselves as input values to a soliton logic gate. The most important fact of all is that these two types of collisions possess the property of sequencing, so they can be cascaded. Using this definition we can go a bit further and consider the collision between solitons, as the inner process of the soliton logic gate and the two recovered with their original state after the collision solitons, as the output values of the logic gate. So, basically, we split the whole process of a collision into two important parts. The first part consists of the logic gate length, bounded between initially the point at which solitons begin to propagate through the medium, and the point at which the two solitons collide, creating a characteristic for their phase values "Collision Envelope". The second part starts from the point of collision, extending all the way up to the point where the two solitons recover their initial time positions in reverse order after the collision.

2   The Half–Adder Processor Scheme

The half–adder processor scheme, first introduced in [3], forms the essential central building block on which the overall FFT soliton computational scheme is wrapped around. The system reads the collision envelopes at distance and time specified points and uses this information to generate solitons with an appropriate phase value to represent the output of each "gate". The phase values of two of the output solitons determine the "sum" and "carry" outputs at the end of the computation process whilst all other solitons are superfluous to this calculation. By definition the half–adder (the sum implementation) is given by:

$$\overline{\overline{(X \cdot \bar{Y})} \cdot \overline{(\bar{X} \cdot Y)}} \tag{1}$$

In Fig. 3 the equivalent soliton scheme, originally presented in [3], is reproduced for convenience. The points highlighted in this schematic representation by means of a bold circle indicate functional points at which a soliton collision, part of a gate, takes place; while, X and Y denote the initial input data. Full "gate" arrangements have been named and numbered (e.g. NAND (*), indicates the first NAND in the computational arrangement, NAND (**) the second, etc.).

In Figs. 4 and 5, the "Input" and the "Output" of the schematic representation of Fig. 3 is reflected on actual soliton collision simulations. Each individual gate–soliton collision is presented in a separate figure for clarity and comparison purposes. The simulation figures are to be followed in a top–to–bottom approach in the schematic representation of Fig. 3.

In all the figures the input–output "gate" sequence follows the soliton propagation direction. The point at which the soliton propagation begins (point 0 in the propagation scale across the depth of the figure) also reflects the input side of the "gate" and respectively, the point at which the soliton propagation ends (point 100 in the propagation scale across the depth of the figure) reflects the output side of the "gate".

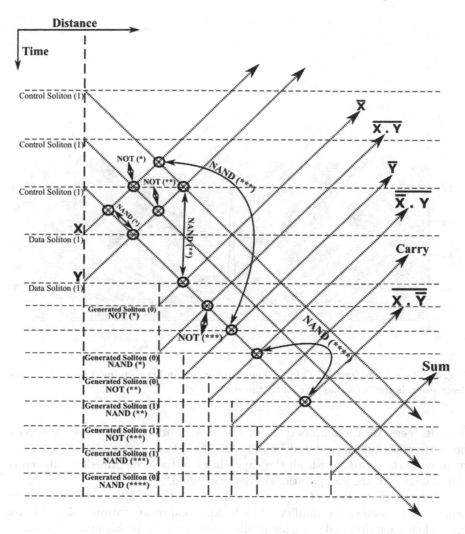

Fig. 3. The half–adder processor.

The half–adder computational arrangement plays a vital role in what is to follow as is this particular arrangement the one that is lying at the heart of the more general "Multiplier" arrangement, about to be presented later on, and required for the realisation in the end of the complete "Butterfly" calculation process which directly leads to the all–optical soliton FFT computational arrangement.

At this point and for the approach used for the presentation of the material to follow in this paper to become clear, we need to stretch–out the fact that the computational complexities involved are extensively simplified if can become apparent that the scheme is flexible enough to be gradually get "packed" in fixed–purpose calculation lengths. This approach doesn't suppress the system

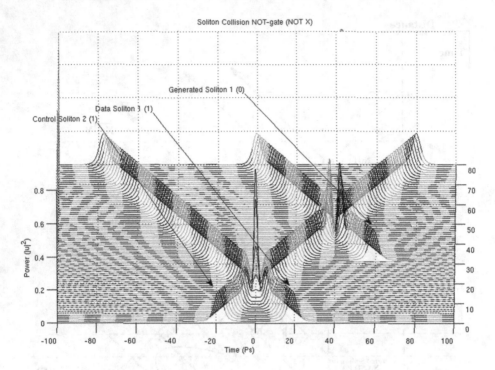

Fig. 4. The soliton "gate" NOT(*). The number in the brackets next to each soliton description is the bit value carried by the soliton.

from its generalisation properties, as the fixed reading points (as these have been identified and introduced in [3,4]) still hold their properties and continue to provide the system with all the capabilities initially identified as inherently characteristic of the computational system at hand.

This systematic type of approach, will give us the ability to investigate the properties (as well as the validity) of each individual computational block in turn and, when the individual parts are finally interconnected to form one "Butterfly" arrangement, to do the same regarding the properties and validity of the overall computational scheme.

3 The Two 2-Bit Numbers Multiplier

In this section we present the "Two 2-bit Numbers Multiplier", which involves a half–adder as its lying–in–its–heart functional unit ("Three–bit Adder Arrangement"). The particular arrangement forms the compact small–scale equivalent of the "Two maximum–number–of–bits Numbers Multiplier", which for general purpose calculations must involve full–adders as well as half–adders in its arrangement.

The reason behind choosing the Two 2–bit Numbers Multiplier is only the fact that the particular arrangement possesses all the functionalities and properties

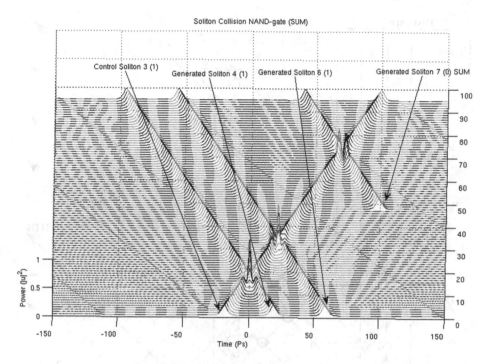

Fig. 5. The soliton "gate" NAND(****). The number in the brackets next to each soliton description is the bit value carried by the soliton.

need to be demonstrated, while at the same time gives us the ability to keep the material presented at a minimum of extension and complexity in this paper.

Starting from the half–adder arrangement, if we now take a closer look in Fig. 3 we will notice that all the output solitons need to be ignored after reading and only the output soliton representing the "carry" value is to be allowed to propagate further on and enter the cascading second half–adder arrangement. Is exactly this soliton–bit that is required for the arrangement to complete the Three–bit Adder Arrangement output calculation as presented in a conventional block diagram in Fig. 6. This "Soliton Suppression" requirement at the very end

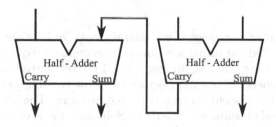

Fig. 6. The three-bit adder.

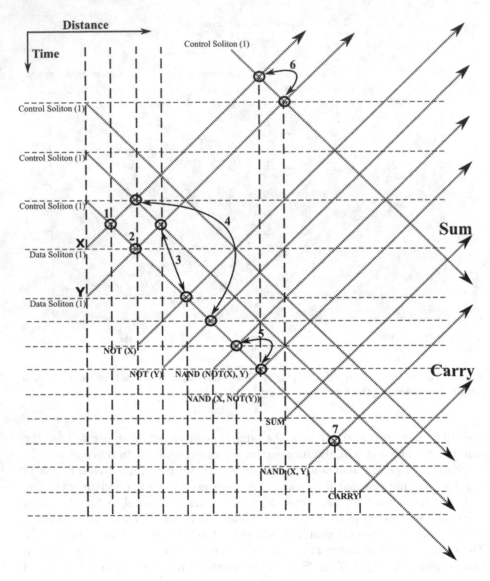

Fig. 7. The alternative half-adder arrangement.

of a computational arrangement is not characteristic only of the computational scheme here presented but rather a common characteristic requirement in soliton computational arrangements as, for example, of the one introduced in [8], where the additional property of not intersecting (solitons crossing paths but not colliding) is also a vital system characteristic requirement. The usual formal term coined for such kind of solitons is "Garbage Solitons" and is chosen to emphasise the fact that these solitons are to play no active role in the cascading calculations following the output of an arrangement. The way this "Soliton Suppression" can

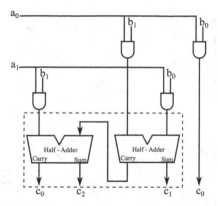

Fig. 8. The "Two 2-bit Numbers Multiplier".

be physically achieved is, in general terms, a technicality, requiring some hands–on experimental work, in order for different methods and their corresponding effects on the overall computational arrangement to be properly studied. For these reasons we postpone, at this point, the explanation of how this "Soliton Suppression" can be accomplished.

In order to present a complete picture of the soliton arrangements as well as the almost unlimited flexibility possessed by the computational system (another reason is that in the view of the author the concept of "Garbage Solitons" is neither entirely satisfactory nor properly defined in its physical terms), in Fig. 7 an alternative soliton arrangement is presented which doesn't need "Soliton Suppression" any more in order for the cascading half–adder arrangement to commence calculation.

In this new arrangement the general soliton pattern remains the same as in the original version, with the only difference that now the third control soliton is starting propagation at a time position shifted to the left (top) by four time slots (in Fig. 7 the original third control soliton propagation route has been maintained as well for comparison purposes). The order in which the individual gates are presenting their results is slightly changed as well. Shifting the third control soliton by four time slots to the left (top) of the arrangement has as a result for the soliton carrying the "carry" value to appear at the end (bottom) of the output soliton order. So, this soliton can now be taken as the first input soliton of the new half–adder arrangement (literally, as it possesses the same propagation angle as the original input solitons to the half–adder arrangement) which, by use of a second appropriate input soliton and three control solitons, as required by the scheme, can provide us with the final computational result, without the need to include any kind of "Soliton Suppression" procedure.

Having established and demonstrated the Three–bit Adder Arrangement, we can now build around it the full Two 2–bit Numbers Multiplier. The overall arrangement requires the addition of another four AND gates, to accommodate

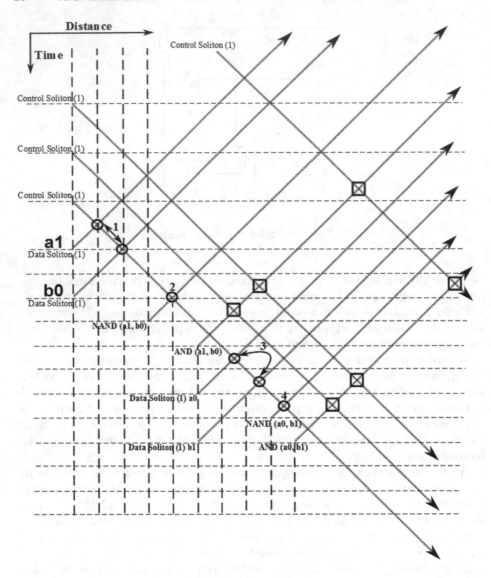

Fig. 9. Part of the "Two 2-bit Numbers Multiplier" (including two of the initial AND gates and the half-adder arrangement without the corresponding generated solitons).

initial bit multiplications. The conventional diagram arrangement for the multiplier is as presented in Fig. 8.

In Fig. 9 part of the Two 2–bit Numbers Multiplier is presented. For illustration purposes Generated Solitons in Fig. 9 are shown to be closer together than they should be in an actual computational arrangement without loosing in computational properties or upsetting the result. Circular soliton collision points indicate collisions taking place during the initial AND gates calculations, while square soliton collision points indicate collisions taking place as part of the half–adder calculation process. The arrangement in Fig. 9 illustrates a certain degree of parallelism in the calculation process, which contributes significantly in increasing the overall computational speed of the arrangement. It comes without saying that the Two 2–bit Numbers Multiplier arrangement illustrated can be extended to cover any bit length required for the multiplication between two individual numbers. Again, the purpose here was to keep the length of the illustration to a minimum.

4   The "Butterfly" Soliton Arrangement

For the remaining part of the "Butterfly" calculation process, we need a soliton arrangement to convert a positive bit–number to a negative one. In order to achieve this we adopt the method of complementing each digit in a bit–number in turn (change 1 for 0 and 0 for 1) and then add 1 to the result. That way, the bit–number taken out of the procedure corresponds to a bit–number representing the negative equivalent of the initial bit–number.

A series of collisions between the solitons carrying the bit–number values and a single control soliton with a phase value opposite to the one possessed by the control soliton that generated the initial bit–number, is enough to produce the bit–number complement. Since all the control solitons used so far in the

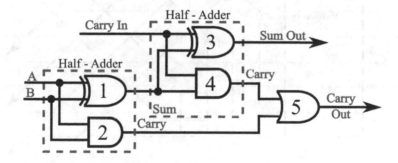

Fig. 10. The full-adder (conventional logic arrangement).

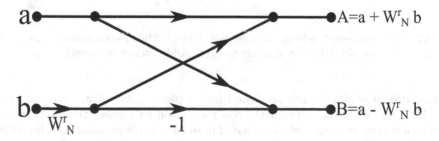

Fig. 11. Basic "Butterfly" computation in the decimation–in–time FFT algorithm.

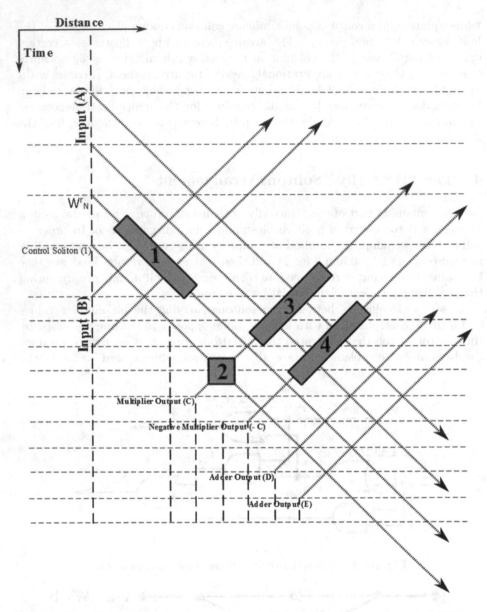

Fig. 12. The "Butterfly" soliton arrangement. [(1) Multiplier arrangement, (2) Negation arrangement, (3) Addition arrangement, (4) Addition arrangement].

computational arrangements presented had a phase value of π, corresponding to a bit value of 1, the appropriate control soliton to achieve the complement calculation must possess a phase value of 0, in turn corresponding to a bit value of 0. The addition of 1 to the complement can be easily achieved by means of full–adder arrangements internally consisting of two interconnecting half–adder arrangements and an OR gate, according to the conventional logic scheme presented in Fig. 10.

After the complement of a bit–number has been calculated, subtracting it from another bit–number requires the addition between the complement calculated and the second bit–number. That way only half–adder and full–adder arrangements are required for the realisation of all the calculations involved in the "Butterfly" arrangement. Addition and subtraction calculations appear at the final stages of the "Butterfly" (Fig. 11), those that actually are giving the result and passing the values calculated to the next processing stage of the overall FFT calculation arrangement.

Having completed the presentation of the individual parts out of which the soliton "Butterfly" arrangement consists of, we can now present the schematic of the overall arrangement required. Figure 12 presents the soliton "Butterfly" arrangement to full extend omitting, by means of a "black box" representation, those parts of the arrangement which have been previously analysed and illustrated. "Adder Output" (D) and "Adder Output" (E) appear at the end of the arrangement as required for the cascading "Butterfly" arrangements to continue further processing the data. All the output soliton propagation routes shown are indicative, since in an actual calculation of bit–numbers more than one solitons will represent the output bit–number of each block of calculation. As it is the case with the conventional Radix–2 FFT algorithm the first and the second decimation process results in a "shuffling" of the input data sequence, which has a well–defined order.

5 Conclusions

In this paper we surveyed the possibilities of an all–optical soliton FFT calculation and shown how this can become possible within the boundaries of the optical soliton 3NLSE domain. The outcome of this investigation is leading the way towards a fast all–optical soliton FFT calculation with the FFT phasors (roots of unity) to be represented directly by solitons of corresponding phase values, currently under extensive research by the author. In such a scheme the 8–point FFT phasors, for example, can be directly represented as: $W_8^0 \rightarrow$ *Soliton phase value* $= 2\pi$, $W_8^1 \rightarrow$ *Soliton phase value* $= \frac{\pi}{4}$, $W_8^2 \rightarrow$ *Soliton phase value* $= \frac{\pi}{2}$, $W_8^3 \rightarrow$ *Soliton phase value* $= \frac{3\pi}{4}$, $W_8^4 \rightarrow$ *Soliton phase value* $= -2\pi$, $W_8^5 \rightarrow$ *Soliton phase value* $= \frac{5\pi}{4}$, $W_8^6 \rightarrow$ *Soliton phase value* $= \frac{6\pi}{4}$, $W_8^7 \rightarrow$ *Soliton phase value* $= \frac{7\pi}{4}$, $W_8^8 \rightarrow$ *Soliton phase value* $= 2\pi$, while the soliton phase values of π and 0 remain reserved to represent digit 1 and digit 0 respectively for the control and data solitons involved. This additional ability, when properly specified, will provide the overall computational scheme with a separate, well defined, and of a smaller fixed length FFT calculation arrangement without the need for it to consist of individual calculation arrangements based on the scheme's "gates".

References

1. Jakubowski, M.H., Steiglitz, K., Squier, R.K.: Computing with solitons multi-valued logic. Special Issue on Collision Based Computing **6**, 5–6 (2001)
2. Jakubowski, M.H., Steiglitz, K., Squier, R.K.: When can solitons compute? Complex Syst. **10**(1), 1–21 (1996)
3. Bakaoukas, A.G., Edwards, J.: Computing in the 3NLS domain using first order solitons. Int. J. Unconventional Comput. (IJUC) **5**(6), 489–522 (2009). ISSN: 1548–7199
4. Bakaoukas, A.G., Edwards, J.: Computing in the 3NLS domain using first and second order solitons. Int. J. Unconventional Comput. **5**(6), 523–545 (2009). ISSN: 1548–7199
5. Tooli, T.: Reversible computing. In: de Bakker, J., van Leeuwen, J. (eds.) Automata, Languages and Programming. LNCS, vol. 85, pp. 632–644. Springer, Heidelberg (1980)
6. Fredkin, E., Toffoli, T.: Conservative logic. Int. J. Theor. Phys. **21**, 219–253 (1981)
7. Ablowitz, M.J., Segur, H.: Solitons and the Inverse Scattering Transform. SIAM, Philadephia (1981)
8. Rand, D., Steiglitz, K.: Computing with Solitons, July 1 2007
9. Pelinovsky, D.E., Afanasjev, V.V., Kivshar, Y.S.: Nonlinear theory of oscillating, decaying, and collapsing solitons in the generalised nonlinear schrödinger equation. Phys. Rev. E **53**(2), 1940–1953 (1996)
10. Hasegawa, Akira: Optical Solitons in Fibers. Springer, New York (1990)
11. Fibich, G., Wang, X.-P.: Stability of solitary waves for nonlinear schrödinger equations with inhomogeneous nonlinearitie. Physica D **96**(108), 96–108 (2003). Elsevier
12. Miller, P.D., Akhmediev, N.N.: Do solitons exchange conserved quantities during collisions? Phys. Rev. Lett. **76**(1), 38–41 (1996)
13. Micallef, R.W., Kivshar, Y., Love, J.D., Burak, D., Binder, R.: Generation of spatial solitons using non-linear guided modes. Opt. Quantum Electron. **30**, 751–770 (1998). Chapman & Hall
14. Ostrowsky, D.B., Reinisch, R. (eds.): Guided Wave Nonlinear Optics. Kluwer, Dordrecht (1992)
15. Akhmediev, N.N., Ankiewicz, A.: Solitons: Nonlinear Pulses and Beams, Chap. 12. Chapman & Hall, London (1997)

Babbage Meets Zuse: A Minimal Mechanical Computer

Raúl Rojas[✉]

Department of Mathematics and CS,
Freie Universität Berlin, Arinimallee 7, 14195 Berlin, Germany
rojas@inf.fu-berlin.de

Abstract. This paper shows how to build a computer consisting of a few mechanical elements. Two large gears are needed, one for the data, and another for the program memory. Only one logical computing element is required. The idea of a simple computer with minimal computing logic goes back to Konrad Zuse, who called it the "logic machine". Charles Babbage was the first one to design a universal mechanical computer. Here, we combine Babbage's gears and wooden pegs with Zuse's idea.

1 Introduction

A conventional computer requires a memory for the data and a processor for transforming the data. The physical structure of the processor is fixed. If we think of a microprocessor just as a logic circuit, then we have a repeating cycle: some bits enter the circuit, are transformed, and are stored internally. Then the microprocessor starts again with a new cycle of operations. Figure 1 shows the structure of a logical circuit representing a microprocessor.

The complete logic circuit can require the coordination of several intermediate binary results, so that the complete operation cycle needs to be broken in k subcircuits. Inside each subcircuit the order and exact timing of the operations is irrelevant, and the only rule is that a logical element needs to have its two inputs ready before it can produce a result. In the complete circuit, the single logical element used is the NAND operation, which is a complete basis for all binary logical operations. The k subcircuits are separated by internal buffers, which store the partial results and allow each subcircuit to synchronize. As Fig. 1 shows, we can number the logic elements, assigning each gate a sequential ID (only the NANDs in the first subcircuit have been numbered for this example). The input to each element, and its output, can be also uniquely numbered (in this example, only the inputs and outputs of the two logic elements to the upper left have been labeled). The labels for input and output of a logical element are "addresses" of one-bit cells where we can store those bits. The complete circuit operates from left to right: the bits are processed always one step further, and when the circuit is finished, it restarts a new cycle using the results from the previous cycle. An external memory represents only bits of data that can be also used. Intermediate results can be stored in that memory. Each memory address can store exactly one bit.

© Springer International Publishing Switzerland 2016
M. Amos and A. Condon (Eds.): UCNC 2016, LNCS 9726, pp. 25–34, 2016.
DOI: 10.1007/978-3-319-41312-9_3

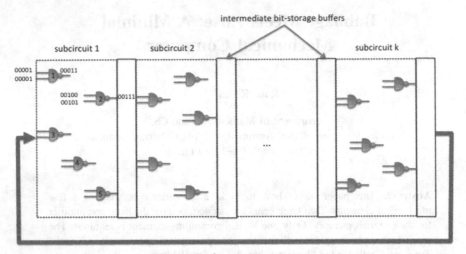

Logic circuit of a microprocessor

Fig. 1. The circuit of a microprocessor divided in stages of computation. The memory buffers between stages are used to handle synchronization between the computations of different subcircuits, if needed. There is only one logic gate, the NAND. The NANDS are numbered. The connections are also numbered and represent addresses where bits can be stored before being used by a NAND computation, or as a result thereof.

We can simulate the microprocessor of Fig. 1 running, by loading the necessary input bits from the addresses given by the labels in the connections. We can compute first the result for NAND number one, then for NAND number two and so on, in each subcircuit. When we are finished with one subcircuit we start the next one, and so on. Inside subcircuits there are no feedback loops (hardware loops, for example for a multiplication, can be unrolled). Computation proceeds in an orderly fashion, from left to right. Inside subcircuits we only have to take care of computing partial results before another gate needs this result as an input. Partial outputs can be stored in the addresses given by the labels of the connections. When the last subcircuit is finished, the stored partial results of subcircuit k can serve as the new input for the first subcircuit, and the whole processor starts a new cycle again.

Where is the memory for data? We can think of the intermediate storage buffers just as a single thing, the complete data-memory. Every label in the complete circuit refers to that data-memory. If we prefer, we can use the lower addresses for the internal needs of the microprocessor and the higher addresses for real data.

One important aspect to take into account is that the arithmetical operations addition, subtraction and multiplication are deterministic. That is, there is no need to have alternative computational paths for their computation. They start and finish, and can be computed with a circuit which is always going forward. However, in a microprocessor we could have the case that one of two computational paths is selected by a bit x. It would be similar to an

"IF (x==1) THEN (compute A) else (compute B)"

kind of question (where, for simplicity, the result of each alternative computation would be the single bit c). Since we do not want to handle conditional jumps in the circuit, the solution is to execute both branches of the computation and only select at the end:

a = result of computing A
b = result of computing B
$c = (x \text{ AND } a) \text{ OR } ((\text{NOT } x) \text{ AND } b)$

This is what microprocessors do when they still don't have the value of the bit x. They apply "speculative execution" computing both possible results, selecting the appropriate one afterwards. In the case of nested "IFs" we need to apply such a scheme recursively. The division algorithm, for example, can be implemented in this way, so that we can simulate a processor able to compute all arithmetical operations and execute them in a loop. I have proved elsewhere that it is possible to build a universal computer exploiting this scheme [1]. From the example above, it should be clear that we only have to simulate circuits doing a blind forward computation, even when the high-level processing view contains alternative computational paths.

2 Zuse's "Logistische Maschine"

It was during the design of his machines Z1, Z2, and Z3 (1936–1941) that the German inventor Konrad Zuse gradually became aware that the instruction set of a digital computer could be reduced to sequences of logical operations acting on single bits and pairs of bits.[1] Addition of two eight-bit numbers, for example, can be reduced to the manipulation of each bit in the numbers' binary representations, executing the necessary sequence of negations, conjunctions and disjunctions in the appropriate order. In other words: one can add two 32-bit numbers going bit column by bit column, from right to left, using both numbers, adding each binary column, and propagating the carry to the left. In Zuse's "algebraic machines", such as the Z3, the four elementary arithmetical operations were implemented in hardware as bit-parallel operations. The two elementary bit-parallel operations provided by the CPU were addition/subtraction of two numbers and shifting. Complex operations were implemented from sequences of this elementary "microinstructions". A rotating dial just selected one microinstruction after the other, one per cycle. The division operation in the Z3, for example, required 18 cycles.

Therefore, since an instruction can be reduced to simpler microinstructions, it occurred to Zuse that a minimal computer, that is, one able to work only on at most two bits at a time, could execute each of the four arithmetical operations, provided that we can write the corresponding program. Zuse called it the "logistische Maschine" (he used Logistik as synonym for Logik). This idea forms part of Zuse's obsession with what today would be called a high-level programming language, the "Plankalkül".

---

[1] This is the essential difference between "bit-parallel" and "bit-sequential" computers. John von Neumann's EDVAC [1] design was for a bit-sequential computer, which would read and act on registers one bit at a time. Most of today's computers are bit-parallel, and so were Zuse's computers.

In this language, designed by Zuse from 1941 to 1945, all data structures are arrays or tuples of single bits, each of which can be accessed individually by a program (being indexed elementary components of a data structure). Therefore, it was natural to think of a machine capable of handling single bits sequentially and capable of emulating the parallel algebraic machines in software, at a minimal cost. The idea of designing a "logical machine" was thus closely connected with the conception of the Plankalkül [2].

Konrad Zuse applied in 1944 (and again in 1947) for a patent for the logical machine [3]. It was Zuse's custom to apply early for patents of his ideas. However, the war and the closure of the German Patent Office for several years made it impossible for him to profit from such early applications. Most of the patents were denied when the patent office opened again, and those which were granted had no commercial impact. The patent for the "logistische Machine" was granted in Austria in 1952, but had no commercial implications for Zuse's company [4].

The logical machine was extremely simple: it consisted of an addressable memory for storing single bits, a tape reader, and a small CPU. In today's terminology, we would say that the word-length was one bit. The processor could read and store single bits in memory. The program was stored on the punched tape using a binary code, and the tape could be as long as desired. There was also the theoretical possibility of gluing together both ends of the punched tape in order to produce a single "loop" of instructions.

The processor of the logical machine had only two registers A and B: each of them could be loaded with a single bit from a memory address. The first time a bit was loaded to the processor, it was stored in register A and a flag (named Pr by Zuse) was set. The second bit loaded from the processor went automatically to register B as commanded by the flag set before.

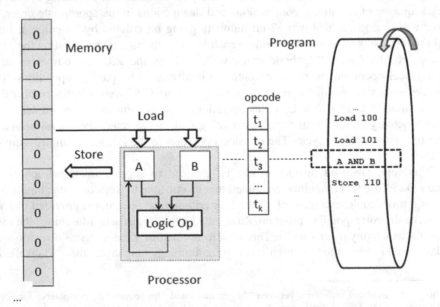

Fig. 2. Block diagram of the Logical Machine

The processor could only execute two register operations: A AND B, or A OR B, that is, the conjunction of the two one-bit registers or their disjunction. The contents of each register could be negated before the conjunction/disjunction. The opcode of the instruction being executed specified completely all such combinations.

The machine operated by retrieving first a command from the punched tape. There were three types of commands: logical operation (AND, OR), load from memory, and store to memory. The result of a load operation went to register A or B, as explained before, the result of a store operation went to register A (which was flagged as occupied). A store operation sent the contents of register A to the desired address and declared the register empty (so that it could be loaded again).

A processor cycle consisted of five subcycles numbered I, II, III, IV and V. A conducting line labelled III, for example, received a voltage only during subcycle III. The operation of the relays was synchronized by activating them only at such specified times. Bits could be stored over long periods using "self-halting" relays, that is, relays with two solenoids. When the first solenoid was energized, the relay closed, which in turn energized a second solenoid which kept the relay closed as long as there was power available. A "clear" signal just disconnected both solenoids from the power supply. In Zuse's diagrams, the relays are always drawn in the "zero" position. A switch to the position "one" moved the relay to the other contact (see the diagrams below).

It was the insight of Konrad Zuse, that we can now build a simulator for the complete computer by using a processor with a single logic element [3, 4]. This is what he called the "logistische Maschine" (although in his design he used two logic gates, and two negations, but we can use only one gate). The "logic machine" has a microprocessor with just two registers for two bits. The memory contains one bit at each memory address. The processor can execute just a NAND of two bits. The result can be stored back to the data-memory.

The microprocessor of Fig. 2 could be simulated by a long program of the following form:

	Comments
...	
LOAD addr-1	Load first input of NAND x to register 1
LOAD addr-2	Load second input of NAND x to register 2
STORE addr-3	Store result in addr-3
LOAD addr-4	Load first input of NAND y to register 1
LOAD addr-5	Load second input of NAND y to register 2
STORE addr-6	Store result in addr-6
...	

The program would handle each NAND, in each subcircuit, one by one. The two input bits are loaded first from the appropriate addresses (here addr-1 and addr-2 for the first NAND). The one and only NAND in the hardware of the logic machine is triggered automatically by the presence of the two input bits (like in a dataflow computer), so that afterwards, the output just needs to be stored at the appropriate address. Once a NAND is finished, the next one is simulated. Once a subcircuit has been simulated completely, we start with the next subcircuit, and so on.

It is then clear that the only hardware we need for the "logistische Maschine" is the following:

- An addressable memory for holding individual bits,
- Two one-bit registers for holding the inputs to a NAND,
- One single NAND in the processor, operating with the two one-bit registers,
- An output buffer for the NAND which holds the result to be stored in the memory,
- A read-only memory for storing the program.

It should be clear that with such a machine, any finite microprocessor operating on a finite external memory can be simulated. The size of the necessary program is finite, because the number of NANDS in the microprocessor is finite.

Nevertheless, although the hardware is now extremely simple, it is still unsatisfactory that we need to decode addresses during the simulation, in order to load or store the appropriate bits. This would require additional logic. Also, decoding the instruction set, although extremely small, requires some logic. Notice also that the program is a giant loop. When an operation cycle is finished, the microprocessor starts again. The program never stops, since a microprocessor never stops either (and goes into idle cycles, if necessary). You have to pull the plug in order to stop your computer (although modern computers pull the plug themselves, automatically).

3 Minimizing the Instruction Set

We can now try to make everything simpler by reducing the instruction set. Since each NAND needs two inputs, and produces one result, the program above can be just written as:

	Comments
...	
addr-1	Load first input of NAND x to register 1
addr-2	Load second input of NAND x to register 2
addr-3	Store result in addr-3
addr-4	Load first input of NAND y to register 1
addr-5	Load second input of NAND y to register 2
addr-6	Store result in addr-6
...	

Every three addresses represent the execution of a NAND in an implicit manner. The first two addresses are inputs, the third one is an output. Now we only need to decode addresses. But we don't want to spend logic for decoding addresses. So we just decide that all addressing starts from address 0, when the simulation starts. If the simulation of the first NAND looks like the following sequence of three addresses (written in decimal for simplicity):

	Comments
...	
4	Load first input of NAND x from address 4
5	Load second input of NAND x from address 5
7	Store result in address 7

But if we have a pointer pointing to address 0 in memory, we can just advance the pointer as needed:

...	Comments
advance pointer	pointer at address 1
advance pointer	pointer at address 2
advance pointer	pointer at address 3
advance pointer	pointer at address 4
memory	first input
advance pointer	pointer at address 5
memory	second input
advance pointer	pointer at address 6
advance pointer	pointer at address 7
memory	store result

We thus introduce a "memory" operation which loads data to each one the two one-bit registers, the first two times it is called, and which stores back to memory when the result has been computed.

All addressing is done through the memory pointer we just created. It is like in a Turing Machine, where we have a one-bit per cell long tape and a read/write head moving to the left or to the right of the tape.

You would think that it would be necessary to have a "move back pointer" instruction, in order to displace the pointer back whenever lower addresses are needed. But we are going to do the following: the same way that the program code consists of a long loop, the memory will be "circular". That is, since the memory is finite, once the pointer arrives to the last memory location, it starts back again at address 0, whenever it is further advanced. In that way, we never need to move the pointer back. The price we pay is that we are stuck with a finite memory, but that is not important since we are simulating a conventional computer and before we start, we can "buy" as much memory as needed for certain applications.

4   Enter Charles Babbage

The mathematician Charles Babbage (1791–1871) is one of the heroes in the history of computing. He designed the "Analytical Engine", a mechanical device he first described in 1837, and which would have been the first computer in the world – if it had been finished [5]. Babbage redesigned the components of the Analytical Engine several times. The main problem was connecting all the numerous mechanical components to each other and getting the synchronization right. Although the mechanical manufacturing possibilities of his day were probably appropriate for the task, he was the solitary designer of the machine. The task was much more than a single person could handle, and the Analytical Engine remained an unfinished dream. The machine could, theoretically, perform all arithmetical operations, also read and store numbers from and to memory, and conditional branching was present in the instruction set.

In Babbage's machines, numbers were stored using gears. If the gear can assume ten different states, for example, the position of a gear can be used to represent decimal digits. But Babbage also considered gears with 20 or 40 states. In that case, the states could be numbered from 0 to 9, starting again at zero, if the gear provided more than ten states. The largest gear in the Analytical Engine could assume 40 states (that is four times the digits from 0 to 9).

We will also use two big gears to store the data and the program in a mechanical version of Zuse's logic machine. Figure 3 shows the resulting contraption.

The clock gear advances the program gear one step at a time (the teeth of the gears are not shown in Fig. 3). The program gear advances the memory gear in lockstep with itself. There are "pegs" attached to the program gear, which are detected at the red lower window. If a peg is detected, the processor is activated to read/write from/to memory. The position from which the memory is read is shown with a red window in the lower part of the memory gear. We are assuming that a multiplexer allocates each read bit to the first or second register, depending on the order they were read. When the operation has been triggered, the result is stored at the memory location defined by the next peg in the program gear.

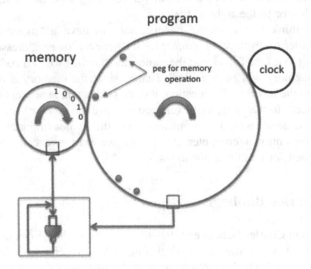

Fig. 3. The mechanical minimal logic machine. The clock gear advances one tooth in every step. The program and memory gear are coupled and advance at the same speed. Pegs in the program gear activate memory operations. The bits are stored in bistable mechanical elements on top of the memory gear. The two one-bit registers and the NAND gate can be built from binary mechanical components such as those used by Konrad Zuse for the Z1 computer [6, 7].

Notice that with this arrangement, moving to the next address can require a full turn of the memory gear, especially if we want to store the result in the same address of the last bit we have read. In the worst case, every address used requires a full turn of the memory gear with N teeth, and the number of teeth between successive pegs in the program gear could be N. Typically, the program gear will have many times the number of teeth that the memory gear has.

The bits in the memory gear could be stored using a bistable mechanical element on top of the memory gear. And the processor could be built with binary mechanical elements similar, for example, to the ones Konrad Zuse used to build his first computer, the Z1.

Such a mechanical arrangement is thus, from an abstract point of view, equivalent to modern computers, with their finite memories. It cannot compete with the infinite tape of a Turing machine, but that was not the purpose of this exercise.

5   Conclusions

No company is going to offer the mechanical minimal logic machine any time soon. Our objective in this paper was to show that from an abstract point of view, a simple device can do what traditional computers do. Of course, the amount of time needed for every single logic computation is prohibitive and this machine would be much slower than any real computer (also, because it is a mechanical design).

The program simulates a microprocessor which can execute any instructions stored in the data memory. That is, although the program in the program gear is fixed, the microprocessor circuit can decode instructions stored in data memory. We can thus have a stored program in main memory making the machine more flexible. The same way a user cannot modify the Intel processor of a PC, the user cannot modify the program gear. But the user can still write self-modifying programs, and can design any programming language he or she would like to have for high-level programming.

Of course there are ways of reducing the execution overhead of the machine, for example, by allowing the memory gear to backtrack. This would require additional mechanical elements and we thus prefer to keep the main idea simple.

There is an old result in programming that states that any program can be written using a single loop in the code. This is an independent proof of that result, since the program gear is just that, a single loop of code.

So, what do you need to simulate a conventional computer? Two big gears, plus one gear for the clock, and one NAND, plus some additional mechanical elements used to coordinate the operation of the one-gate processor and its registers. Many different mechanical embodiments are possible and I look forward to the first mechanical realization of the Babbage-Zuse computer. Such a machine is, in principle, as good as any other real computer – only the size of the gears is going to be the paramount problem for a realization!

References

1. Rojas, R.: How to make Zuse's Z3 a universal computer. Ann. Hist. Comput. **20**(3), 51–54 (1998)
2. Zuse, K., Plankalkül, D.: Berichte der GMD, Nr. 63, Sankt Augustin (1972)
3. Zuse, K.: Patent Application Z394, Zuse Papers 005/017 (1944)

4. Zuse, K.: Vorrichtung zum Ableiten von Resultatangaben mittels Grundoperatione des Aussagenkalküls, Patent N. 172288 (Austrian Patent Office) (1952)
5. Babbage, Ch.: On the analytical engine. In: Passages from the Life of a Philosopher, London (1864)
6. Rojas, R.: The Z1: architecture and algorithms of Konrad Zuse's first computer, June 2014. arXiv:1406.1886v1
7. Rojas, R.: The design principles of Konrad Zuse's mechanical computers, March 2016. arXiv: 1603.02396

Generative Power of Matrix Insertion-Deletion Systems with Context-Free Insertion or Deletion

Henning Fernau[1], Lakshmanan Kuppusamy[2(⊠)], and Indhumathi Raman[3]

[1] Fachbereich 4 – Abteilung Informatikwissenschaften,
Universität Trier, 54286 Trier, Germany
fernau@uni-trier.de
[2] School of Computing Science and Engineering,
VIT University, Vellore 632 014, India
klakshma@vit.ac.in
[3] School of Information Technology and Engineering,
VIT University, Vellore 632 014, India
indhumathi.r@vit.ac.in

Abstract. Matrix insertion-deletion systems combine the idea of matrix control (as established in regulated rewriting) with that of insertion and deletion (as opposed to replacements). We improve on and complement previous computational completeness results for such systems, showing (for instance) that matrix insertion-deletion systems with matrices of length two, insertion rules of type $(1, 1, 1)$ and context-free deletions are computationally complete. We also show how to simulate (Kleene stars of) metalinear languages with several types of systems with very limited resources. We also generate non-semilinear languages using matrices of length three with context-free insertion and deletion rules.

Keywords: Matrix ins-del systems · Computational completeness · Metalinear languages

1 Introduction

It is assumed that inserting or deleting words in between parts of sentences often take place when processing natural languages. This concept also frequently occurs in DNA processing and RNA editing; see [2, 3, 26]. Based on the insertion operation, Marcus introduced *external contextual grammars* [19] as an attempt to mathematically model natural language phenomena. A different variety of linguistically motivated contextual grammars are the *semi-contextual grammars* studied by Galiukschov [10], which can be viewed as insertion grammars. The deletion operation as a basis of a grammatical derivation process was introduced in [14]. Insertion and deletion together were first studied in [15] and the corresponding grammatical mechanism is called *insertion-deletion system* (abbreviated as ins-del system). Informally, if a string η is inserted between two parts w_1 and w_2 of a string $w_1 w_2$ to get $w_1 \eta w_2$, we call the operation *insertion*, whereas

© Springer International Publishing Switzerland 2016
M. Amos and A. Condon (Eds.): UCNC 2016, LNCS 9726, pp. 35–48, 2016.
DOI: 10.1007/978-3-319-41312-9_4

if a substring δ is deleted from a string $w_1 \delta w_2$ to get $w_1 w_2$, we call the operation *deletion*. Suffixes of w_1 and prefixes of w_2 are called *contexts*.

Several variants of ins-del systems have been considered in literature and among them the important variants (from our perspective) are *ins-del P systems* [1], *context-free ins-del systems* [20], *graph-controlled ins-del systems* [7,8,13], *matrix insertion systems* [18], *matrix ins-del systems* [16,25], etc. We refer to the survey article [28] for more details of variants of ins-del systems.

In a matrix ins-del system, the insertion-deletion rules are given in matrix form. If a matrix l is chosen for derivation, then all the rules in the matrix l are applied in order and no rule of the matrix is exempted. In a size $(k; n, i', i''; m, j', j'')$ of a matrix insertion-deletion system, the parameters (from left to right) denote the maximum number of rules in any matrix, the maximal length of the inserted string, the maximal length of the left context for insertion, and the maximal length of the right context for insertion; a similar list of three parameters concerning deletion follows. We denote the languages classes generated by matrix ins-del systems of size s by MAT(s). It is shown in [25] that the following matrix ins-del systems are computationally complete: MAT($3; 1, 1, 0; 1, 1, 0$), MAT($3; 1, 1, 0; 1, 0, 1$), MAT($2; 1, 1, 0; 2, 0, 0$), MAT($2; 2, 0, 0; 1, 1, 0$), MAT($8; 1, 1, 1; 1, 0, 0$), MAT($8; 1, 0, 0; 1, 1, 1$).
Here, we prove that the following classes of languages are also computationally complete: MAT($2; 1, 0, 1; 2, 0, 0$), MAT($2; 2, 0, 0; 1, 0, 1$), MAT($3; 1, 0, 1; 1, 0, 1$), MAT($3; 1, 0, 1; 1, 1, 0$), MAT($2; 1, 1, 1; 1, 0, 0$), as well as MAT($4; 1, 0, 0; 1, 1, 1$). The last two results improve the results available in [25]. Moreover, the following language families all strictly contain the families of linear and metalinear languages: MAT($2; 2, 1, 0; 1, 0, 0$), MAT($2; 2, 0, 1; 1, 0, 0$), MAT($3; 1, 1, 0; 1, 0, 0$), and MAT($3; 1, 0, 1; 1, 0, 0$). We also prove that matrix ins-del systems of the above sizes simulate the Kleene stars of linear and metalinear languages, as well.

2   Preliminaries

We assume that the readers are familiar with the standard notations used in formal language theory. However, we now recall a few important notations here.

Let $\mathbb{N}$ denote the set of positive integers, and $[1 \ldots k] = \{i \in \mathbb{N} : 1 \leq i \leq k\}$. Given an *alphabet* (finite set) Σ, Σ^* denotes the free monoid generated by Σ. The elements of Σ^* are called *strings* or *words*; λ denotes the empty string. For a string $w \in \Sigma^*$, $|w|$ denotes the length of a string w and w^R denotes the reversal (mirror image) of w. Likewise, L^R and $\mathcal{L}^R$ are understood for languages L and language families $\mathcal{L}$. RE denotes the family of the recursively enumerable languages, LIN is the class of the linear languages and MLIN, the family of metalinear languages, is the smallest language class containing LIN and is closed under concatenation. Notice that LIN is neither closed under concatenation nor under Kleene closure; MLIN is not closed under Kleene closure. We will occasionally make use of the fact that linear rules are, w.l.o.g., of the form $A \to aB$ or $A \to Ba$ or $A \to \lambda$ for distinct nonterminals A, B and terminals a.

For the computational completeness results, we are using the fact that type-0 grammars in the special Geffert normal form are known to characterize the recursively enumerable languages. According to [8], a type-0 grammar $G = (N, T, P, S)$ is said to be in *special Geffert normal form*, SGNF for short, if

- N decomposes as $N = N' \cup N''$, where $N'' = \{A, B, C, D\}$ and N' contains at least the two nonterminals S and S',
- the only non-context-free rules in P are the two erasing rules $AB \to \lambda$ and $CD \to \lambda$,
- the context-free rules are of the following forms:
  $X \to Yb$ or $X \to bY$ where $X, Y \in N'$, $X \neq Y$, $b \in T \cup N''$, or $S' \to \lambda$.

How to construct this normal form is described in [8] and is based on [11]. Also, the derivation of a string is done in two phases. First, the context-free rules are applied repeatedly and the phase I is completed by applying the rule $S' \to \lambda$ in the derivation. In phase II, only the non-context-free erasing rules are applied repeatedly and the derivation ends. It is to be noted that as these context-free rules are more of a linear type, it is easy to see that there can be at most only one nonterminal from N' present in the derivation of G. Also, note that $X \neq Y, X, Y \in N'$ in the context-free rules.

Sometimes, we also use the well-known Penttonen normal form [24] for a type-0 grammar. For Parikh images, semilinear and non-semilinear languages, we refer to [23].

2.1 Insertion-Deletion Systems

We now give the basic definition of insertion-deletion systems, following [15, 26].

Definition 1. An *insertion-deletion system* is a construct $\gamma = (V, T, A, R)$, where V is an alphabet, $T \subseteq V$ is the terminal alphabet, A is a finite language over V, R is a finite set of triplets of the form $(u, \eta, v)_{ins}$ or $(u, \delta, v)_{del}$, where $(u, v) \in V^* \times V^*$, $\eta, \delta \in V^+$.

The pair (u, v) is called the *context*, η is called the *insertion string*, δ is called the *deletion string* and $x \in A$ is called an *axiom*. If $u = v = \lambda$ for a rule, then the corresponding insertion/deletion can be done freely anywhere in the string and is called context-free insertion/deletion. An insertion rule will be of the form $(u, \eta, v)_{ins}$, which means that the string η is inserted between u and v. A deletion rule will be of the form $(u, \delta, v)_{del}$, which means that the string δ is deleted between u and v. Applying $(u, \eta, v)_{ins}$ corresponds to the rewriting rule $uv \to u\eta v$, and $(u, \delta, v)_{del}$ corresponds to the rewriting rule $u\delta v \to uv$. Consequently, for $x, y \subset V^*$ we write $x \Rightarrow y$ if y can be obtained from x by using either an insertion rule or a deletion rule.

2.2 Matrix Insertion-Deletion Systems

A matrix insertion-deletion system [16, 25] is a construct $\Gamma = (V, T, A, R)$ where V is an alphabet, $T \subseteq V$, A is a finite language over V, R is a finite set of matrices $\{r_1, r_2, \ldots r_l\}$, where each r_i, $1 \leq i \leq l$, is a matrix of the form

$$r_i = [(u_1, \alpha_1, v_1)_{t_1}, (u_2, \alpha_2, v_2)_{t_2}, \ldots, (u_k, \alpha_k, v_k)_{t_k}]$$

with $t_j \in \{ins, del\}$, $1 \leq j \leq k$. For $1 \leq j \leq k$, the triple $(u_j, \alpha_j, v_j)_{t_j}$ is an ins-del rule. Consequently, for $x, y \in V^*$ we write $x \Longrightarrow_{r_i} y$ if y can be obtained from x by applying all the rules of a matrix r_i, $1 \leq i \leq l$, in order.

By $w \Longrightarrow_* z$, we denote the relation $w \Longrightarrow_{r_{i_1}} w_1 \Longrightarrow_{r_{i_2}} \cdots \Longrightarrow_{r_{i_k}} z$, where for all j, $1 \leq j \leq k$, we have $1 \leq i_j \leq l$. The language generated by Γ is defined as $L(\Gamma) = \{w \in T^* \mid x \Longrightarrow_* w, \text{ for some } x \in A\}$.

If a matrix ins-del system has at most k rules in a matrix and the size of the underlying ins-del system is $(n, i', i''; m, j', j'')$, then we denote the corresponding class of language by $\mathrm{MAT}(k; n, i', i''; m, j', j'')$. We now discuss a few examples of matrix ins-del system and they are used later in proving some theorems.

Example 1. The language $L_{cd} = \{a^n b^m c^n d^m \mid m, n \geq 1\}$ of cross-serial dependencies can be generated by a binary matrix insertion-deletion system as follows: $\Gamma_{cd} = (\{a, b, c, d\}, \{a, b, c, d\}, \{abcd\}, R)$, where $R = \{r_1, r_2\}$ with: $r_1 = [(a, a, \lambda)_{ins}, (c, c, \lambda)_{ins}]$, $r_2 = [(b, b, \lambda)_{ins}, (d, d, \lambda)_{ins}]$. We note that the rules $r_1' = [(\lambda, a, a)_{ins}, (\lambda, c, c)_{ins}]$, $r_2' = [(\lambda, b, b)_{ins}, (\lambda, d, d)_{ins}]$ also generate L_{cd}. This shows that $L_{cd} \in \mathrm{MAT}(2; 1, 1, 0; 0, 0, 0) \cap \mathrm{MAT}(2; 1, 0, 1; 0, 0, 0)$. We refer to [27] for further variants and a discussion of the linguistic relevance of this type of example. □

Example 2. Lemma 3 in [18] shows (in our terminology) that $L_{ts} = \{a^n b a^n c a^n \mid n \in \mathbb{N}\} \in \mathrm{MAT}(3; 1, 1, 1; 0, 0, 0)$, using a single matrix of insertion rules only. □

We note that the above discussed languages L_{cd}, L_{ts} and L_{cd}^R are non context-free languages.

3   Auxiliary Results

In order to simplify the proofs of some of our main results, the following observations are helpful.

Theorem 1. *For all non-negative integers k, n, i', i'', m, j, j'', we have that*

$$\mathrm{MAT}(k; n, i', i''; m, j', j'') = [\mathrm{MAT}(k; n, i'', i'; m, j'', j')]^R.$$

Proof. To an ins-del rule $r = (x, y, z)_\mu$ with $\mu \in \{ins, del\}$, we associate the reversed rule $\rho(r) = (z^R, y^R, x^R)_\mu$. Let $\Gamma = (V, T, A, R)$ be a matrix insertion-deletion system. Map a matrix $l = [r_1, \ldots, r_k] \in R$ to $\rho(l) = [\rho(r_1), \ldots, \rho(r_k)]$ in $\rho(R)$. Define $\Gamma^R = (V, T, A^R, \rho(R))$. Then, an easy inductive argument shows that $L(\Gamma^R) = (L(\Gamma))^R$. Observing the sizes of the system shows the claim. □

From Theorem 1, we can immediately deduce the following two corollaries:

Corollary 1. *Let k, n, i', m, j' be non-negative integers. The family of languages $\mathrm{MAT}(k; n, i', i'; m, j', j')$ is closed under reversal.*

Corollary 2. *Let $\mathcal{L}$ be a language class that is closed under reversal. Then, for all non-negative integers $k, n, i', i'', m, j', j''$, we conclude that*

1. *$\mathcal{L} = \mathrm{MAT}(k; n, i', i''; m, j', j'')$ if and only if $\mathcal{L} = \mathrm{MAT}(k; n, i'', i'; m, j'', j')$.*
2. *$\mathcal{L} \subseteq \mathrm{MAT}(k; n, i', i''; m, j', j'')$ if and only if $\mathcal{L} \subseteq \mathrm{MAT}(k; n, i'', i'; m, j'', j')$.*

4   Computational Completeness Results

An easy consequence from Corollary 2 are the following completeness results:

Theorem 2. *(i)* $\mathrm{MAT}(2; 1, 0, 1; 2, 0, 0) = \mathrm{RE}$, *(ii)* $\mathrm{MAT}(2; 2, 0, 0; 1, 0, 1) = \mathrm{RE}$, *(iii)* $\mathrm{MAT}(3; 1, 0, 1; 1, 0, 1) = \mathrm{RE}$, *(iv)* $\mathrm{MAT}(3; 1, 0, 1; 1, 1, 0) = \mathrm{RE}$.

Proof. We recall that the families $\mathrm{MAT}(2; 1, 1, 0; 2, 0, 0)$, $\mathrm{MAT}(2; 2, 0, 0; 1, 1, 0)$, $\mathrm{MAT}(3; 1, 1, 0; 1, 1, 0)$, and $\mathrm{MAT}(3; 1, 1, 0; 1, 0, 1)$ are known to equal RE (cf. [25]). As RE is closed under reversal, the theorem follows from Corollary 2.   □

In the following, we discuss further completeness results which are improvement over some of the existing results in terms of the maximum number of rules (i.e., maximal length of the matrix). More specifically, in [25], matrices of length 8 are used, which we reduce to 2 and 4 here. The other measure sizes in the results stay the same. Our simulations also show different resource needs for restricting insertions compared to restricting deletions.

Theorem 3. $\mathrm{MAT}(4; 1, 0, 0; 1, 1, 1) = \mathrm{RE}$.

Proof. Consider a type-0 grammar $G = (N, T, P, S)$ in SGNF. The rules from P are labelled injectively with labels from $[1 \ldots |P|]$. The nonterminal alphabet decomposes like $N = N' \cup N''$, $N'' = \{A, B, C, D\}$, $S, S' \in N'$, according to SGNF. We construct a matrix ins-del system $\Gamma = (V, T, \{S\}, M)$ with $V = N \cup T \cup \{p, p', q, q', f, g\}$.

The set of matrices M of Γ is defined as follows.

We simulate the rule $p\colon X \to bY$, $X, Y \in N'$, $b \in N'' \cup T$, by the following rules:

$$p1 = [(\lambda, p, \lambda)_{ins},\ (\lambda, p', \lambda)_{ins}, (p', X, p)_{del}, (\lambda, b, \lambda)_{ins}]$$
$$p2 = [(\lambda, Y, \lambda)_{ins},\ (b, p, Y)_{del},\ (\lambda, p', \lambda)_{del}]$$

We simulate the rule $q\colon X \to Yb$, $X, Y \in N'$, $b \in N'' \cup T$, by the following rules:

$$q1 = [(\lambda, q, \lambda)_{ins},\ (\lambda, q', \lambda)_{ins}, (q, X, q')_{del}, (\lambda, b, \lambda)_{ins}]$$
$$q2 = [(\lambda, Y, \lambda)_{ins},\ (Y, q, b)_{del},\ (\lambda, q', \lambda)_{del}]$$

A rule $f\ :\quad AB\quad \to\quad \lambda$ is simulated by the following rules $[(\lambda, f, \lambda)_{ins}, (\lambda, A, f)_{del}, (f, B, \lambda)_{del}, (\lambda, f, \lambda)_{del}]$.
A rule $g\ :\quad CD\quad \to\quad \lambda$ is simulated by the following rules $[(\lambda, g, \lambda)_{ins},\ (\lambda, C, g)_{del}, (g, D, \lambda)_{del}, (\lambda, g, \lambda)_{del}]$.
A rule $h : S' \to \lambda$ is simulated by $[(\lambda, S', \lambda)_{del}]$.

We now proceed to prove that $L(\Gamma) = L(G)$. We initially prove that $L(G) \subseteq L(\Gamma)$ by showing that Γ correctly simulates the application of the above rules p, q, f, g, h.

Working of $p : X \to bY$: Let $S \Longrightarrow_* \alpha X \beta \Longrightarrow_* \alpha bY\beta \Longrightarrow_* w$ be a derivation of some string $w \in L(G)$. We now show that this derivation can be simulated by $p : X \to bY$ as follows: Consider the string $\alpha X \beta$ and we now apply the rules of matrix $p1$. The markers p and p' are randomly inserted in the first two rules. However the third rule is applicable only when p' and p are inserted before and after the non-terminal X. After X has been deleted, b is then inserted in a context-free manner. At this point, we note that matrix $p1$ cannot be applied again since there is only one non-terminal of N' (in this case, X) and this is deleted. On applying matrix $p2$, Y is inserted anywhere and then p is deleted in the contexts of b and Y. The importance of p' here is to make sure that the left context of p is the introduced b only. Finally, p' is deleted.

Working of $q : X \to Yb$: Similar to the working of the above p rule.

The working of the rules f, g, h are simple and hence on starting at S and by repeatedly applying the rules p, q, f, g, h, we eventually get $S \Longrightarrow_* w$. This proves that $L(G) \subseteq L(\Gamma)$. To prove the reverse relation $(L(\Gamma) \subseteq L(G))$, we observe that the rules of Γ are applied in groups and each group of rules corresponds to one of p, q, f, g, h. This observation completes the proof.   □

We could use ideas similar to in the previous simulation to show that RE equals $\mathrm{MAT}(3; 1, 1, 1; 1, 0, 0)$. However, with a different simulation strategy, we can obtain a stronger result.

Theorem 4. $\mathrm{MAT}(2; 1, 1, 1; 1, 0, 0) = \mathrm{RE}$.

Proof. Let $G = (N, T, P, S)$ be a type-0 grammar in Penttonen normal form [24] where the context-free rules are of the form $X \to YZ, X \to a, \ X \to \lambda$ and the non-context-free rule is of the form $XY \to XZ$ where $X, Y, Z \in N, \ a \in T$. The rules from P are labelled injectively with labels from $[1 \ldots |P|]$. We now construct a matrix ins-del system $\Gamma = (V, T, \{S\}, R)$ with $V = N \cup T \cup \{p, p', p'', q, q', f, f'\}$ and the set of matrices R is defined as follows.

We simulate the rule $p : X \to YZ$, where $X, Y, Z \in N$, by the following rules:

$$p1 = [(\lambda, p, X)_{ins}, (X, p'', \lambda)_{ins}]$$
$$p2 = [(\lambda, X, \lambda)_{del}, (p, p', p'')_{ins}]$$
$$p3 = [(p, Y, p')_{ins}, (\lambda, p, \lambda)_{del}]$$
$$p4 = [(p', Z, p'')_{ins}, (\lambda, p', \lambda)_{del}]$$
$$p5 = [(\lambda, p'', \lambda)_{del}]$$

We simulate the rule $q : X \to a, X \in N, \ a \in T$ by the following rules:

$$q1 = [(\lambda, q, X)_{ins}, (X, q', \lambda)_{ins}]$$
$$q2 = [(\lambda, X, \lambda)_{del}, (q, a, q')_{ins}]$$
$$q3 = [(\lambda, q, \lambda)_{del}, (\lambda, q', \lambda)_{del}]$$

We simulate the rule $f : XY \to XZ$, where $X, Y, Z \in N$ by the following rules:

$$f1 = [(Y, f', \lambda)_{ins}, (X, f, Y)_{ins}]$$
$$f2 = [(\lambda, Y, \lambda)_{del}, (f, Z, f')_{ins}]$$
$$f3 = [(\lambda, f, \lambda)_{del}, (\lambda, f', \lambda)_{del}]$$

A rule $h : X \to \lambda X \in N$ in P is simulated by the simple rule $[(\lambda, X, \lambda)]$.

We now proceed to prove that $L(\Gamma) = L(G)$. We initially prove that $L(G) \subseteq L(\Gamma)$ by showing that Γ correctly simulates the application of the above rules p, q, f, g, h.

Working of $p : X \to YZ$: Using the rule $p1$, p and p'' are inserted to the sides of X and using $p2$, the X for which the rule to be applied is removed. The contexts p and p'' in rule 2 of $p2$ make sure that the correct X is deleted. Then, using the matrix $p3$ and $p4$ (they can be applied in any order), the corresponding Y and Z are introduced at the appropriate position. The markers are deleted using the rule $p3, p4$ and $p5$. Though the rule $p1$ can be applied several times, applying it repeatedly will end up with strings having nonterminals, thus, such words will not be counted in the language.

Working of $q : X \to a$: Using the matrix $q1$, the nonterminals q and q' will mark which nonterminal to be deleted. Then, using $q2$ the nonterminal X for which the rule $X \to a$ to be applied is deleted.and a is introduced in the place of the deleted symbol X. With the remaining matrix $q3$, the used markers q, q' are deleted.

Working of $f : XY \to XZ$: To simulate such a rule, it is to be noted that if we replace Z in the place of Y, then it is sufficient. To do so, by using the matrix $f1$, we introduce markers f and f' on the left of Y and on the right of Y respectively. Using $f2$, Z is replaced by Y and f, f' are deleted by using the rule $f3$.

To prove the reverse relation $(L(\Gamma) \subseteq L(G))$, we observe that the rules of Π are applied in groups and each group of rules corresponds to one of p, q, f, h. This observation completes the proof. $\qquad\square$

It is known [21] that LIN is incomparable with $\text{MAT}(1; 1, 1, 1; 0, 0, 0)$. First of all, this shows that the previous result is optimal with respect to the allowed resources. Second, this arouses some interest in simulating linear languages with parsimonious resources. We follow this second line of research in the following.

5   Linear Languages

Theorem 5. $\text{LIN} \subsetneq \text{MAT}(2; 2, 1, 0; 1, 0, 0)$.

Proof. Consider a linear grammar $G = (N, T, P, S)$ with rules of the form $A \to aB$, $A \to Ba$ and $A \to \lambda$ for $A, B \in N$, $A \neq B$, and $a \subset T$. We construct a matrix insertion-deletion system $\Gamma = (V, T, \{S\}, R)$ with $V = N \cup T$. The set of matrices of R of Γ is defined as follows; notice that $|P| = |M|$.
$A \to aB$ is simulated by the matrix $[(A, aB, \lambda)_{ins}, (\lambda, A, \lambda)_{del}]$.
$A \to Ba$ is simulated by the matrix $[(A, Ba, \lambda)_{ins}, (\lambda, A, \lambda)_{del}]$.
$A \to \lambda$ is simulated by the matrix $[(\lambda, A, \lambda)_{del}]$.
Since the working of the above rules is simple and straightforward, we conclude $L(\Gamma) = L(G)$. The strictness of the inclusion follows from Example 1. $\qquad\square$

As LIN is closed under reversal, Corollary 2 yields:

Theorem 6. LIN $\subsetneq$ MAT$(2; 2, 0, 1; 1, 0, 0)$.

Theorem 7. LIN $\subsetneq$ MAT$(3; 1, 1, 0; 1, 0, 0)$.

Proof. We only give the three rules that work similar to the rules of Theorem 5.
$A \rightarrow aB$ is simulated by the matrix $[(A, B, \lambda)_{ins}, (A, a, \lambda)_{ins}, (\lambda, A, \lambda)_{del}]$.
$A \rightarrow Ba$ is simulated by the matrix $[(A, a, \lambda)_{ins}, (A, B, \lambda)_{ins}, (\lambda, A, \lambda)_{del}]$.
$A \rightarrow \lambda$ is simulated by the matrix $[(\lambda, A, \lambda)_{del}]$.   □

As LIN is closed under reversal, Corollary 2 yields:

Theorem 8. LIN $\subsetneq$ MAT$(3; 1, 0, 1; 1, 0, 0)$.

As LIN is not closed under Kleene star, it is interesting to note that matrix ins-del system of the above discussed sizes can also simulate the family of L^* where $L \in$ LIN. We present this in the following theorems.

Theorem 9. *If $L \in$ LIN, then $L^* \in$ MAT$(2; 2, 1, 0; 1, 0, 0)$.*

Proof. Theorem 5, $L \in$ MAT$(2; 2, 1, 0; 1, 0, 0)$. Let $\Gamma = (V, T, \{S\}, R)$ be the corresponding matrix ins-del system for L. We now construct a matrix ins-del system Γ' for L^* as follows: Let $\Gamma' = (V', T, \{\#S\}, R')$ where $V' = V \cup \{\#, g, g'\}$ and R' is the set of following matrices:
The rule $X \rightarrow aY$ is simulated by the matrix $[(X, aY, \lambda)_{ins}, (\lambda, X, \lambda)_{del}]$.
The rule $X \rightarrow Ya$ is simulated by the matrix $[(X, Ya, \lambda)_{ins}, (\lambda, X, \lambda)_{del}]$.
The rule $X \rightarrow a$ is simulated by the following matrices:

$$g1 = [(X, gg', \lambda)_{ins}, (\lambda, X, \lambda)_{del}]$$
$$g2 = [(g, a, \lambda)_{ins}, (\lambda, g, \lambda)_{del}]$$
$$g3 = [(\lambda, g', \lambda)_{del}, (\#, S, \lambda)_{ins}]$$
$$g4 = [(\lambda, \#, \lambda)_{del}, (\lambda, S, \lambda)_{del}]$$

The sequence of matrices $g1, g2, g3$ simulates the rule $g : X \rightarrow a$ and then continues to simulate the linear grammar again. This is achieved by appropriately inserting S to the right of $\#$ This enables us to start the process of simulation again for any desired number of times. The matrix $g4$ implements the stopping condition. From these arguments, it is easy to see that $L(\Gamma') = L^*$.   □

As LIN is known to be closed under reversal and as $(L^*)^R = (L^R)^*$, the family of languages that can be written as L^*, with $L \in$ LIN, is closed under reversal, as well. Hence, by Corollary 2, we conclude the following result.

Theorem 10. *If $L \in$ LIN, then $L^* \in$ MAT$(2; 2, 0, 1; 1, 0, 0)$.*

Small changes to the previous arguments (e.g., simulating $X \rightarrow aY$ by the matrix $[(X, Y, \lambda)_{ins}, (X, a, \lambda)_{ins}, (\lambda, X, \lambda)_{del}]$ and $X \rightarrow a$ by the matrices $g1' = [(X, g', \lambda)_{ins}, (X, g, \lambda)_{ins}, (\lambda, X, \lambda)_{del}], g2, g3$ and $g4$) lead to the following results.

Theorem 11. *If $L \in$ LIN, then $L^* \in$ MAT$(3; 1, 1, 0; 1, 0, 0)$.*

Theorem 12. *If $L \in$ LIN, then $L^* \in$ MAT$(3; 1, 0, 1; 1, 0, 0)$.*

6   Metalinear Languages

We now extend our simulations to the case of MLIN.

Theorem 13. MLIN $\subsetneq$ MAT$(2; 2, 1, 0; 1, 0, 0)$.

Proof. If $L \in$ MLIN happens to be a linear language, we can proceed as in Theorem 5. So, we assume that $L \in$ MLIN $-$ LIN is given. We can think of the work of a metalinear grammar G with $L(G) = L \subseteq T^*$ (generating the concatenation of k linear languages $L(G_1), \ldots, L(G_k)$ with start symbols $S_1, \ldots, S_k$, respectively, and k pairwise disjoint nonterminal alphabets $N_1, \ldots, N_k$) as follows: starting with $S_1 S_2'$ as the axiom, first, G_1 generates a terminal word. Then, $S_2' \to S_2 S_3'$ is executed, and starting from S_2, G_2 generates a terminal word. This strategy continues, until $S_{k-1}' \to S_{k-1} S_k'$ is executed, followed by the generation of a terminal word by G_{k-1} and finally $S_k' \to S_k$ initiates the last grammar G_k to append a terminal word.

We now formally construct a matrix ins-del system $\Gamma = (V, T, \{S_1 S_2'\}, R)$ for G. For $1 \leq i \leq k$, let V_i be the alphabet resulting from the construction of matrix ins-del system Γ_i for G_i according to Theorem 5. Let $V = \bigcup_{i=1}^{k} (V_i \cup \{S_i'\} \cup \{t_i, t_i', t_i''\})$. Let R_i be the rule set of G_i. Starting with the axiom $S_i S_{i+1}'$, all strings of $L(G_i)$ are derived from S_i similar to Theorem 5. For a clearer understanding, we present the simulation of rules of R_i here:
The rule $p_i : X \to aY$ in R_i, is simulated by $p_i.1 = [(X, aY, \lambda)_{ins}, (\lambda, X, \lambda)_{del}]$.
The rule $q_i : X \to Ya$ in R_i is simulated by $q_i.1 = [(X, Ya, \lambda)_{ins}, (\lambda, X, \lambda)_{del}]$.
We simulate for $1 \leq i \leq k - 2$, the rule $t_i : X \to a$ in R_i of G_i as follows:

$$t_i.1 = [(X, t_i a, \lambda)_{ins}, (\lambda, X, \lambda)_{del}]$$
$$t_i.2 = [(\lambda, t_i, \lambda)_{del}, (S_{i+1}', t_i' S_{i+2}', \lambda)_{ins}]$$
$$t_i.3 = [(\lambda, t_i', \lambda)_{del}, (S_{i+1}', S_{i+1} t_i'', \lambda)_{ins}]$$
$$t_i.4 = [(\lambda, t_i'', \lambda)_{del}, (\lambda, S_{i+1}', \lambda)_{del}]$$

Namely, consider by induction a sentential form $w_1 \cdots w_{i-1} \alpha X \beta S_{i+1}'$, where $w_1 \in L(G_1)$, $\ldots$, $w_{i-1} \in L(G_{i-1})$, and $\alpha\beta \in T^*$ such that the sentential form $\alpha X \beta$ is derivable in G_i, starting from S_i. Applying now t_i in this situation results in $w_1 \cdots w_{i-1} \alpha a \beta S_{i+1}'$. We want to continue by replacing S_{i+1}' with $S_{i+1} S_{i+2}'$. Conversely, in Γ we have:

$$\underbrace{w_1 \cdots w_{i-1}}_{w'} \alpha X \beta S_{i+1}' \Longrightarrow_{t_i.1} w' \alpha t_i a \beta S_{i+1}' \Longrightarrow_{t_i.2} w' \alpha a \beta S_{i+1}' t_i' S_{i+2}' \Longrightarrow_{t_i.3}$$

$$w' \alpha a \beta S_{i+1}' S_{i+1} t_i'' S_{i+2}' \Longrightarrow_{t_i.4} w' \alpha a \beta S_{i+1} S_{i+2}'.$$

Notice that the special symbols t_i, t_i', t_i'' that are introduced and checked in the matrices $t_i.j$ prevent any other sequence of matrix applications from happening but the intended one, as explained above. For $i = k - 1$, we take the same matrices, but interpreting $S_{i+2}' = S_{(k-1)+2}' = S_{k+1}'$ as the empty word. The rule $t_k : X \to \lambda$ is simulated by the matrix $t_k.1 = [(\lambda, X, \lambda)_{del}]$. This completes the proof, as the claimed strictness of the inclusion immediately follows from Example 1. $\qquad\square$

As MLIN is closed under reversal, Corollary 2 yields:

Theorem 14. MLIN $\subsetneq$ MAT$(2; 2, 0, 1; 1, 0, 0)$.

Theorem 15. MLIN $\subsetneq$ MAT$(3; 1, 1, 0; 1, 0, 0)$.

Proof. Due to Theorem 7, we can assume that $L \in$ MLIN $-$ LIN. Consider the working of a metalinear grammar G as discussed in the initial lines of Theorem 13. We now formally construct a matrix ins-del system $\Gamma = (V, T, \{S_1 S_2'\}, R)$ for G. For $1 \leq i \leq k$, let V_i be the alphabet resulting from the construction of matrix ins-del system Γ_i for G_i according to Theorem 5. Let $V = \bigcup_{i=1}^{k} (V_i \cup \{S_i'\} \cup \{t_i, t_i'\})$. Let R_i be the rule set of G_i. Starting with the axiom $S_i S_{i+1}'$, all strings of $L(G_i)$ are derived from S_i similar to Theorem 5. For a clearer understanding, we present the simulation of rules of R_i here:
The rules $X \rightarrow aY$ and $X \rightarrow Ya$ of R_i in G_i are simulated by the matrices $[(X, Y, \lambda)_{ins}, (X, a, \lambda)_{ins}, (\lambda, X, \lambda)_{del}]$ and $[(X, a, \lambda)_{ins}, (X, Y, \lambda)_{ins}, (\lambda, X, \lambda)_{del}]$ respectively. The working of these matrices is straightforward.
We simulate for $1 \leq i \leq k - 2$, the rule $t_i : X \rightarrow a$ in R_i of G_i as follows:

$$t_i.1 = [(X, a, \lambda)_{ins}, (X, t_i, \lambda)_{ins}, (\lambda, X, \lambda)_{del}]$$
$$t_i.2 = [(\lambda, t_i, \lambda)_{del}, (S_{i+1}', S_{i+2}', \lambda)_{ins}, (S_{i+1}', t_i', \lambda)_{ins}]$$
$$t_i.3 = [(\lambda, t_i', \lambda)_{del}, (S_{i+1}', S_{i+1}, \lambda)_{ins}, (\lambda, S_{i+1}', \lambda)_{del}]$$

Namely, consider by induction a sentential form $w_1 \cdots w_{i-1} \alpha X \beta S_{i+1}'$, where $w_1 \in L(G_1), \ldots, w_{i-1} \in L(G_{i-1})$, and $\alpha, \beta \in T^*$ such that the sentential form $\alpha X \beta$ is derivable in G_i, starting from S_i. Applying now t_i in this situation results in $w_1 \cdots w_{i-1} \alpha a \beta S_{i+1}'$. We want to continue by replacing S_{i+1}' with $S_{i+1} S_{i+2}'$. Conversely, in Γ we have: $w_1 \cdots w_{i-1} \alpha X \beta S_{i+1}' \Longrightarrow_{t_i.1} w_1 \cdots w_{i-1} \alpha t_i a \beta S_{i+1}'$. Notice that the special symbols t_i and t_i' prevent any other sequence of matrix applications from happening but the intended one, as explained above. For $i = k - 1$, we take the same matrices, but interpreting S_{i+2}' as the empty word. The rule $t_k : X \rightarrow a$ is simulated by $t_k.1 = [(X, a, \lambda)_{ins}, (\lambda, X, \lambda)_{del}]$. The strictness of the inclusion immediately follows from Examples 1 and 2. $\qquad \square$

As MLIN is closed under reversal, Corollary 2 yields:

Theorem 16. MLIN $\subsetneq$ MAT$(3; 1, 0, 1; 1, 0, 0)$.

Theorem 17. *If $L \in$ MLIN, then $L^* \in$ MAT$(2; 2, 1, 0; 1, 0, 0)$.*

Proof. By Theorem 13, $L \in$ MAT$(2; 2, 1, 0; 1, 0, 0)$. Let $\Gamma = (V, T, \{S\}, R)$ be the corresponding matrix ins-del system for L. We now construct a matrix ins-del system Γ'' for L^* as follows: Let $\Gamma'' = (V'', T, \{\#S_1 S_2', \lambda\}, R'')$ where $V'' = V \cup \{\#, g_i, g_i', g_i''\}$ and R'' is the set of matrices $\{ [(X, aY, \lambda)_{ins}, (\lambda, X, \lambda)_{del}],$ $[(X, Ya, \lambda)_{ins}, (\lambda, X, \lambda)_{del}], M\}$ where M contains the matrices collected in Table 1. The working of the matrices in this case is similar to the working of the matrices in Theorem 13. When $i = k$, $\alpha X \beta \Longrightarrow_{g_i.1} \alpha a g_i \beta$. At this point, we have a choice of applying the matrix $g_i.2$ or $g_i.4$. In the former case, we have

$\#S_1S_2'$ in the string and this enables us to simulate L again and this can be done as many number of times as desired. The latter case is the stopping condition. Since the axiom set of the grammar contains λ, L^* is generated. $\square$

As MLIN is known to be closed under reversal and as $(L^*)^R = (L^R)^*$, the family of languages that can be written as L^*, with $L \in$ MLIN, is closed under reversal, as well. Hence, by Corollary 2, we conclude the following result.

Theorem 18. *If $L \in$ MLIN, then $L^* \in$ MAT$(2; 2, 0, 1; 1, 0, 0)$.*

Theorem 19. *If $L \in$ MLIN, then $L^* \in$ MAT$(3; 1, 1, 0; 1, 0, 0)$.*

Proof. By Theorem 15, $L \in$ MAT$(3; 1, 1, 0; 1, 0, 0)$. Let $\Gamma = (V, T, \{S\}, R)$ be the corresponding matrix ins-del system for L. We now construct a matrix ins-del system Γ'' for L^* as follows: Let $\Gamma'' = (V'', T, \{\#S_1S_2', \lambda\}, R'')$ where $V'' = V \cup \{\#, f_i, f_i'\}$ and R'' is the set of matrices: $\{ [(X, Y, \lambda)_{ins}, (X, a, \lambda)_{ins}, (\lambda, X, \lambda)_{del}],$ $[(X, a, \lambda)_{ins}, (X, Y, \lambda)_{ins}, (\lambda, X, \lambda)_{del}],$ M' $\}$ where M' is the following set of f_i matrices.

$$f_i.1 = [(X, f_i, \lambda)_{ins}, (X, a, \lambda)_{ins}, (\lambda, X, \lambda)_{del}] \text{ for } 1 \leq i \leq k$$

$$f_i.2 = \begin{cases} [(\lambda, f_i, \lambda)_{del}, (S_{i+1}', f_i', \lambda)_{ins}, (S_{i+1}', S_{i+2}', \lambda)_{ins}] \text{ for } 1 \leq i \leq k-2 \\ [(\lambda, f_i, \lambda)_{del}, (S_{i+1}', f_i', \lambda)_{ins} \text{ for } i = k-1 \\ [(\lambda, f_i, \lambda)_{del}, (\#, S_2', \lambda)_{ins}, (\#, S_1, \lambda)_{ins}] \text{ for } i = k \end{cases}$$

$$f_i.3 = \begin{cases} [(\lambda, f_i', \lambda)_{del}, (S_{i+1}', S_{i+1}, \lambda)_{ins}, (\lambda, S_{i+1}', \lambda)_{del}] \text{ for } 1 \leq i \leq k-1 \\ [(\lambda, f_i, \lambda)_{del}, (\lambda, \#, \lambda)_{del}] \text{ for } i = k. \end{cases}$$

The working of the matrices in this case is similar to the working of the matrices in Theorem 15. When $i = k$, $\alpha X \beta \Longrightarrow_{f_i.1} \alpha f_i a \beta$. At this point, we have a choice of applying the matrix $f_i.2$ or $f_i.3$. In the former case, we have $\#S_1S_2'$ in the string and this enables us to simulate L again and this can be done as many number of times as desired. The latter case is the stopping condition. We note that this grammar generates L^+. However, since the axiom set of the grammar contains λ, L^* is generated. $\square$

Table 1. The simulation of the Kleene star of a metalinear language

$$g_i.1 = [(X, ag_i, \lambda)_{ins}, (\lambda, X, \lambda)_{del}] \text{ for } 1 \leq i \leq k$$

$$g_i.2 = \begin{cases} [(\lambda, g_i, \lambda)_{del}, (S_{i+1}', S_{i+2}'g_i', \lambda)_{ins}] \text{ for } 1 \leq i \leq k-2 \\ [(\lambda, g_i, \lambda)_{del}, (S_{i+1}', g_i', \lambda)_{ins}] \text{ for } i = k-1 \\ [(\lambda, g_i, \lambda)_{del}, (\#, S_1S_2', \lambda)_{ins}] \text{ for } i = k \end{cases}$$

$$g_i.3 = [(\lambda, g_i', \lambda)_{del}, (S_{i+1}', S_{i+1}g_i'', \lambda)_{ins}] \text{ for } 1 \leq i \leq k-1$$

$$g_i.4 = \begin{cases} [(\lambda, g_i'', \lambda)_{del}, (\lambda, S_{i+1}', \lambda)_{del}] \text{ for } 1 \leq i \leq k-1. \\ [(\lambda, g_i, \lambda)_{del}, (\lambda, \#, \lambda)_{del}] \text{ for } i = k. \end{cases}$$

As argued above, the family of languages that can be written as L^*, with $L \in$ MLIN, is closed under reversal, so that Corollary 2 yields:

Theorem 20. *If $L \in$ MLIN, then $L^* \in$ MAT$(3; 1, 0, 1; 1, 0, 0)$.*

7 Conclusions and Further Research Directions

In this paper, using matrix ins-del systems having either context-free insertion or deletion rules, we have obtained some (improved) computational completeness results and simulated linear and metalinear languages with small resource needs. We have also shown how to extend these simulations to cover Kleene stars of linear and metalinear languages without any additional size requirements.

The examples we considered so far might suggest that matrix ins-del systems with context-free insertion-deletion rules of small size only describe *mildly context-sensitive* languages. This is not the case in some sense [22], as we show in the below proposition. However, this observation deserves further study. Also, closure properties of these language classes are mostly unknown.

Proposition 1. MAT$(3; 1, 0, 0; 1, 0, 0)$ *contains non-semilinear languages.*

Proof. We can translate the vector addition system with states as given by Hopcroft and Pansiot [12] into some MAT$(3; 1, 0, 0; 1, 0, 0)$ system Γ. The axiom is Ac. We take the following rules:

$$m_1 = [(\lambda, A, \lambda)_{del}, (\lambda, c, \lambda)_{del}, (\lambda, A', \lambda)_{ins}],$$
$$m_2 = [(\lambda, A', \lambda)_{del}, (\lambda, b, \lambda)_{ins}, (\lambda, A, \lambda)_{ins}],$$
$$m_3 = [(\lambda, A, \lambda)_{del}, (\lambda, B, \lambda)_{ins}],$$
$$m_4 = [(\lambda, B, \lambda)_{del}, (\lambda, b, \lambda)_{del}, (\lambda, B', \lambda)_{ins}],$$
$$m_5 = [(\lambda, B', \lambda)_{del}, (\lambda, c, \lambda)_{ins}, (\lambda, B'', \lambda)_{ins}],$$
$$m_6 = [(\lambda, B'', \lambda)_{del}, (\lambda, c, \lambda)_{ins}, (\lambda, B, \lambda)_{ins}),$$
$$m_7 = [(\lambda, B, \lambda)_{del}, (\lambda, a, \lambda)_{ins}, (\lambda, A, \lambda)_{ins}], \text{ and}$$
$$m_8 = [(\lambda, A, \lambda)_{del}].$$

In the terminology of Hopcroft and Pansiot, the first two matrices simulate transition t_1; matrix m_3 simulates transition t_2; matrices m_4, m_5, m_6 simulate transition t_3; matrix m_7 simulates transition t_4. The matrix m_8 only serves to terminate if the simulates system was in a certain state. Lemma 2.8 in [12] shows that, with terminal alphabet $T = \{a, b, c\}$, $L(\Gamma) = \{w \in T^* \mid |w|_b + |w|_c \leq 2^{|w|_a}\}$, which is not semilinear. □

These observations motivated us to study Parikh images of languages described by matrix ins-del systems, focusing on context-free insertion-deletion rules, see [6].

We now present some further concrete research directions below.

– Proving a non-trivial simulation result for the family of context-free languages by context-free matrix ins-del systems with small size is left open.

- Most completeness results were obtained by simulating phrase structure grammars in Penttonen or in Geffert normal form. The reader might wonder if it would be more efficient to simulate other ins-del mechanisms, like graph-controlled ins-del systems, where also good computational completeness results are known, with only small descriptional complexities. One of the drawbacks in this approach is that the computational resources are counted quite differently, so that a small graph-controlled ins-del system would not lead to a small matrix ins-del system. Supposedly, this situation would change if other types of descriptional complexity measures would be used. For instance, apart from [17] and the literature quoted therein, we are not aware of any studies on the nonterminal complexity of controlled ins-del systems. In the case of controlled context-free grammars, it was then quite easy to transfer results between different forms of regulations, see [4,5,9] and the papers quoted therein.
- A further direction of future study could be aspects of parsing controlled ins-del systems. Also this area seems to be largely neglected, although it is clear that this is of much importance if it comes to finally applying these generative devices in language processing.

Acknowledgements. The second author acknowledges the project SR/S3/EECE/054/2010, Department of Science and Technology, New Delhi, India, for setting the platform to work in this domain.

References

1. Alhazov, A., Krassovitskiy, A., Rogozhin, Y., Verlan, S.: P systems with minimal insertion and deletion. Theor. Comput. Sci. **412**(1–2), 136–144 (2011)
2. Benne, R. (ed.): RNA Editing: The Alteration of Protein Coding Sequences of RNA. Molecular Biology. Ellis Horwood, Chichester (1993)
3. Biegler, F., Burrell, M.J., Daley, M.: Regulated RNA rewriting: modelling RNA editing with guided insertion. Theor. Comput. Sci. **387**(2), 103–112 (2007)
4. Fernau, N.: Nonterminal complexity of programmed grammars. Theor. Comput. Sci. **296**, 225–251 (2003)
5. Fernau, H., Freund, R., Oswald, M., Reinhardt, K.: Refining the nonterminal complexity of graph-controlled, programmed, and matrix grammars. J. Automata Lang. Comb. **12**(1/2), 117–138 (2007)
6. Fernau, H., Kuppusamy, L.: Parikh images of matrix ins-del systems. In: Cai, J.-Y., Cui, J., Sun, X. (eds.) TAMC 2016. LNCS. Springer, Heidelberg (2016)
7. Fernau, H., Kuppusamy, L., Raman, I.: Descriptional complexity of graph-controlled insertion-deletion systems. In: Câmpeanu, C., Manea, F., Shallit, J.O. (eds.) DCFS 2016. LNCS, vol. 9777, pp. 111–125. Springer, Heidelberg (2016)
8. Freund, R., Kogler, M., Rogozhin, Y., Verlan, S.: Graph-controlled insertion-deletion systems. In: McQuillan, I., Pighizzini, G. (eds.) Proceedings Twelfth Annual Workshop on Descriptional Complexity of Formal Systems, DCFS, vol. 31. EPTCS, pp. 88–98 (2010)
9. Freund, R., Păun, G.: On the number of non-terminal symbols in graph-controlled, programmed and matrix grammars. In: Margenstern, M., Rogozhin, Y. (eds.) MCU 2001. LNCS, vol. 2055, pp. 214–225. Springer, Heidelberg (2001)

10. Galiukschov, B.S.: Semicontextual grammars (in Russian). Mat. logica i mat. ling., Kalinin Univ., pp. 38–50 (1981)
11. Geffert, V.: How to generate languages using only two pairs of parentheses. J. Inf. Process. Cybern. EIK **27**((5/6)), 303–315 (1991)
12. Hopcroft, J.E., Pansiot, J.-J.: On the reachability problem for 5-Dimensional vector addition systems. Theor. Comput. Sci. **8**, 135–159 (1979)
13. Ivanov, S., Verlan, S.: Universality of graph-controlled leftist insertion-deletion systems with two states. In: Durand-Lose, J., Nagy, B. (eds.) MCU 2015. LNCS, vol. 9288, pp. 79–93. Springer, Heidelberg (2015)
14. Kari, L.: On insertion and deletion in formal languages. PhD thesis, University of Turku, Finland (1991)
15. Kari, L., Thierrin, G.: Contextual insertions/deletions and computability. Inf. Comput. **131**(1), 47–61 (1996)
16. Kuppusamy, L., Mahendran, A., Krishna, S.N.: Matrix insertion-deletion systems for bio-molecular structures. In: Natarajan, R., Ojo, A. (eds.) ICDCIT 2011. LNCS, vol. 6536, pp. 301–312. Springer, Heidelberg (2011)
17. Kuppusamy, L., Raman, I., Krithivasan, K.: On succinct description of certain context-free languages by ins-del and matrix ins-del systems. Int. J. Found. Comput. Sci. (2016, to appear)
18. Marcus, M., Păun, G.: Regulated Galiukschov semicontextual grammars. Kybernetika **26**(4), 316–326 (1990)
19. Marcus, S.: Contextual grammars. Revue Roumaine de Mathématiques Pures et Appliquées **14**, 1525–1534 (1969)
20. Margenstern, M., Păun, G., Rogozhin, Y., Verlan, S.: Context-free insertion-deletion systems. Theor. Comput. Sci. **330**(2), 339–348 (2005)
21. Martín-Vide, C., Păun, G., Salomaa, A.: Characterizations of recursively enumerable languages by means of insertion grammars. Theor. Comput. Sci. **205**(1–2), 195–205 (1998)
22. Michaelis, J., Kracht, M.: Semilinearity as a syntactic invariant. In: Retoré, C. (ed.) LACL 1996. LNCS (LNAI), vol. 1328, pp. 329–345. Springer, Heidelberg (1997)
23. Parikh, R.J.: On context-free languages. J. ACM **13**(4), 570–581 (1966)
24. Penttonen, M.: One-sided and two-sided context in formal grammars. Inf. Control (now Inf. Comput.) **25**, 371–392 (1974)
25. Petre, I., Verlan, S.: Matrix insertion-deletion systems. Theor. Comput. Sci. **456**, 80–88 (2012)
26. Păun, G., Rozenberg, G., Salomaa, A.: DNA Computing: New Computing Paradigms. Texts in Theoretical Computer Science. An EATCS Series. Springer, Heidelberg (1998)
27. Stabler, E.: Varieties of crossing dependencies: structure dependence and mild context sensitivity. Cogn. Sci. **28**, 699–720 (2004)
28. Verlan, S.: Recent developments on insertion-deletion systems. Comput. Sci. J. Moldova **18**(2), 210–245 (2010)

Evolving Carbon Nanotube Reservoir Computers

Matthew Dale[1,3]([✉]), Julian F. Miller[2,3],
Susan Stepney[1,3], and Martin A. Trefzer[2,3]

[1] Department of Computer Science, University of York, York, UK
[2] Department of Electronics, University of York, York, UK
[3] York Centre for Complex Systems Analysis, York, UK
md596@york.ac.uk

Abstract. Reservoir Computing is a useful general theoretical model for many dynamical systems. Here we show the first steps to applying the reservoir model as a simple computational layer to extract exploitable information from physical substrates consisting of single-walled carbon nanotubes and polymer mixtures. We argue that many physical substrates can be represented and configured into working reservoirs given some *pre-training* through evolutionary selected input-output mappings and targeted input stimuli.

Keywords: Material computation · Evolution-*in-Materio* · Reservoir Computing · Unconventional computing · Evolvable hardware

1 Introduction

Reservoir Computing (RC) [6,11] has been proposed as an expressive model and as a computationally inexpensive method for training rich high-dimensional dynamical systems, ranging from simulated and biological neural networks to novel hardware-based implementations [9]. RC exploits the emergent complexity of dynamic networks to perform information processing tasks.

An input-driven Reservoir Computer is typically divided into three parts: the input, the "reservoir", and the readout. This separation provides a representation that exploits the complex projection of the input into a high-dimensional state space. This rich state space is created from a *black-box* network and is harnessed using only a simple output training mechanism.

Most reservoirs are hand-crafted to a task, so there is often a need for expert domain knowledge to design an optimal system. However, due to the system partitioning, some element of semi-autonomous *pre-training* is possible, avoiding the need for manual search for efficient reservoirs. This pre-training concept appears in the RC literature [9], but is typically used only for simulated reservoirs. We hypothesise that pre-training can be highly advantageous when moving into the physical domain.

© Springer International Publishing Switzerland 2016
M. Amos and A. Condon (Eds.): UCNC 2016, LNCS 9726, pp. 49–61, 2016.
DOI: 10.1007/978-3-319-41312-9_5

Evolution-in-Materio (EIM) [12,13] explores the concept of *configuring* matter for computation, originally outside the context of RC. The training procedure uses an evolutionary algorithm to configure a rich continuous complex material to perform desired tasks. This usually takes the form of evolving a set of signals or static voltages and their connection locations on an electrode array interfacing the computational material. The aim is to evolve an input-output mapping that carries out a desired computational mapping. Its rationale is that physical systems contain enormous amounts of complexity, and that evolution exhibits the most efficient method to discover and exploit these physical properties.

Here we investigate the use of computer controlled evolution (CCE) to configure a physical system for RC. We demonstrate that by using a form of evolution-in-materio we can pre-train a physical dynamical system – which might not necessarily be a natural reservoir candidate – into a functional and optimisable reservoir computing system. We demonstrate this on two temporal reservoir computing tasks: the Nonlinear Auto Regressive Moving Average task (NARMA) and the wave generator task, each requiring different internal characteristics. We compare four different carbon nanotube-based materials, a conductive sheet, and an open-circuit system.

2   Reservoir Computing

Reservoir computing exploits the dynamic response of an excitable system given a single- or multi-dimensional input signal. Typically, the reservoir has some nonlinear properties, enabling both dynamic memory and dynamic processing. RC has become a competitive technique for training Recurrent Neural Networks (RNNs) on temporal processing tasks.

The conceptual view of what makes a "reservoir" and the methods used to train them is not limited to simulated neural networks. For example, Optoelectronic and Photonic [1,15,19] reservoir-based systems can be made. Such highly specialised reservoirs require some amount of *pre-* and *post*-processing.

However, other material reservoirs require minimal additional processing. For example, one of the first *physical* reservoirs was simply a bucket of water [5]. A fabricated neuromorphic device called an Atomic Switch Network (ASN) has been modelled as a reservoir [17,18].

There, communication with the reservoir—a configurable memristive network—takes place through a multiple input/output micro-electrode array. The memristive substrate contains a random topology of highly-integrated functionalised silver nanowires that together create emergent behaviours.

We use a basic model reservoir (based on the Echo State Network [6]) consisting of a randomly initialised recurrent *tanh*-based neural network with n nodes. The input(s) to the network $u(n)$ are fed through connection weights W^{in} with a one-to-one mapping to internal nodes. The internal nodes are mapped to each other via the random W matrix, creating the recurrent structure through internal loops. The output of the system $y(n)$ is given by the matrix multiplication of trainable output weights W^{out} and the reservoir's internal states $x(n)$.

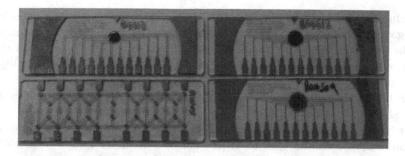

Fig. 1. Substrates under test. Top left, SWCNT/PBMA mixture with a concentration of 1 % SWCNT by weight. Top right, SWCNT/PBMA 0.53 %. Bottom left, gold resistor array. Bottom right, SWCNT/PMMA 0.1 %

We consider *supervised* machine learning tasks where both the training input $u(n)$ and target output $y^{Target}(n)$ are provided. Training is carried out by adjusting W^{out} to reduce the error between the system output $y(n)$ and target output $y^{Target}(n)$. To evaluate the reservoir's performance we partition the data sets into three parts: the *training* set (50 %), the *validation* set (25 %), and the *test* set (25 %). The output weights are trained on the training set, and reservoir fitness is evaluated on the validation set. The final error is calculated using the *Normalised Root Mean Squared Error*(NRMSE) on the test set data.

2.1 Optimising Reservoirs

Simulated Echo State Reservoirs have many parameters. One can change their dynamics and memory capacity by adjusting the global scaling factors for the weights. For example, the *spectral radius* ρ, a scaling parameter for the internal weights W, can dramatically influence the *echo state property* [6] (fading memory capacity) of the system. Other parameters such as topology, neuron sparsity and type of activation function can also be varied. This suggests that a certain amount of optimisation can be done over a "randomly" created reservoir.

A number of optimisation techniques have been explored in simulated networks, but few, if any, have been used in hardware-based reservoirs. This raises the question: can we create and train systems that might not 'naturally' form reservoirs, or are in their untrained state classed as poor reservoirs? We hypothesise that a system with interesting and malleable properties can be configured, or dynamically perturbed, into a state that produces effective reservoir properties.

3 Materials and Hardware

3.1 Materials Under Investigation

The materials used here were fabricated within the NASCENCE consortium [4]. The aim of that project was to investigate candidate materials and techniques for configuring materials for computation. Our work continues this agenda by investigating a substrate's response to reservoir-style training, to demonstrate that the reservoir computing model can be applied to a range of substrates.

Our experimental method is evaluated on 4 different material test subjects (Fig. 1) and two additional system "settings" (*short-circuit* and *open-circuit*) to provide both a description of how much the system as a whole is being evolved and to show what can be achieved with a purely conductive sheet.

The material for each test subject is deposited onto a glass slide with 12 chromium/gold-contact (40 to $50\,\mu m$ contact diameter and 100 to $150\,\mu m$ contact spacing) micro-electrodes arranged in either a circle or square array.

Test subjects one and two are single-wall Carbon Nanotube (SWCNT)/ polymer mixtures with SWCNT concentrations of 0.53 % and 1 % (by weight) mixed with poly-butyl-methacrylate (PBMA) dissolved in Anisole. Test subject three is a 0.1 % SWCNT mixture with poly-methyl methacrylate (PMMA). For each substrate, approximately 20 ml of the mixture is dispensed on the electrode array, then dried. The random formations and settling of SWCNTs within the samples can fluctuate. The conductivity of each material is determined by SWCNT density and electrode contact. The heterogeneous behaviour of the material is the result of the dielectric properties of the polymer and the shifting electronic properties of networks formed from both semi-conducting and metallic SWCNTs.

Test subject four is a reference material: a gold resistor array patterned onto a glass slide with multiple connection points using etch-back photo-lithography. The resistor array is arguably simpler and reasonably stable with known internal resistance values. This test subject investigates if the technique can be applied to more linear mediums and what, if any, are the advantages of SWCNT-based materials over simple resistive networks.

The *open* and *short* circuit settings are added to verify the significance the material has on the evolvability of the system, that is, to pinpoint what is doing the computation. In the open-circuit no material is connected; the system is simply left to find a solution through system noise, or from unknown characteristics within the system. The conductive sheet (copper tape) is used as a short-circuit connection to assess if the material has any advantageous properties beyond conductivity.

3.2   Hardware Platform

The hardware used in this experiment forms a hybrid digital/analogue hardware loop. Computer controlled evolution (CCE) is performed in the digital space on a connected desktop PC using a MATLAB interface. In the analogue/physical space, the material is stimulated using a National Instruments Data Acquisition Card (NI PCI-6723) supplying analogue output signals, which can be routed to any of the electrodes interfacing the material via an Analog Devices (AD75019) 16×16 analogue cross-point switch. An NI DAQ card (NI PCI-6225) is used to record analogue inputs from the electrode array via the cross-point switch in the same manner.

The cross-point switch is used to autonomously assign which electrodes and DAQ card channels are currently in use and what role each electrode performs. Once the evolved configuration is registered on the cross-point switch, bidirectional communication is established between both DAQ cards and the electrodes.

4 Material Configuration

As part of the NASCENCE project a number of stimulation signals have been investigated, such as complex signals like evolved square waves [10,14]. For the purpose of this investigation we are restricting ourselves to static voltages to avoid any interference, or artefacts, that evolution may create in respect to temporal-based tasks.

The electrical configuration of a material is therefore exclusively carried out through the placement and adjustment of static voltages. The aim is to configure the internal characteristics of the material by manipulating its natural dynamics, conductivity and signal processing abilities.

To encode the electrical configuration of the substrate a 21-gene genotype is created. All genes are open to mutation and are subdivided into: electrode assignment (genes 1–12), redundant genes (genes 13–16), values of static input voltages (genes 17–20) and input scaling on $u(n)$ (gene 21). Genes 1–16 are integer values; all other genes are floating point numbers with a precision of 4 decimal places; genes 17–20 range between [−5V, 5V]; gene 21's range is [0V, 2V] for the NARMA task (already pre-scaled by factor of 10) and [0V, 5V] for the wave generator task.

The phenotype of the system is implemented via the cross-point switch assignment. The interfacing equipment is set up so that all accessible inputs and outputs are connected to the switch. The switch then directs which DAQ channels communicate to the electrode array via a 256-bit digital input (SIN) derived from the values in genes 1–12.

This genome design allows evolution to decide both the number of readouts in use and the number of static input voltages the material can receive. At genotype instantiation, and under the mutation operator, a maximum of 10 possible readouts (referred to as measurable *reservoir states*) are possible.

This is due to the input signal $u(n)$ and ground (GND) always being required. A maximum of 4 static input voltages (referred to as "configuration voltages") can also be applied simultaneously. This feature (implemented by redundant genes) allows evolution to converge towards any assignment, such as 6 readouts and 4 configuration voltages, or, 8 readouts and 2 configuration voltages (Fig. 2), as long as the required phenotype size of 12 is always adhered to.

The input scaling gene (scaling $u(n)$) is added as the material may require varying input-data intensities under different electrical configurations. The gene is initialised at the maximum value, then left to evolve.

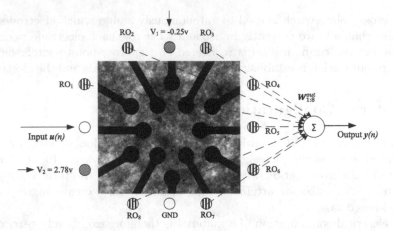

Fig. 2. Physical reservoir representation using electrodes. Each assigned readout electrode (RO_n) forms the reservoir state $x_n(n)$. The configuration voltages (V_n) location and value are decided upon by evolution. The W^{out} matrix is calculated and applied in the digital domain.

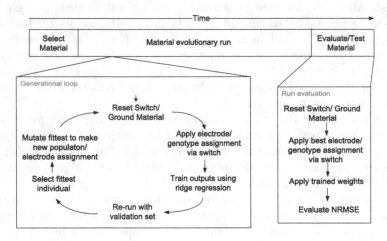

Fig. 3. Reservoir work flow through time: the combined evolutionary-regression training procedure for the hardware-based reservoir. The generational loop is expanded to show the switch assignment process and training/validation process. The final evaluation procedure using the test set is also expanded.

We use an elitist $1+\lambda$ evolutionary strategy with a population of 5 ($\lambda = 4$) for 150 generations across 10 runs. The λ children are mutations of the previous generation's fittest individual. In the case that a child is the same fitness as the parent, the child is selected to pass on its genes. This allows evolution to neutrally sweep the search space if no immediate fitness change is present.

The procedure is shown in Fig. 3. First, a material is selected, equating to a random initialisation of a simulated network. Next, the evolutionary run commences, cycling through the generational loop for every new population. This loop comprises: a physical resetting (grounding) of the material; the application of a new switch assignment (material "configuration") from the genotype for every individual; and a ridge regression (using Tikhonov regularisation) training step on the electrode output weights. The fitness of each individual in the generational loop is calculated on the validation set using NRMSE. The result, calculated on the best individual found in the evolutionary run, is the error calculated on the "unseen" test set.

5   Benchmark Tasks

5.1   Nonlinear Auto-Regressive Moving Average (NARMA) Task

The NARMA task originates from work on training recurrent networks [2]. It evaluates a reservoir's ability to model an n-th order highly non-linear dynamical system where the system state depends on the driving input as well as its own history. The challenging aspect of the NARMA task is that it contains both non-linearity and long-term dependencies created by the n-th order time-lag.

An n-th ordered NARMA experiment is carried out by predicting the output $y(n+1)$ given by Eq. (1) when supplied with $u(n)$ from a uniform distribution of interval $[0, 0.5]$. For the 5-th and 10-th order systems $\alpha = 0.3$, $\beta = 0.05$, $\delta = 10$ and $\gamma = 0.1$.

$$y(n+1) = \alpha y(n) + \beta y(n)\left(\sum_{i=0}^{\delta} y(n-i)\right) + 1.5u(n-\delta)u(n) + \gamma \qquad (1)$$

5.2   Wave Generator Task

The wave generator task requires a rich transformation of an input waveform (a periodic signal) to create a new waveform using temporal features such as phase shifts, delays, harmonic generation, recurrence etc. The task [17] is linked directly to Fourier series analysis. The task is to train a reservoir to produce three different output waveforms given an input sine wave. This is achieved by applying an input sine-wave to one electrode, to produce a square-wave, sawtooth, and cosine waveform of the same frequency, and a sine-wave with double frequency at $y(n)$.

5.3   Memory Capacity

Measuring the short-term memory capacity of a reservoir was first outlined in [7] as a quantitative measurement of the echo state property (fading memory). To determine the memory capacity of a reservoir we measure how many delayed versions of the input $u(n - k)$ the outputs can recall or recover with precision. Applying Eq. (2), we can measure memory capacity by how much variance of the delayed input can be recovered, summed over all delays. This is carried out by training individual output units to recall the input at time k.

$$MC = \sum_{k=1}^{\infty} MC_k = \sum_{k=1}^{\infty} \frac{cov^2(u(n-k), y(n))}{\sigma^2(u(n))\sigma^2(y(n))} \qquad (2)$$

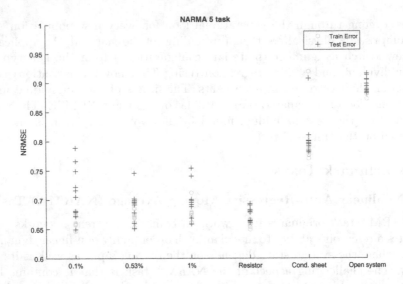

Fig. 4. NARMA-5 plot of train and test error of 10 runs across all materials (lower error is better fitness). All test subjects outperform the open system; all with the exception of some 0.1 % concentration runs outperform the conductive sheet in all runs.

6   Experimental Results

Figure 4 shows the NARMA-5 task results. The materials under test, when using the evolved configurations, outperform both the conductive sheet and the open system. This suggests the material is a significant element to the overall computational system, an assumption made within the literature but formally verified here, and that the computational properties of the material are trainable through evolution.

The resistor array produces better results with a smaller variance than the SWCNT materials on this task. However, this almost reverses for the test error when moving to the harder NARMA-10 task.

Figure 5 shows the NARMA-10 task results. The materials perform modestly on this task given the availability of trainable states (readouts). Although an exact comparison cannot be made, some indication of system performance on this task can be seen by looking at an optoelectronic reservoir [15] consisting of a 50-node psuedo-network reaching an NRMSE ≈ 0.41, and various sized simulated-reservoirs ranging from an NRMSE of 0.4 to 0.9 in [20].

The required memory capacity (MC) for each task correlates to the input lag and is therefore different for the two NARMA tasks. The measured MC does not change, however (Fig. 6). It could be that the material cannot increase its MC, given the small number of readouts available. Nevertheless it is puzzling: the MC should not be limited by the number of readouts, because the internal structure and dynamics of the system do not possess the same limitations.

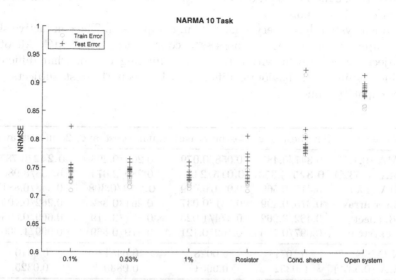

Fig. 5. NARMA-10 plot of train and test error of 10 runs across each material. Despite an increase in complexity the material still shows some computational advantage. The resistor array appears to struggle more on generalisation of the test data on this task.

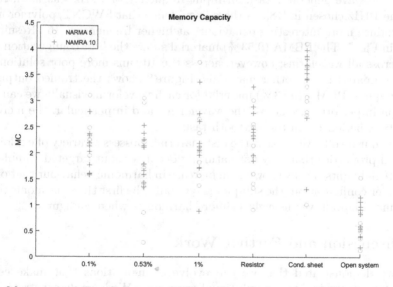

Fig. 6. Memory capacity of all test subjects post-evolutionary configuration, i.e. evaluated on the best configuration found from each run.

Alternatively, the method used to evaluate the material's memory capacity could be too susceptible to noise.

The open system has a very small MC in comparison. The conductive sheet, however, appears on average to possess a consistently larger MC. All of our test subjects appear to fit within this range, making it somewhat difficult to determine significant behavioural differences between the test subjects using memory capacity alone.

Material	Saw(best/avg)	Cos(best/avg)	Square(best/avg)	2Sin(best/avg)
PMMA (0.1%)	0.347/0.487	0.058/0.079	0.266/0.293	**0.242**/0.787
PBMA (0.53%)	**0.325**/4.358	**0.015**/2.915	0.289/2.074	0.255/8.986
PBMA (1%)	0.417/0.569	0.029/0.069	**0.253**/0.308	0.348/0.881
Resistor array	0.375/0.499	0.031/0.037	0.261/0.382	0.262/0.705
Cond. sheet	0.482/3.262	0.374/1.025	0.367/3.619	0.669/0.895
Open system	0.697/0.750	0.102/0.121	0.579/0.669	0.999/1.000
ASN (MSE)	0.1071	0.0028	0.0451	0.0910
PBMA (0.53%)	0.0352	0.0001	0.0830	0.0325

Fig. 7. Wave generator results for an input 1 kHz sine wave. Test Error is given for 10 runs. Additional MSE results are added for the PBMA (0.53 %) against ASN measurements given in [18].

For the wave generator task an input frequency of 1 kHz was used, rather than the 10 Hz chosen in [18], as there is evidence that SWCNT/polymer materials produce more interesting behaviours at higher frequencies [16]. Results are shown in Fig. 7. The PBMA (0.53 %) material shows the best configuration averaged across all waveforms; however, across the 10 runs more poor solutions are found compared to the other materials. Figure 8 shows the trained outputs of the configured PBMA (0.53 %) material for each waveform; visually we can see a variation in performance across the waveforms, and in particular, the increased difficulty experienced on the sawtooth task.

From our results we see that the test materials possess a variety of exploitable electrical properties that may not naturally occur without targeted stimulation. Figure 9 highlights this by showing an increase in harmonic behaviour that occurs only under configuration: the sub-plot shows only the first three harmonics occur when unconfigured, versus eight or more harmonics when configured.

7 Discussion and Further Work

We have demonstrated that we can evolve configurations that make certain substrates into trainable computational reservoirs. We have demonstrated that small, configurable (analogue) devices can be trained to tackle difficult system modelling and temporal tasks. The results provide an insight into the potential of the methodology, which is not limited to carbon-nanotube based materials.

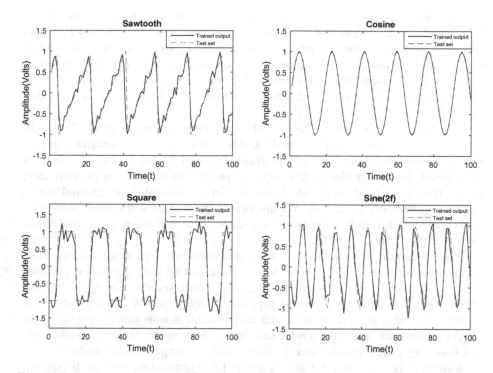

Fig. 8. Trained reservoir output (PBMA 0.53 %) plotted against the desired output for each waveform. All waveforms are trained and outputted simultaneously.

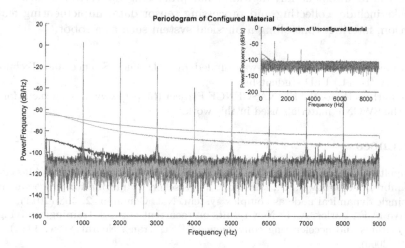

Fig. 9. Power spectral density of readout states on the wave generator task for the PBMA 0.53 % material. The main plot shows an increase in harmonic behaviour when the material is "configured". The subplot shows the unmodified material given an input 1 kHz sine-wave.

However, these results do leave room for improvement. Our results for the NARMA-10 task are modest in comparison to an optoelectronic reservoir (as shown in Sect. 6). However, the latter uses a much larger reservoir (50 nodes) and a different reservoir encoding: representation through a pseudo network using pre/post-processing and a long delay line. For the wave generator task, our configured materials are competitive with or outperform the Atomic Switch Network in [17].

The biggest limitation is the size of our current electrode array. The 6–10 input electrodes (and hence reservoir nodes in the model) is small in comparison to typical numbers of nodes in simulated and hardware-based reservoirs (hundreds). For larger electrode arrays we predict an increase in performance, as the training procedure should have an increased number of internal states and spatial diversity to exploit. We are currently increasing the array size to 64 electrodes, which requires hardware upgrades. This will allow us to undertake more complex temporal tasks.

Other fundamental investigations are still required, such as correlating electrical characteristics to evolved solutions and estimating the information processing capabilities of each material by examining its reservoir *quality*. To do the latter we will exploit a number of proposed metrics [3,8,9]. This involves the quantitative measurement of dynamics and associated reservoir properties. This should provide an improved understanding of how useful these materials are, and how they might behave over a wider range of computational problems.

This work is a first step towards a method in which substrates can be manipulated, or exploited, to extract machine-learning capabilities from an inherently analogue (physical) medium. This can offset the computational load on, or remove the requirement for, digital signal processing for certain tasks. Potential tasks include: collecting and processing sensor data, implementing feature extraction, filtering, controlling a physical system such as a robot.

Acknowledgments. This work was funded by a Defence Science and Technology Laboratory (DSTL) PhD studentship.

The authors thank the EU NASCENCE Project (http://www.nascence.eu) for providing the SWCNT materials used in this work.

References

1. Appeltant, L., Soriano, M.C., Van der Sande, G., Danckaert, J., Massar, S., Dambre, J., Schrauwen, B., Mirasso, C.R., Fischer, I.: Information processing using a single dynamical node as complex system. Nat. Commun. **2**, 468 (2011)
2. Atiya, A.F., Parlos, A.G.: New results on recurrent network training: unifying the algorithms and accelerating convergence. IEEE Trans. Neural Netw. **11**(3), 697–709 (2000)
3. Bertschinger, N., Natschläger, T.: Real-time computation at the edge of chaos in recurrent neural networks. Neural Comput. **16**(7), 1413–1436 (2004)
4. Broersma, H., Gomez, F., Miller, J., Petty, M., Tufte, G.: Nascence project: nanoscale engineering for novel computation using evolution. Int. J. Unconventional Comput. **8**(4), 313–317 (2012)

5. Fernando, C.T., Sojakka, S.: Pattern recognition in a bucket. In: Banzhaf, W., Ziegler, J., Christaller, T., Dittrich, P., Kim, J.T. (eds.) ECAL 2003. LNCS (LNAI), vol. 2801, pp. 588–597. Springer, Heidelberg (2003)
6. Jaeger, H.: The "echo state" approach to analysing and training recurrent neural networks-with an erratum note. Bonn, Germany: German National Research Center for Information Technology GMD Technical Report 148, 34 (2001)
7. Jaeger, H.: Short term memory in echo state networks. Tech. rep. no. GMD report 152. German National Research Center for Information Technology (2001)
8. Legenstein, R., Maass, W.: What makes a dynamical system computationally powerful. In: New Directions in Statistical Signal Processing: From Systems to Brain, pp. 127–154 (2007)
9. Lukoševičius, M., Jaeger, H.: Reservoir computing approaches to recurrent neural network training. Comput. Sci. Rev. **3**(3), 127–149 (2009)
10. Wang, X., Halang, W.: Evaluation. In: Wang, X., Halang, W. (eds.) Discovery and Selection of Semantic Web Services. SCI, vol. 453, pp. 109–126. Springer, Heidelberg (2013)
11. Maass, W., Natschläger, T., Markram, H.: Real-time computing without stable states: a new framework for neural computation based on perturbations. Neural Comput. **14**(11), 2531–2560 (2002)
12. Miller, J.F., Downing, K.: Evolution in materio: looking beyond the silicon box. In: NASA/DoD Conference on Evolvable Hardware 2002, pp. 167–176. IEEE (2002)
13. Miller, J.F., Harding, S., Tufte, G.: Evolution-in-materio: evolving computation in materials. Evol. Intell. **7**(1), 49–67 (2014)
14. Nichele, S., Lykkebo, O.R., Tufte, G.: An investigation of underlying physical properties exploited by evolution in nanotubes materials. In: 2015 IEEE Symposium Series on Computational Intelligence, pp. 1220–1228. IEEE (2015)
15. Paquot, Y., Duport, F., Smerieri, A., Dambre, J., Schrauwen, B., Haelterman, M., Massar, S.: Optoelectronic reservoir computing. Sci. Rep. **2**, 287 (2012). (Article 287)
16. Lykkeb, O.R., Nichele, S., Laketic, D., Tufte, G.: Is there chaos in blobs of carbon nanotubes used to perform computation? In: The Seventh International Conference on Future Computational Technologies and Applications Future Computing 2015, pp. 12–17 (2015)
17. Sillin, H.O., Aguilera, R., Shieh, H., Avizienis, A.V., Aono, M., Stieg, A.Z., Gimzewski, J.K.: A theoretical and experimental study of neuromorphic atomic switch networks for reservoir computing. Nanotechnology **24**(38), 384004 (2013)
18. Stieg, A.Z., Avizienis, A.V., Sillin, H.O., Aguilera, R., Shieh, H., Martin-Olmos, C., Sandouk, E.J., Aono, M., Gimzewski, J.K.: Self-organization and emergence of dynamical structures in neuromorphic atomic switch networks. In: Adamatzky, A., Chua, L. (eds.) Memristor Networks, pp. 173–209. Springer, Heidelberg (2014)
19. Vandoorne, K., Mechet, P., Van Vaerenbergh, T., Fiers, M., Morthier, G., Verstraeten, D., Schrauwen, B., Dambre, J., Bienstman, P.: Experimental demonstration of reservoir computing on a silicon photonics chip. Nat. Commun. **5**, 3541 (2014)
20. Verstraeten, D., Schrauwen, B., D'Haene, M., Stroobandt, D.: An experimental unification of reservoir computing methods. Neural Netw. **20**(3), 391–403 (2007)

Global Network Cooperation Catalysed by a Small Prosocial Migrant Clique

Steve Miller[1](✉) and Joshua Knowles[2]

[1] School of Computer Science, University of Manchester, Manchester, UK
stevemiller.gm@gmail.com
[2] School of Computer Science, University of Birmingham, Birmingham, UK

Abstract. Much research has been carried out to understand the emergence of cooperation in simulated social networks of competing individuals. Such research typically implements a population as a single connected network. Here we adopt a more realistic premise; namely that populations consist of multiple networks, whose members migrate from one to another. Specifically, we isolate the key elements of the scenario where a minority of members from a cooperative network migrate to a network populated by defectors. Using the public goods game to model group-wise cooperation, we find that under certain circumstances, the concerted actions of a trivial number of such migrants will catalyse widespread behavioural change throughout an entire population. Such results support a wider argument: that the general presence of some form of disruption contributes to the emergence of cooperation in social networks, and consequently that simpler models may encode a determinism that precludes the emergence of cooperation.

Keywords: Evolution of cooperation · Evolutionary game theory · Public goods game · Complex networks

1 Introduction

A considerable amount of scientific work has been undertaken to explain the apparently paradoxical existence of cooperative behaviour in a world defined by the competitive basis of natural selection [1]. The question of how cooperation may emerge within a competitive environment is, by definition, predicated on cooperation being originally absent from the population. On such a basis, the original appearance of cooperation occurs as a random event, more specifically, a mutant behaviour in (rare) individual(s). We then consider whether such a mutation will be extinguished, or will achieve fixation throughout a population. Within investigations of network-reciprocated cooperation [2,3], models which abstract social networks to test mechanisms for the emergence of cooperation broadly follow approaches (implicitly) of this nature (see [4] for a review of such investigations).

The overwhelming majority of research studies in this field have considered a population to be one single connected network. However in the real world,

© Springer International Publishing Switzerland 2016
M. Amos and A. Condon (Eds.): UCNC 2016, LNCS 9726, pp. 62–74, 2016.
DOI: 10.1007/978-3-319-41312-9_6

multiple (relatively) discrete dynamic networks exist within populations, and at times, members of one social network may migrate to another. This is an aspect of cooperation in real-world scenarios which requires understanding, yet has thus far received little attention. In the work that follows, we isolate the key elements of such a scenario: namely, we have a primary network of interest, predicated on defector behaviour, and we consider the arrival of a very small group of connected individuals that have emigrated from a cooperative network.

Our investigations here also derive from a second motivating principle. In earlier work [5], we have described how population size fluctuation has a positive impact, in promoting the emergence of cooperation in networks. Commenting on this (ibid.), we suggested the possibility that the observed effect may be viewed as a generalised response to perturbation of networks, and that population size fluctuation may be only one way, amongst several, of perturbing a network to thus yield similar results. This notion hints at a potential issue: that models of cooperation which are overly deterministic, or lacking in noise, may preclude the cooperative phenomena we seek to investigate. In the work that follows we consider whether our findings add further support to this thinking.

2 Background

Here we highlight a few key elements of game theory relevant to this work. We then briefly consider existing research forming the basis for our investigations.

Within the context of evolutionary game theory, a variety of games are used to model social behaviours. A model of particular interest for investigating cooperation is the public goods game (PGG), otherwise referred to as the tragedy of the commons [6] or the n-person prisoner's dilemma. This game, being based on group-wise rather than pair-wise behaviour, is arguably more analogous to the complexity of real-world social interactions, than the standard prisoner's dilemma (PD), which only models interactions between paired individuals [7].

In the PGG, each participant can choose to contribute, or not, a fixed amount to a central 'pot'. This pot is then increased by a multiplier and redistributed amongst all participants, regardless of whether they contributed. The rational analysis of this game demonstrates that the selfish choice (defection), is the option which maximises an individual's payoff, however if all individuals exercise the same rationality, none will contribute and the public good will be minimised, hence we have a 'social dilemma'. Whilst the rational analysis predicts tragedy, real-world examples of cooperation (contributing to the public good) are abundant. It is this discrepancy between game theoretic predictions and empirical findings which research attempts to redress.

The PGG can be implemented within *evolving* social networks [8], using an approach where each member of the network in turn, initiates a PGG within a group which consists of the individuals it is directly connected to—its 'neighbourhood'. Any given individual in the network will be a neighbour of several other nodes, hence in addition to the PGG that a particular node initiates itself, it will also be a participant in PGGs initiated by others. It is this participation of an individual in multiple games with multiple opponents, i.e. *group-wise* interaction, which differentiates the PGG from its cousin in game theory—the prisoner's dilemma (PD). In the PD, an individual is able to retaliate or reciprocate in response to their partner's behaviour. In the PGG however, participants are not able to effectively target retaliation directly against defectors, since such retaliation (i.e. not contributing to the public good) harms cooperator and defector neighbours equally. The classical result for the PGG is that cooperation becomes less likely as neighbourhood size increases. This result can be appreciated intuitively, by considering that the more the neighbourhood size increases, (i.e. the closer it gets to having all members of the network participating), the more the game approximates the mean field scenario, where defection is the Nash equilibrium [9].

The above approach has been extended to demonstrate the emergence of cooperation, amongst evolving populations of individuals playing PGG, in *dynamic randomly growing* networks [10]. This development differs from earlier work in its use of two evolutionary elements, rather than one. The two elements are:

1. *Strategy updating*: This is the primary evolutionary mechanism, present in [8] and common to the majority of evolutionary game theoretic models used to investigate cooperation in networks. It represents intrinsic effects within the population, specifically, direct competition between two competing neighbours. This mechanism's effect is directly responsible for the spread of those strategies which confer greater fitness upon individuals. It does not however, in any way, affect the network topology.
2. *Population size fluctuation*: This secondary evolutionary mechanism [11] represents widespread 'environmental' effects that are explicitly extrinsic to the population. In the real world, examples might be disease, predation, food shortages, drought, many of which may be seasonal. Here a proportion of the less fit members of a society are periodically 'killed off'. Specifically, in the case of our implementation, individuals are removed from the population, along with the positions they occupied within the network due to their connections. This (fitness-based) process causes changes in the network topology, but it does not implement the spread of behaviours from one individual to another.

In the following, we investigate how a variety of network simulations, all predicated on originally non-cooperative behaviour, are affected by the arrival of a very small ($n \leq 3$) group of cooperative migrants. We initially describe, in detail, the implementation of our models. We then provide 'behaviour profiles' for a range of network scenarios and growth mechanisms, followed by deeper scrutiny of phenomena within the actual simulations that are of particular interest.

3   Methods

Our work is based on methodology presented in [8,10,12]. We here give a full description of our approach for completeness.

Our model describes agents located at the nodes of networks. Each node in the network has a 'neighbourhood', defined by the nodes its edges connect to. A PGG occurs for each neighbourhood and hence a network of N nodes will result in N PGGs. Each agent in the network has a behaviour encoded by a 'strategy' variable: 'cooperate' or 'defect', which determines whether it contributes to PGGs, or not, respectively.

The general outline of the evolutionary process, for one generation, is as follows:

1. *Play public goods games*: In a round-robin fashion, each agent initiates a PGG involving its neighbours. An agent's fitness score is the sum of payoffs from all the individual PGGs that it participates in.
2. *Update strategies*: Selection occurs. Agents with low scores will have their strategies replaced, on a probabilistic basis, by comparison with the fitness scores of randomly selected neighbours.
3. *Remove nodes*: If the network has reached the nominal maximum size, it is pruned by a tournament selection process that removes less fit agents.
4. *Grow network*: A specified number of new nodes are added to the network, each connecting to m randomly selected distinct existing nodes via m edges.

In the following, we provide more detail on each of the four steps:

Play public goods games. Each node of the network, in turn, initiates a PGG. Within a single PGG, all cooperator members of a neighbourhood contribute a cost c to 'the pot'. The resulting collective investment I is multiplied by r, and rI is then divided equally amongst all members of the neighbourhood, regardless of strategy.

Since an agent contributes a cost c to each game they participate in, their overall contribution, in one generation, is therefore $c(k+1)$ where k is the number of neighbours (degree). The single game individual payoffs of an agent x are given by the following equations, for scenarios where x is a defector (P_D) and a cooperator (P_C) respectively:

$$P_D = crn_c/(k_x + 1) \ , \tag{1}$$

$$P_C = P_D - c \ , \tag{2}$$

where c is the cost contributed by each cooperator, r is the reward multiplier, n_c is the number of cooperators in the neighbourhood based around x, and k_x is the degree of x.

Update strategies. Each node i selects a neighbour j at random. If the fitness of node i, f_i is greater or equal to the neighbour's fitness f_j, then i's strategy is unchanged. If the fitness of node i, f_i is less than the neighbour's fitness, f_j, then i's strategy is replaced by a copy of the neighbour j's strategy, according to a probability proportional to the difference between their fitness values. Thus poor scoring nodes have strategies displaced by those of more successful neighbours.

Hence, at generation t, if $f_i(t) < f_j(t)$ then i's strategy is replaced with that of the neighbour j with the following probability:

$$\Pi_{U_i}(t) = \frac{f_j(t) - f_i(t)}{fd\_max(k_i(t), k_j(t))} \ , \tag{3}$$

where k_i and k_j are degrees of node i and its neighbour j respectively. The purpose of the denominator is to normalise the difference between the two nodes, with $fd\_max(k_i(t), k_j(t))$ representing the largest achievable fitness difference between the two nodes given their respective degrees. In the absence of a mathematical approach to calculate this, we run simulations for all 4 combinations (of the 2 strategy types at the 2 nodes), to establish maximum possible difference.

Grow network. We add 10 new nodes (7 on the first generation), with randomly allocated strategies, per generation. Each new node uses m edges to connect to existing nodes. Duplicate edges and self-edges are not allowed. The probability $\Pi(t)$ that an existing node i receives one of the m new edges is given by the following equations, for random attachment (RA), degree-based preferential attachment (PA), and fitness-based evolutionary preferential attachment (EPA) [12], respectively:

$$\Pi_{RA_i}(t) = \frac{1}{N(t)} \ , \tag{4}$$

where $N(t)$ is the number of nodes available to connect to at time t in the existing network. (Given that in our model each new node extends $m = 2$ new edges, and multiple edges are not allowed, N is therefore sampled *without replacement*.)

$$\Pi_{PA_i}(t) = \frac{k_i(t)}{\sum_{j=1}^{N(t)} (k_j(t))} \ , \tag{5}$$

where $k_i(t)$ is the degree of an existing node i and $N(t)$ is the number of nodes available to connect to at time t in the existing network.

$$\Pi_{EPA_i}(t) = \frac{1 - \epsilon + \epsilon f_i(t)}{\sum_{j=1}^{N(t)} (1 - \epsilon + \epsilon f_j(t))} \ , \tag{6}$$

where $f_i(t)$ is the fitness of an existing node i and $N(t)$ is the number of nodes available to connect to at time t in the existing network. The parameter $\epsilon \in [0, 1)$ is used to adjust selection pressure. (We used $\epsilon = 0.99$ for 'strong' EPA.)

Growth only occurs at times when the network is below a nominal maximum size (we used $N_{max} = 1000$ nodes). For all added nodes, other than migrants, we set $m = 2$.

Remove nodes (for fluctuation simulations). Whenever the network achieves or exceeds the nominal maximum size, it is pruned by a percentage X. This is achieved by tournament selection using a tournament size equivalent to 1 % of the network. Tournament members are selected randomly from the network. The tournament member having the least fitness is the 'winner' and is added to a short list of nodes to be deleted. Tournament selection continues until the short list of $X\%$ nodes for deletion is fully populated.

The nodes on the short list (and all of their edges) are removed from the network. Any nodes that become isolated from the network as a result of this process are also deleted. (Failure to do this would result in small numbers of single, disconnected, non-playing nodes, having static strategies and zero fitness values.) When there are multiple nodes of equivalent low fitness value, oldest nodes are deleted first. Where $X = 0$, no deletions occur; in this case, on reaching maximum size, the network structure becomes static.

Migrant Clique Attachment. At generation 300, the migrant group connects to the existing primary network. Our migrant groups are small complete networks i.e. cliques, consisting of between 1 to 3 nodes (specific details in results section), all having cooperator strategies. Initial connection to the primary network is via only one of the nodes in the clique. This node extends either 1 or 2 edges (specific details in results section) to existing network nodes chosen at random. Once connected, the migrants are treated as a part of the primary network and are exposed to all elements of the evolutionary process described above.

General Simulation Conditions. In networks grown from founder members, initial nodes were populated with defector strategies. In 'pre-existing' networks, all nodes were populated with defectors. Strategy types of subsequently added nodes were allocated independently, uniformly at random (cooperators and defectors with equal probability). All networks had an overall average degree of approximately $k = 4$, hence an average neighbourhood size of $g = 5$ (since neighbourhood includes self). Simulations were run until 20,000 generations. Final 'fraction of cooperators' values we use are means, averaged over the last 20 generations of each simulation. Each simulation consisted of 25 replicates. We used a shrinkage value of $X = 2.5\%$ for all fluctuation simulations. Simulation data is recorded after step 2 (*Update strategies*).

4   Results and Discussion

We initially present our results using an approach common for investigations in this field. We aggregate data from multiple differing sets of simulations, plotting final fraction of cooperators against the variable, η, which is the PGG reward multiplier normalised with respect to the average neighbourhood size in the network. In Fig. 1a we present such 'behaviour profiles' for results from the 'simplified scenario' of pre-existing networks. These networks have initially random graph topology [13] and are initialised entirely with defectors. Figure 1b, illustrates the 'more realistic' scenario where we consider networks grown from their origins, in this case from 3 founder defector members. In both network scenarios we provide profiles for the three attachment mechanisms of RA, PA and EPA.

For the simpler scenario of pre-existing networks, initialised with all defectors (Fig. 1a) and having a fixed network size, we naturally observe zero cooperation

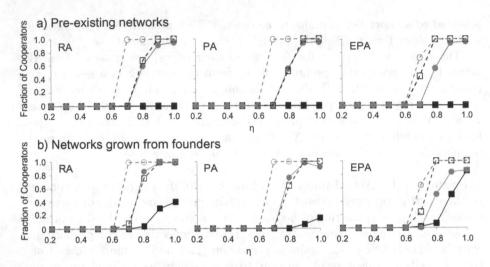

Fig. 1. Behaviour profile plots illustrating the impact of a migrant cooperator clique on the emergence of cooperation for three different attachment mechanisms: RA, PA and EPA. (**a**) shows pre-existing networks having initially random graph topology and initialised entirely with defectors. (**b**) shows networks grown from 3 defector founders. Final fraction of cooperators present is plotted against η (the PGG reward multiplier r normalised with respect to average neighbourhood size, $g = 5$). Migrant cliques consist of 3 connected cooperators, one of which attaches to the existing network randomly by 2 nodes. Green lines with circle markers are simulations featuring migrants. Black lines with square markers are controls (no migrants). Solid lines represent simulations that are fixed in their network topology. (In the case of **b**, topology becomes fixed upon population achieving maximum size.) Dashed lines represent fluctuating simulations (colour figure online).

(solid black lines) for all attachment mechanisms. In comparison, the migrant scenario (solid green line) precipitates cooperation once the temptation of the reward achieves a particular threshold ($\eta > 0.7$). In the case of fluctuating network size, we see that the migrants promote higher levels of cooperation than those seen in their absence (compare green dashed with black dashed lines), except in the case of EPA, where levels of cooperation have already been elevated by the increased network heterogeneity associated with this mechanism (see [14] for detailed information on the role of network heterogeneity in cooperation).

When we consider the more complex scenario of networks grown from founders (Fig. 1b), we see that our earlier findings still hold. Again, above a reward threshold ($\eta > 0.6$), the arrival of the migrants promotes widespread cooperation. We see this effect for networks that become static on reaching specified maximum size and also in those that fluctuate in size thereafter. We note that in the case of fluctuating models, we see little difference in final outcomes when comparing pre-existing networks with those grown from founders (compare corresponding coloured dashed lines in Figs. 1a and b). As described in earlier research [11], the fluctuation mechanism, by deleting low fitness nodes from within the network, can overcome the limitations of 'fossilised' (zero-fitness, defector-dominated) regions of the network in a manner that is not achievable by strategy updating between neighbours. Importantly, cooperation can be supported by a fluctuating population size, without the requirement for highly heterogeneous network topology: the fluctuation mechanism drives networks to a topology that has only moderately heterogeneous connectivity (in the form of a compressed exponential degree distribution) [10].

Whilst the behaviour profile plots above allow us to neatly characterise and compare different experimental simulations, they describe derived data which for the most part is of limited interest, whilst potentially masking more interesting phenomena. More specifically, as the value of the reward variable (η) is maximised/minimised, the dilemma becomes diminished and the dominant behaviour of populations becomes consistent and highly predictable. We suggest that in presenting abstracted representations of real-world scenarios, such regions of the behaviour profiles are of limited relevance.

It is the *mid-range* values of the reward variable that represent the social dilemma in its strongest form. We suggest that these regions are of particular importance in investigating the emergence of cooperation, since they represent the much more realistic challenge faced in nature by individuals attempting to *balance* cost versus reward, and in addition, where noise may likely be a confounding or contributory factor. Where we see transitions in population behaviour, where a mixture of competing behaviours exists, where the choice of cooperate or defect is not clear cut, and where noise may be present—these are the areas we are interested in.

We now explore the behaviour of our populations, in these regions of interest, by focusing on the behaviour of replicate simulations as they transition from defection to cooperation. From Figs. 1a and b, we see the widest variety of outcomes in the region approximately around where $\eta = 0.8$. Figure 2 illustrates individual time plots of simulations based on this value, for the simplified case of pre-existing networks initialised with defectors. The plots show simulations with the effects of fluctuation and immigration enabled, disabled, and acting in concert. We summarise from inspection of these plots that:

i The fluctuation mechanism on its own enables a majority of replicates to transition to cooperation. Similar levels of cooperation are achieved by all of those replicates that transition. Transition times however remain variable with some replicates failing to transition over the time period studied.

ii The isolated effect of migrant arrival drives higher levels of cooperation amongst replicates. In the case of this effect though (in contrast to our previous observation), it is the *levels* of cooperation achieved which are variable.

iii The combined impact of migrants together with fluctuating population size, results in all replicates transitioning to cooperation with consistency in both final levels of cooperation achieved, and also in transition times (all replicates transition within 200 generations of the arrival of the migrants).

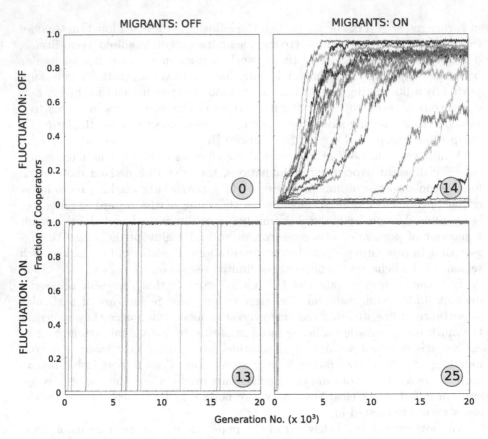

Fig. 2. Simulation time plots (25 replicates) illustrating the effects of migrant clique arrival and fluctuation, in pre-existing random networks initialised with defectors, with $\eta = 0.8$. Plots show number of cooperators over 20,000 generations. Migrant groups are complete networks of 3 cooperator nodes, 1 of which connects to 2 randomly selected existing network nodes. Network growth is by random attachment. All other details are as described in Methods section. Number of replicates transitioned to cooperation is shown in circle inset.

In Fig. 3 we illustrate similar time plots, in this case for the more complex scenario featuring networks grown from founder populations of 3 defectors. We observe that the findings seen earlier, for the simplified case of pre-existing networks, still hold: fluctuation alone promotes consistent levels of increased cooperation albeit with variable transition times; migrants alone promote cooperation albeit to varying levels; the combination of cooperator migrants and fluctuation brings consistency to both transition times and levels of cooperation achieved.

These findings are also robust to attachment mechanisms. For both of the network models illustrated above, in addition to random attachment (as represented in Figs. 2 and 3), the same observations also held when tested using both degree-based attachment (PA), and fitness-based attachment (EPA).

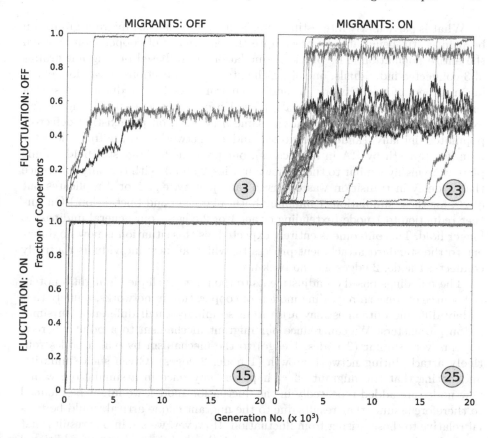

Fig. 3. Simulation time plots (25 replicates) illustrating the effects of migrant clique arrival and fluctuation, for networks grown from 3 defector founders, with $\eta = 0.8$. Plots show number of cooperators over 20,000 generations. Migrant groups are complete networks of 3 cooperators nodes, 1 of which connects to 2 randomly selected existing network nodes. Network growth is by random attachment. All other details are as described in Methods section. Number of replicates transitioned to cooperation is shown in circle inset.

The ability of the of the migrant clique to invade defector networks appears to arise from benefits conferred on the connecting migrant by the 'back-up' provided from its fellow migrants. These back-up migrants are initially immune to both strategy updating and the impact of defectors in reducing their payoff values (being as they are initially not directly connected to the network). The back-up migrants can boost the payoff (fitness) of a connecting migrant, so that during strategy updating, it can thus readily convert the existing network node it connects to, into a cooperator. Beyond initial possible payoff calculations, which can be established analytically, it becomes harder to pin down the details of the further spread of cooperation. However, it is clear from our investigations that in the case of migrant-triggered cooperation, it is this back-up which is key.

What is particularly interesting here, is just how small the migrant group can be, whilst still being able to precipitate the emergence of cooperation through the entire population. The previous simulations were based on migrant groups of 3 connected individuals, one of which extends 2 connections to random existing members of the network. In additional work, we have reduced the size of the migrant group to 2 individuals, of which one connects only 1 edge to an existing network node. Tested at the same η (= 0.8), on pre-existing defector-populated initially random networks, and on networks grown from defector founders (growth by RA in both cases), our previous findings still hold. (Time plots were highly similar to those shown in Figs. 2 and 3, with the only difference that a delay in transition was observed infrequently, e.g. 1 or 2 replicates out of 25, for those simulations combining both migration and fluctuation.) On further reduction to 1 node (extending either 1 or 2 edges), our general findings no longer hold. This outcome is entirely expected, as this situation is now no different to the standard attachment process by which all new individuals routinely connect—1 node, 2 edges, i.e. no back-up.

These findings based on adjustments to the migrant clique highlight a potential source of concern regarding models of cooperation in networks, namely that widely differing outcomes may arise from seemingly small differences in simulation parameters: We can reduce our migrant mechanism to a point where it appears very similar (2 nodes, 1 edge) to the mechanism by which nodes routinely attach during network growth (1 node, 2 edges). Given such similarity, and noting that the migrant effect happens only once in a simulation, whilst new nodes are added repeatedly in the fluctuation model, we might be inclined to therefore assume that results due to the migrant clique arrival would be trivial relative to those arising from fluctuation. However, we see in our results that the isolated, seemingly trivial, migrant event clearly brings about an additional change to populations, which is not achieved in its absence. The small difference between these two very similar mechanisms results in markedly different behavioural dynamics. Importantly, despite their apparent similarities, the attachment mechanism used for routine network growth clearly cannot create the additional opportunities for cooperation that the migrant clique's arrival can enable.

These results combined with findings of previous research, reinforce our belief that fluctuations in the network, or migrant cliques, or alternative mechanisms to perturb the system, bring an added dimension to models of cooperation in networks that simpler mechanisms fail to provide: It is these noisy perturbations of the network that disrupt the 'status quo' and catalyse the spread of cooperation throughout the population. If this assumption is correct then there is a risk that simpler, more deterministic models of cooperation in networks may lack the disruptive elements that promote cooperation and may thus preclude or impede its emergence.

5   Conclusion

Using various models of cooperation, based on the public goods game, we have investigated a scenario where individuals migrate, from a cooperative network, to join one that does not demonstrate cooperation. Under certain conditions, notably around the region where the social dilemma is at its strongest, we find quite striking results: The effect of a few concerted migrants catalyses a marked behavioural change, precipitating the widespread emergence of cooperation throughout the entire population. Of particular interest is our finding that the migrant group size can be extremely small and needs only to form one initial connection in order to initiate a marked response. The actions of a seemingly trivial group of concerted cooperators initiate changes throughout a population that is orders of magnitude larger than the migrant group.

We have hypothesised that perturbation, in the form of population size fluctuation, and also in the form of invading migrants, can promote cooperation. We have demonstrated this to be the case for both of these effects in isolation, and to a greater extent, in concert. Clearly other methods, or combinations of methods, for perturbing or disrupting networks exist that may yield similarly interesting results.

Our results reinforce previous work proposing that perturbations of networks, or possible alternative forms of disruption, are an important contributory feature in the emergence of cooperation. Taken generally, such observations suggest the potential for oversimplified or strictly deterministic models of cooperation in social networks, to limit or exclude the phenomena they seek to investigate. We highlight, in particular, that from a combination of two mechanisms studied here, there emerged a consistency in outcome that is unlikely to have been anticipated from studying simpler models of each mechanism in isolation.

Acknowledgements. This work has been funded by the Engineering and Physical Sciences Research Council (Grant reference number EP/I028099/1).

References

1. Axelrod, R., Hamilton, W.D.: The evolution of cooperation. Science **211**, 1390–1396 (1981)
2. Nowak, M.A., May, R.M.: Evolutionary games and spatial chaos. Nature **359**, 826–829 (1992)
3. Nowak, M.A.: Five rules for the evolution of cooperation. Science **314**, 1560–1563 (2006)
4. Perc, M., Szolnoki, A.: Coevolutionary games: a mini review. BioSystems **99**, 109–125 (2010)
5. Miller, S., Knowles, J.: Population fluctuation promotes cooperation in networks. Sci. Rep. **5** (2015). (Article Number 11054)
6. Hardin, G.: The tragedy of the commons. Science **162**, 1243–1248 (1968)
7. Perc, M., Gómez-Gardeñes, J., Szolnoki, A., Floría, L.M., Moreno, Y.: Evolutionary dynamics of group interactions on structured populations: a review. J. R. Soc. Interface **10**, 20120997 (2013)
8. Santos, F.C., Santos, M.D., Pacheco, J.M.: Social diversity promotes the emergence of cooperation in public goods games. Nature **454**, 213–216 (2008)
9. Nash, J.: Non-cooperative games. Ann. Math. **54**, 286–295 (1951)

10. Miller, Steve, Knowles, Joshua: The emergence of cooperation in public goods games on randomly growing dynamic networks. In: Squillero, Giovanni, Burelli, Paolo (eds.) EvoApplications 2016. LNCS, vol. 9597, pp. 363–378. Springer, Heidelberg (2016). doi:10.1007/978-3-319-31204-0_24
11. Miller, S., Knowles, J.: A minimal model for the emergence of cooperation in randomly growing networks. In: Proceedings of the European Conference on Artificial Life 2015 (ECAL 2015), vol. 13, pp. 114–121 (2015)
12. Poncela, J., Gómez-Gardeñes, J., Floría, L.M., Sánchez, A., Moreno, Y.: Complex cooperative networks from evolutionary preferential attachment. PLoS one **3**, e2449 (2008)
13. Erdős, P., Rényi, A.: On random graphs. Publicationes Mathematicae Debrecen **6**, 290–297 (1959)
14. Santos, F.C., Pacheco, J.M.: A new route to the evolution of cooperation. J. Evol. Biol. **19**, 726–733 (2006)

Model-Based Computation

Cameron Beebe[1,2(✉)]

[1] Graduate School of Systemic Neurosciences,
Research Center for Neurophilosophy and Ethics of Neurosciences,
LMU Munich, Munich, Germany
cameronbeebs@gmail.com
[2] Munich Center for Mathematical Philosophy,
LMU Munich,
Munich, Germany

Abstract. A brief analysis of analog computation is presented, taking into account both historical and more modern statements. I will show that two very different concepts are tangled together in some of the literature—namely continuous valued computation and analogy machines. I argue that a more general concept, that of *model-based* computation, can help us untangle this misconception while also helping to evaluate two particularly interesting kinds of computational claims. The first kind concerns computational claims about the brain, in the spirit of Searle's *Is the Brain a Digital Computer?* The second kind concerns what has recently been called *analog simulation*, most notably in systems reproducing effects analogous to Hawking Radiation. Some final comments discuss how a model-based notion of computation helps us understand in a more concrete way the differences found among alternative models of computation.

Keywords: Model-based · Computation · Analog · Simulation

1 Introduction

The scope of this present article is not formal, but conceptual. I wish to provide a general discussion on the notion of computation, motivated by the fact that there has been some conceptual confusion present in the literature concerning analog computation. By an analysis of this confusion and the general 'computational landscape', I hope to contribute to our understanding of some recent claims by introducing what is called *model-based computation*. I argue that this is a natural development for the notion of computation, and is well-motivated from the analysis of analog computation provided.

A first step will be to provide evidence that there is a conceptual confusion present in discussions of analog computation. This will help establish what analog computation is *not*, and motivate the discussion in subsequent sections of what it *is*—and how a more general notion of model-based computation accommodates it. We begin with two statements from Nielsen and Chuang's bible of quantum information theory, which I quote at length for the unfamiliar reader:

© Springer International Publishing Switzerland 2016
M. Amos and A. Condon (Eds.): UCNC 2016, LNCS 9726, pp. 75–86, 2016.
DOI: 10.1007/978-3-319-41312-9_7

"In the years since Turing, many different teams of researchers have noticed that certain types of analog computers can efficiently solve problems believed to have no efficient solution on a Turing machine. At first glance these analog computers appear to violate the strong form of the Church-Turing thesis. Unfortunately for analog computation, it turns out that when realistic assumptions about the presence of noise in analog computers are made, their power disappears in all known instances; they cannot efficiently solve problems which are not efficiently solvable on a Turing machine. This lesson — that the effects of realistic noise must be taken into account in evaluating the efficiency of a computational model — was one of the great early challenges of quantum computation and quantum information, a challenge successfully met by the development of a theory of quantum error-correcting codes and fault-tolerant quantum computation. Thus, unlike analog computation, quantum computation can in principle tolerate a finite amount of noise and still retain its computational advantages" [8, p. 5].

"One might suspect that quantum computers are just analog computers, because of the use of continuous parameters in describing qubit states; however, it turns out that the effects of noise on a quantum computer can effectively be digitized" [8, p. 164].

Two things should be noted immediately. First, there seems to be an assumed notion of analog computation as a delicate and noise-intolerant business. I argue that this stems from the core misconceptions that continuous valued 'organs' (that is, components performing specialized functions) are not only essential to analog computation (they are not) but that a device which has such organs is *synonymous* with analog computation.[1] This is simply not the case, as we will see shortly.

The reader may also wish to see argument 6 from Scott Aaronson's page on skeptics of quantum computation, where he claims "We know that analog computers are not that reliable, and can go haywire because of small errors." [1] Aaronson proceeds to respond to the question of "why a quantum computer should be any different, since you have these amplitudes which are continuously varying quantities." In his response, he makes the very conflation at question here, namely that analog computation is synonymous with continuous value computation.

These claims against analog computation do not hold up to closer scrutiny. We will see in the next section that they are not supported by a basic analysis of analog computation. In the literature, we actually find some clarification with respect to what an analog computer was initially conceptualized as. See e.g. Ulmann [11]. Rather than being defined by the continuity of parameters, it was defined through *analogy*—and in fact von Neumann [7, p. 293] among others even refers to two classes of computing machines, analogy and digital machines. The term *analogy machines* sounds much different to our modern ears than analog

---

[1] We will see shortly that von Neumann, among others, used the term organ.

computer, but I argue it more accurately represents the landscape of computation. Particularly in modern computer science where alternative or specialized computing devices have become more common, it is important to have a clear conceptual overview of this landscape.

Thus, in the next section I introduce what I think is a much clearer conception of analog computation. I then proceed to outline some thoughts on what I call 'model-based computation' respecting this conception. Afterwards, I evaluate two discussions in light of this notion of model-based computation. The first includes computational claims about the brain and the current notion of hierarchical generative models in cognitive science. We will see that hierarchical generative models unsurprisingly describe model-based computation as outlined in this present work (in particular analog computation). The second discussion will focus on analog models in physics, in particular the notion of analog simulation recently put forth in Dardashti et al. [3]. Relevant aspects of the notion of model-based reasoning will also be briefly discussed. In the conclusion I will draw attention to the importance of this discussion on the developing market place of alternative computing.

2 What Is Analog Computation?

Enormous credit is due to Bernd Ulmann for providing us with a clear assessment of what analog computation *is*. I quote at length since I believe his comments are very informative and are incapable of compression without loss.

"First of all it should be noted that the common misconception that the difference between *digital computers* on one side and *analog computers* on the other is the fact that the former use discrete values for computations while the latter work in the regime of continuous values is wrong! In fact there were and still are analog computers that are based on purely digital elements. In addition to that even analog electronic analog computers are not working on continuous values — eventually everything like the integration of a current boils down to storing (i.e., counting) quantized electrons in a capacitor.

If the type of values used in a computation — discrete versus continuous — is not the distinguishing feature, what else could be used to differentiate between *digital* and *analog* computers? It turns out that the difference is to be found in the structure of these two classes of machines: A digital computer in our modern sense of the word has a fixed structure concerning its constituent elements and solves problems by executing a sequence (or sequences) of instructions that implement an algorithm. These instructions are read from some kind of memory, thus a better term for this kind of computing machine would be *stored-program digital computer* since this describes both features of such a machine: Its ability to execute instructions fetched from a memory subsystem and working with numbers that are represented as streams of digits.

An analog computer on the other hand is based on a completely different paradigm: Its internal structure is not fixed — in fact, a problem is solved on such a machine by changing its structure in a suitable way to generate a *model*, a so-called *analog* of the problem. This analog is then used to *analyze* or *simulate* the problem to be solved. Thus the structure of an analog computer that has been set up to tackle a specific problem represents the problem itself while a stored-program digital computer keeps its structure and only its controlling program changes" [11, p. 2].

It seems elementary to quote an introductory textbook, yet in the previous section we have seen that the misconception Ulmann speaks of is prevalent even at the highest levels of theoretical computer science. Going back to von Neumann, we find the beginning of the next most essential aspect of analog computation (and computation in general)—that computation depends on the *use* of a system. We also see evidence that the misconception concerning analog computers has been around for quite some time:

"The electromechanical relay, or the vacuum tube, when properly used, are undoubtedly all-or-none organs. Indeed, they are the prototypes of such organs. Yet both of them are in reality complicated analogy mechanisms, which upon appropriately adjusted stimulation respond continuously, linearly or non-linearly, and exhibit the phenomena of "breakdown" or "all-or-none" response only under very particular conditions of operation" [7, pp. 297–298].

We should be careful in parsing this particular quote, since von Neumann uses 'analogy' and 'continuously' in the same sentence. I think that even he has made the mistake of conflating analogy with continuity. In other places he seems to maintain the distinction, but since then the misconception in computer science at large seems to have only gotten worse. However, what we see is that 'proper use' is essential to defining computation. We will return in more detail to this in later sections, but for now we can state more accurately what we mean by an analog computer.

Definition 1 (Analog Computer). *An analog computer is a device whose internal structure is malleable and contains similarities to the class of problems it is used to solve. Additionally, these similarities by themselves should form a sufficient* **model** *of the relevant class of problems such that (in our proper use of the device) the organs involved function in a way that is consistent with our understanding of the target problems.*

While some analog computers under this definition can indeed be considered as (ideally) implementing differential equations or having continuous organs, this must be recognized as only a subset of potential uses of such a computer. In other words, the definition does not explicitly endorse smoothness or rule out digital systems. What is more important for the notion of analog computation, and for developing a richer conception of computation, is that the user and the architecture both play important roles in their relationship to a *model*. The user has to develop a model, or recognize similarities, or utilize analogical reasoning to set up the system in such a way that it can solve the problems at hand. Thus, in the remainder of this article, the reader should note that when I use the term 'analog', even as an adjective, it does not refer to continuity in any way.

Our view of the architecture will reflect this modeling procedure, meaning that as von Neumann notes an 'all-or-nothing' organ might be liable to be characterized under other usages as a more or less continuous valued organ. What should be clear at this stage is that analog computation utilizes a *model* to frame the use of the device. Historically, this seems to have been in particular models incorporating similarity and analogy. However, I argue this is just one type of a more general category of what can be called *model-based computation*. At this point I diverge slightly from Ulmann's statements [11], although the central premise is, I think, present in his work already quoted and thus I am offering more of a naturally implied extension than a meaningful divergence.

3   Model-Based Computation

The notion of model-based computation is rather quite simple alongside those definitions already provided for analog computation by Ulmann [11]. It is just slightly more general, in that the model used may or may not incorporate similarities or analogies to the extent that analog models do.[2] That is, even if there are similarities in the device, these similarities may not be sufficient by themselves to form a model of the target problem class. Analog computation is then a special case more accurately thought of as shorthand for analog-model computation. It might be that good examples of model-based computation are in fact using analog models, but it is arguably a small class within the computational landscape compared to any potential model-based computation—if only for the reason that analog models are a restricted class of models in general.

But what is a model? This question has been widely addressed in the philosophy of science community, and a few brief notes might be helpful before moving forward. There are a variety of different kinds of models which are used in science. There are toy models, idealized models, scale models, mathematical models, and many more kinds of models. Each of these kinds may have overlap with other kinds, they are not exclusive of each other. All models, it seems, need a target object or set of data which is to be represented or accounted for in some way in the model. See Frigg and Hartmann [5] for more on models in science. Model-based computation may involve many of the same aspects as other models in science.

Definition 2 (Model-Based Computer). *A model-based computer is a device which may have a malleable internal structure, and which represents in some relevant way a target problem class. The relevant representation in the*

---

[2] Although it may be an open question whether all models are in fact rooted in analogy or similarity, I will not focus on such an argument here.

*device should form a model which, under proper use, functions in a manner that
is consistent with our understanding of the target problem class.*

It is useful to go one step further in this section, to discuss model-based
simulation. This will be helpful before encountering analog simulation in later
sections. Model-based simulation is a refined form of model-based computation,
in which the dynamics of the device are relevant for the user or target problem
(as opposed to just a functional relation). Generally, the dynamics of a model-
based computer may or may not model what we know about the dynamics of
the target system. Yet, they may still be relevant for the User for simulational
purposes. Simulation operates on a richer model that deems relational aspects
(such as temporal relations) of the device relevant. One can have static relevant
features represented in a model which, after use, has an output which functionally represents a useful computation concerning a target problem. However, the
dynamics of using the model may be irrelevant to the kind of dynamics present
in the target system. In this case we would not say that there is model-based
simulation present.

Just reading the output of a slide rule, for example, does not seem to involve
simulation but just accomplishes a computation with the model. Take two equal
length sticks with logarithmic scales on them lined up side by side. Multiplication
can be calculated by sliding one of the sticks relative to the other by a factor.
That is, 2 times 4 could slide one stick by 2 on the logarithmic scale (representing
a multiplication of 2). Then, one looks up the other factor and reads off the
corresponding value on the other stick. In this case, 4 would be lined up with 8,
the result of the calculation.[3]

The dynamics of sliding the stick does not seem to model an algorithm for
multiplying some integers. The model in this case involves not only the physical ruler, but also the reasoning and mathematics involved to create the scales
represented on the ruler. The preparation of the computing device has utilized
pre-computed knowledge (i.e. $\log(xy) = \log(x) + \log(y)$) to functionally output
values consistent with an algorithm for multiplication, but the sliding dynamics are not relevant for the computation. I think it is quite reasonable to expect
that model-based computation generally will not include relevant dynamics with
the target system. When it does, a stronger notion of model-based simulation
is applicable. We will see later an example of analog simulation in which the
dynamics are relevant *and* similar.

3.1   Benefits?

In the present work I am remaining qualitative in my analysis of the 'computational landscape', however some general comments may be of interest concerning

---

[3] It is also interesting to note that a slide rule is typically called an analog computer.
Under the misconception of analog computer as necessarily involving continuous
variables, what role does continuity play in the use of a slide rule? It is arguable
that the continuously adjustable aspect of the device is incidental to the actual use
and function of the computer since outputs are also not real numbers.

any formal results associated with analogy machines or model-based computation. If there is any genuine 'speed-up' to be found compared to classical computation, I think it will be primarily the result of two sources. The first potential source is simply due to the architecture and type of values processed in the given system.

The second, and likely more important, source of potential speed-up in model-based computing is that it fronts certain information in the 'premises' of the set-up. In other words, some computational work has already been done in the set-up of the system. The model is, as it were, pruning off certain forks in reasoning or avoiding certain lengthy calculations that do not need to be investigated or reported by the program. As a simple example, just consider Deutsch's problem and finding out whether a black box implements a balanced or constant function of four possible functions $f : \{0, 1\} \to \{0, 1\}$.

A classical computer requires two evaluations of the black box, sending both a 0 and 1 through. We learn not only whether it is constant or balanced, but also *which* of the functions is performed. A quantum computer can, by throwing out the irrelevant information of the specific function and encoding the global property of the function cleverly into the phase, tell us in one go whether the box implements a constant or balanced function. Our model of the problem works with the architecture to cleverly set up the computation such that it tells us only what we need to know and nothing more.[4]

Any complexity claims should always be aware of these 'fronted' or indirectly utilized resources. If we haven't recognized these resources adequately, we might be mislead by certain claims of speed-up or complexity. In statements such as the following from Rubel, for example, we can see that these resources are alluded to by mentioning that the scientist has a 'feel' for the computing device:

"It is fashionable nowadays to downgrade analog computers, largely because of their unreliability and lack of high accuracy (roughly one-tenth of one percent at best). But analog computers, besides their versatility, are extremely fast at what they do, which is solving differential equations. In principle, they act instantaneously and in real time. Further, in contrast to the situation in digital computing, the operator of an analog computer has an extremely good "feel" for what the computer is doing. Analog computers are still unrivaled when a large number of closely related differential equations must be solved" [9, pp. 78–79].

While Rubel is specifically referring to analog computers, I think the statement is generally applicable to model-based computation. It is this 'feel' that I think imparts some of the benefits to model-based computation, since one has already done some work in constructing the model and in understanding how to work with the particular architecture. Many models provide the user with a 'feel' for the target problem or system, even with the acknowledgement that in reality

---

[4] This is of course an idealization, which should not be a problem since Turing machines are idealizations—actual physical architectures of course deviate from this idealization.

there are certain features of the model which are non-representative or known to be false. See e.g. Frigg and Hartmann [5, §4.2]. By utilizing a model in computation, the features of the model (such as idealization, etc.) have restricted the computational possibilities to things which fit the use—thus streamlining any process to just those which are relevant for the User. For this reason, a model-based computer (or analog computer) will not necessarily be a general purpose computer.

4   Computational Claims About the Brain

We now move to an analysis of the first kind of computational claim to be discussed in this paper. In Searle's [10], he equates the question *Is the Brain a Digital Computer?* with *Are Brain Processes Computational?*. After the preceding discussion, this seems like a mistake.[5] Digital computers are of course computational, but something that is computational is *not* necessarily *digital*. A digital computer may be repurposed in another context (with another user) to implement another form of computation, as noted by von Neumann:

> "By an all-or-none organ we should rather mean one which fulfills the following two conditions. First, it functions in the all-or-none manner under certain suitable operating conditions. Second, these operating conditions are the ones under which it is normally used; they represent the functionally normal state of affairs within the large organism, of which it forms a part. Thus the important fact is not whether an organ has necessarily and under all conditions the all-or-none character—this is probably never the case—but rather whether in its proper context it functions primarily, and appears to be intended to function primarily, as an all-or-none organ" [7, p. 298].

To be fair, Searle's discussion does touch upon some very legitimate issues with these questions. However, it is not clear that his discussion translates easily for the notion of model-based computation advocated for here. I want to agree with Searle's (and von Neumann's) comments on *use* being fundamental to computation, but avoid the framing of computation as equivalent to *digital* computation. Digital computation is but one *subset* of potential user-dependent contexts which may constitute a computational device. Not only does a model-based notion of computation help clear this issue up, but it importantly emphasizes at its core the user-dependent context which is so central to the notion of computation generally. This helps us grasp better what alternative models of computation are doing for us, namely that they are subjectively pruning away irrelevance or emphasizing certain relevancies.

Then, what would it mean if we asked *Is the Brain a Model-based Computer?*, and is this different still from Searle's second question *Are Brain Processes Computational?* In the scope of this present paper I cannot answer all of the interesting questions brought up in this topic, but I can discuss one recent approach in cognitive science that arguably fits the notion of model-based computer.

---

[5] Even more so than Searle himself might have admitted.

4.1   Bayesian Brain and Generative Modeling

There is a growing use of Bayesian probabilistic methods and hierarchical generative models (HGM) in cognitive science. See e.g. Friston [6] and Clark [2]. Some of this literature can be taken as arguing that the brain be considered a model-based computer as we have defined it here: that it is a device whose evolution in time effectively performs computations based on a pre-established *model*. Take Friston's description as an example:

> "The Bayesian brain hypothesis uses Bayesian probability theory to formulate perception as a constructive process based on internal or generative models. The underlying idea is that the brain has a model of the world that it tries to optimize using sensory inputs. [...] In this view, the brain is an inference machine that actively predicts and explains its sensations" [6, p. 129].

This approach is argued by the authors to have the capacity of unifying several areas of cognitive science. Whether the specifically Bayesian approach is the final unifier may still be at question. Nonetheless, the approach not only fits the model-based account of computation I have advocated here, but even seems to fit the more restricted sense of analog computation since the modeling that the brain is doing is related via similarity to the external world. The brain, under this view, is constantly simulating the world and adjusting its model according to the errors experienced. The HGM is amplifying relevant or similar features of a model via feedback with the environment, while dissimilar features fall out of focus (and, under the Bayesian approach, obtain lower probabilities).

Under this framework, we would answer 'yes' to the question of whether the brain is a model-based computer, and also 'yes' to the question of whether brain processes are computational. However, this may be a bit premature since we have noticed that computation is dependent on a user—and what would be *using* this model-based computer? This is no trivial problem, and in fact relates to longstanding mind/brain problems and what is called the "homunculus fallacy" (HF). See e.g. Searle [10, §V]. Can the model-based conception of computation add anything new to this problem?

Without being overly conclusive, I suggest that the hierarchical generative model of cognition may be a good step towards addressing the user problem. The reason, we will see, is that it simply accepts a finite regress and offers a more general notion of model-based computation.[6] While this isn't solving the problem (or avoiding the fallacy) in the traditional sense, it is simply not so unreasonable to suppose that the brain—as a computational system—involves complex hierarchical modeling of the external world. The representations in this model will no doubt still succumb to HF objections, but not in a naive way.

---

[6] Attempting to mitigate or explicitly accepting the HF is a required step, since as Searle notes, "... The homunculus fallacy is endemic to computational models of cognition and cannot be removed by the standard recursive decomposition arguments." [10, p. 36] What can be done, I argue, is to put a new spin on the issue.

The slightly more sophisticated view does not succumb to an infinite regress traditionally associated with the homunculus fallacy, since there are finite levels in the hierarchy. The homunculus could just be the topmost level in the hierarchical generative model, and it 'uses' the computations from lower levels in the hierarchy. Now, a reader familiar with the HF will likely object and say that the topmost level of the hierarchy is still problematic, since it is not 'used' by a higher level user. I do not know a way out of this objection, nor whether it will be useful to reconcile. I can only say that the entire integrated 'body + HGM' system definitely seems to use the HGM, for all of the reasons why people think HGM is a good model of cognition in the first place.

In any case, it seems that a sophisticated model-based notion of computation does not do worse for computational claims about the brain than what has been accomplished previously. The brain doesn't need to be a digital computer, or a general purpose analog computer. However, it is clear that a brain-like system which utilizes a model (i.e. does model-based computation) of the external environment to generate minimum error or minimum surprise is much different than Searle's formulation of these issues.

5   Analog Simulation in Physics

For our second kind of computational claim to be discussed, we move to physics. A few recent publications in the physical sciences (along with some philosophy of physics) have drawn attention to the use of analog models in scientific reasoning. One notable example is that of fluid systems displaying analogous phenomena to Hawking radiation (the phenomena of photons escaping the event horizon of a black hole). See Unruh [12]. These models have been argued, under strict conditions, to be performing analog *simulation* by Dardashti et al. [3]. Importantly, these systems seem to allow us more access to black hole phenomena than would otherwise be possible.

The reader should already be anticipating the main point of this section: these sort of systems are *analog computers* in the clearest sense—they are based on strict similarity conditions, and as alluded to earlier are prime examples of model-based computation (specifically analogy-based). They are simulating while also displaying formal and physical similarities with the target computational problem. The type of simulation these systems do is arguably providing even stronger results than traditional simulation in which the architecture of the computing device is irrelevant to the simulated problem. However, because of the background knowledge involved in constructing a table-top system, we might be less surprised at the outputs because we have a good 'feel' for what the system can do.

The strict models used in analog simulation are based on formal similarities (such as isomorphisms) between the systems of equations describing both the computing device (i.e. a table top fluid system) and the target system (i.e. a black hole). We mentioned earlier that for model-based simulation, the dynamics of the computation are relevant (but may not be similar). For analog simulation, the dynamics of the device must preserve relevant similarities with the dynamics of the target system. This brings us to the last important step in this short paper, namely re-connecting our discussion with previous work concerning model-based *reasoning*.

5.1 Model-Based Reasoning in Science

The literature concerning model-based reasoning is, to my knowledge, mainly discussing model-based reasoning in science. See e.g. Frigg and Hartmann [5, §3]. The systems discussed in the previous section are good examples. These models are used by scientists to reason about target systems. The scientist may, for example, use the model to justify a theory of Hawking radiation or to suggest new experimental questions. There seems to be a second sense of model-based reasoning present elsewhere, however.

This other sense of model-based reasoning is in diagnostics, or in artificial intelligence systems which have a model of the environment. See Davis and Hamscher [4]. Now, this might sound very close to the notion of HGM as model-based computation I discussed previously. However I think it is important to distinguish between model-based reasoning as somehow providing rules or guidelines in an argument or in an artificial inference system, with model-based computation as I have construed it. Model-based computation can be a part of model-based reasoning, but it isn't clear that model-based computation *is* model-based reasoning.

Reasoning is an active process (one might even say conscious), whereas computation—aside from the User's set up of a problem or the interpretation of an output — seems to be passively implemented. Model-based reasoning may likely be involved in constructing a particular computing device, but it isn't clear that what the device is doing should also be considered model-based reasoning. Or, it isn't clear that our *use* of the device as a model-based computer constitutes model-based reasoning as understood by previous work on the subject. Nonetheless, it seems to be that a more in-depth analysis of these two notions may be fruitful.

6 Conclusion

A model-based notion of computation helps us understand *why* certain architectures or models might perform better on, for example, optimization problems. Take D-Wave's supercooled annealing chip, for example. Its usefulness derives from a combination of architectural features and model-based considerations in the set-up of the device, and these determine the types of problems that it will be useful for. It is worth investing in because it exploits a combination of precomputed modeling considerations with an architecture that also reflects these considerations.

Model-based computation seems to be a worthwhile notion to entertain when discussing alternative computing approaches. It does not represent any kind of dramatic proposal to re-draw complexity classes or endorse any view on hyper-computation. In fact, it is clear from the discussion that complexity claims should be wary of fronted resources by the modeling process. As a conceptual tool, model-based computation helps us get a better grasp on the landscape of computation. I have argued that this tool is useful for analyzing and understanding various kinds of computational claims. Perhaps it can also help us keep track of the emerging market for specialized computing devices.

Acknowledgments. I would like to thank Bernd Ulmann for introducing me to my own errors on the foundations of analog computation, and for motivating this present analysis.

References

1. Aaronson, S.: Lecture 14: skepticism of quantum computing. http://www.scottaaronson.com/democritus/lec14.html
2. Clark, A.: Whatever next? predictive brains, situated agents, and the future of cognitive science. Behav. Brain Sci. **36**(3), 181–204 (2013)
3. Dardashti, R., Thébaut, K., Winsberg, E.: Confirmation via analogue simulation: what dumb holes could tell us about gravity. Br. J. Philos. Sci. (2015). http://bjps.oxfordjournals.org/content/early/2015/05/22/bjps.axv010.abstract (online)
4. Davis, R., Hamscher, W.: Model-based reasoning: troubleshooting. Memorandum AI Memo 1059, Artificial Intelligence Laboratory, Advanced Research Projects Agency, Office of Naval Research (1988)
5. Frigg, R., Hartmann, S.: Models in science. In: Stanford Encyclopedia of Philosophy (2012). http://plato.stanford.edu/entries/models-science/ (Fall 2012)
6. Friston, K.: The free-energy principle: a unified brain theory? Nat. Rev. Neurosci. **11**(2), 127–138 (2010)
7. Neumann, J.V.: The general and logical theory of automata. In: Taub, A.H. (ed.) John von Neumann Collected Works, vol. V: Design of Computers, Theory of Automata and Numerical Analysis, pp. 288–326. Pergamon Press, Oxford (1963)
8. Nielsen, M., Chuang, I.: Quantum Computation and Quantum Information. Cambridge University Press, Cambridge (2010)
9. Rubel, L.A.: The brain as an analog computer. J. Theor. Neurobiol. **4**, 73–81 (1985)
10. Searle, J.R.: Is the brain a digital computer? Proc. Addresses Am. Philos. Assoc. **64**(3), 21–37 (1990)
11. Ulmann, B.: Analog Computing. De Gruyter, Berlin (2013)
12. Unruh, W.G.: Dumb holes: analogues for black holes. Philos. Trans. R. Soc. A **366**, 2905–2913 (2008)

In Vitro Implementation of a Stack Data Structure Based on DNA Strand Displacement

Harold Fellermann, Annunziata Lopiccolo,
Jerzy Kozyra, and Natalio Krasnogor[✉]

Interdisciplinary Computing and Complex Biosystems Research Group,
School of Computing, Newcastle University, Newcastle-upon-Tyne, UK
natalio.krasnogor@newcastle.ac.uk

Abstract. We present an implementation of an in vitro signal recorder based on DNA assembly and strand displacement. The signal recorder implements a stack data structure in which both data as well as operators are represented by single stranded DNA "bricks". The stack grows by adding push and write bricks and shrinks in last-in-first-out manner by adding pop and read bricks. We report the design of the signal recorder and its mode of operations and give experimental results from capillary electrophoresis as well as transmission electron microscopy that demonstrate the capability of the device to store and later release several successive signals. We conclude by discussing potential future improvements of our current results.

1 Introduction

DNA nanotechnology is now a well established method for arranging and controlling matter on the nanoscale [1]. Because of the relative ease with which molecular folding and molecular interactions can be designed by choosing appropriate nucleic acid sequences, DNA is a prominent substrate for designing artificial reaction networks with designed functionality. In particular, it has been shown that arbitrary chemical reaction networks can be translated into equivalent toehold mediated DNA strand displacement systems up to a constant scaling factor that accounts for the relatively slow speed of DNA reorganization reactions [2]. Among the broadest application areas of such designed chemistries is the area of molecular computing, where complex reaction networks consisting of dozens of molecular players with well defined interactions can be readily synthesized and tested in the laboratory.

Recent years have seen theoretical designs and molecular realizations of conventional and unconventional molecular computational circuits. The majority of this work has been concerned with implementing logic gates such as Boolean gates [3,4], join-and-fork gates [5,6] and seesaw gates [7,8], and wiring these gates together to create circuits of increasing complexity, such as molecular adders [9], static lookup tables [10] and game-playing molecular automata [11].

H. Fellermann and A. Lopiccolo—Contributed equally to this work.

© Springer International Publishing Switzerland 2016
M. Amos and A. Condon (Eds.): UCNC 2016, LNCS 9726, pp. 87–98, 2016.
DOI: 10.1007/978-3-319-41312-9_8

This approach toward molecular computing, which closely mimics electrical engineering, is somewhat disconnected from algorithmic computer science, where algorithms are built by composing data and operations. Indeed, DNA computing has so far seen few designs for DNA data structures – with Qian et al.'s theoretical design of a DNA based stack machine being one noteworthy exception [12].

Here, we present the *in vitro* implementation and experimental characterization of a DNA data structure, namely a *stack*, where data and operations form the core of the molecular interaction network. Our design shares similarities with the one presented by Qian et al. but has been optimized for maximal robustness among all molecular interactions and minimal occurrence of undesirable reactions. The stack data structure is here employed as a signal recorder and its recording and readout fidelity is characterized experimentally. We understand this contribution as a stepping stone toward *in vitro* implementations of more general data structures, as well as computationally universal stack machines. To the best of our knowledge, our work provides the first experimental results on a DNA based stack in particular, and DNA based data structures in general.

2   A Stack Data Structure Built from DNA

A stack is an abstract data structure that serves as a linear collection of elements, with two principal operations: *push* adds an element to the stack, and *pop* removes the most recently added element that was not yet removed. Formally, this is achieved through the interface

$$push : \text{stack} \times \text{element} \longrightarrow \text{stack}$$
$$pop : \text{stack} \longrightarrow \text{stack} \times \text{element}$$

with the invariant

$$pop(push(\text{stack}, \text{element})) = \text{stack}, \text{element}$$

to guarantee *last-in-first-out* operation.

Fully implementing this data type in DNA requires molecular realizations of the assembled stack, all potential elements, as well as the push and pop operations. We achieve this by associating each data element and each operation with a single stranded DNA (ssDNA) strand with partial secondary structures. We call those strands "bricks". The stack data structure is built from bricks via hybridization of complementary DNA domains. More precisely, the stack forms a double stranded DNA (dsDNA) assembly with essentially no single stranded regions but one active toehold domain, that offers an entry for operation. Data bricks form the top strand and push bricks form the bottom strand of this dsDNA assembly.

To prevent run-away processes that might occur when adding bricks in realistic concentrations, we design the device to toggle between two states in all modes of operation. We refer to these as *data state* and *operator state*.

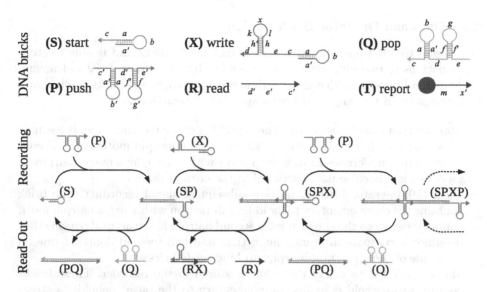

Fig. 1. Schematic of the DNA recorder. The top row shows schematics of the individual ssDNA bricks. Arrows indicate 5' → 3' direction. Below are the modes of operation to record (middle row) and read out (bottom row) signals from the stack.

When the stack is in data state, it will accept a single data brick. Upon binding this data element, the device toggles into the operator state in which it cannot further interact with data bricks, but instead awaits a new operator brick such as *push*. Again, only a single operator brick is accepted, and by interacting with it, the stack toggles back into the data state.

Our design differs from the one proposed by Qian et al. [12] in several important aspects:

1. We implement all data and operations as single DNA strands, whereas Qian et al. employ bricks of up to three DNA strands.
2. Our assembled DNA stack is entirely double stranded and does not feature any dangling single stranded overhangs, which are used by Qian et al. to store the actual data elements.
3. Instead, in our design data is encoded in internal secondary structure motifs in the double strand, namely in hairpin loops that form holiday junctions.
4. Our modes of operation are based on DNA interactions that are effectively irreversible at the operating temperature. Qian et al.'s design, in contrast, employs only reversible interactions and relies on detailed balance to drive the device from one configuration into another.

We have taken these design decisions, in order to minimize the amount of required distinct DNA sequences and to obtain maximally robust modes of operation, especially when envisioning ultimate *in vivo* applications.

2.1 Data and Operator Brick Design

Our signal recorder operates with six distinct DNA bricks and is able to store combinations of two different signals, encoded by two types of data elements. Two further bricks are added for experimental analysis. See Fig. 1 for a schematic representation of the employed bricks and their interactions.

- *Start* (S): data brick designating the beginning of the recorder tape. It features a toehold domain for interaction with *push* and a hairpin motif at the 5' end. This hairpin undergoes branch migration with a complementary hairpin in *push* but is otherwise not functional in the current design.
- *Push* (P): operator brick to initiate subsequent signal recording. The brick contains the complementary toehold for interaction with *start*, a hairpin motif complementary to the one in *start*, a second hairpin for structural reasons that does not participate in branch migration, and two toehold domains, one on each side of the structural hairpin, to bind *write* bricks.
- *Write* (X/Y): data bricks that can be stored in the recorder. These bricks contain two toehold domains complementary to the push toeholds, a structural hairpin that does not undergo branch migration, plus the same toehold domain and 5' hairpin that form the *start* brick. Toehold domains and branch migration hairpins are identical for all types of *write* bricks. Thus, they can only differ in their structural hairpin motif. Since these hairpins do not participate in hybridization or branch migration, they can be functionalized to host any desired functionality such as recognition sites for DNA binding proteins.

  We employ two different types of *write* bricks, denoted as *write-X* and *write-Y*. *Write-Y* features a longer hairpin stem than *write-X* (twenty-five base pairs against ten base pairs) and has a different sequence in its stem loop. Although we currently employ binary data (X or Y), the approach is intrinsically n-ary.
- *Pop* (Q): data brick that undoes the rightmost *push* operation. This brick is the exact complement of *push*
- *Read* (R): operator brick that removes the rightmost *write* operation. The brick is the complement of all toehold domains used in *write*'s. Notably, it does not contain any domains that interact with the structural hairpin of *write* bricks.
- *Report* (T): non-essential bricks for experimental analysis. Report bricks do not participate directly in the operations of the stack recorder. Instead, they interact with the data domains of structural hairpins in the *write* bricks. *Report* bricks can be added to the device in any configuration since their binding sites in the data hairpins are always accessible and since they do not interfere with the operating modes of the device.

  In this study, we use linear *report* strands that are 5' biotinylated via a 2.6 nm tetra-ethyleneglycol (TEG) spacer. We functionalized these *report* bricks with streptavidin coated gold nanoparticles of different diameters, which allows for easy recognition using transmission electron microscopy (TEM).

Domain sizes have been chosen with the following objectives: toeholds are long enough to span a single helical turn when hybridized with their complements (10 nt) which should promote irreversible hybridization. Hairpin loops that participate in branch migration are long enough to promote stable stems (6 base pair stems with 4–5 nt loops) but short enough to obtain quick branch migration times. The structural hairpin loop of *write* bricks together with the unpaired domain of *report* are long enough to accommodate 5 nm and 10 nm diameter nanoparticles in close vicinity to the device.

2.2 Modes of Operation

DNA hybridization, branch migration and strand displacement are the three processes governing all DNA interactions involved in the system. All reactions are energetically downhill, driven by the binding energy of the closing toehold domains.

Recording. A schematic of the recording process is shown in Fig. 1 middle row. Starting from an empty stack, which is represented by the *start* brick (S), the device is toggled into its data state by providing a *push* operator (P). The *start-push* interaction begins by irreversibly binding toehold c and continues via branch migration among the two complementary *aba'* domains. The stack is now in its data state (SP), where a single open toehold region ($d'e'$) can recruit a *write* brick (X or Y). The *write* will partially hybridize with the $d'e'$ *push* toeholds, thus toggling the stack back into its operator state (SPX). In this state, the stack exposes the same toehold-hairpin interface that characterizes the *start* brick, which allows the device to undergo subsequent rounds of recording.

Note that the assembled stack is essentially double stranded with a single exposed toehold domain. Because the structural hairpins of neither the *push* nor the *write* participate in branch migration, the stack will form holiday junctions for each recorded data element. As data specific domains are encoded in the loop regions of this holiday junction, the recording cycle is independent on the actual data written.

Read-Out. While recording proceeds from left to right in the schematic, read-out will proceed from right to left, thereby undoing any recording in the last-in first-out manner required by the stack specification. The read-out cycle is schematically presented in the bottom row of Fig. 1.

In operator state (SPX), providing a *read* brick (R) will peel the last recorded *write* brick off the stack, thereby toggling the device back into the data state (SP). This reaction proceeds in two steps: first, the *read* brick hybridizes to the stack at its unique exposed c domain. Secondly, the dangling $d'e'$ domains of the *read* brick initiate a three-way branch migration with the $d'e'$ domains of the adjacent *push* brick against the de domains of the *write* brick, until the *push* strand is completely displaced.

Note that the data hairpin of the *write* brick does not participate in the branch migration. This ensures that a unique *read* brick can interact with any *write* brick, ensuring that data elements can be read from the recorder without a need to know which information has been stored. The resulting *read-write* complex (RX) does not expose any single stranded domains and will not participate in further DNA interactions.

In its data state (SP), the stack can either be extended again with another data element by switching to the recording operation, or reading can be completed by toggling the stack back into its operator state. The latter is done by providing a *pop* brick (Q) that will interact with and peel off the exposed *push* brick. Analogue to the previous reaction, *pop-push* interactions are composed of their initial irreversible toehold hybridization, subsequent branch migration and eventual strand displacement. Again, the resulting *push-pop* complex (PQ) is completely double stranded and will not participate in further DNA interactions.

3   Methods

3.1   Primary Sequence Specification

In the past we have successfully utilized evolutionary algorithms for evolving nano scale and self-assembling systems [13–15]. Thus we resorted to genetic algorithms to obtain nucleic acid sequences for all specified domains in the DNA stack specification. The fitness function of our algorithm (a) minimizes the total Hamming distance between the bricks target secondary structures and their folding predictions from ViennaRNA [16], and (b) maximizes the binding energies of all desired pair interactions while minimizing binding energies of all undesired pair interactions. Table 1 lists the nucleotide sequences of all domains, found by the highest-scoring genotype of our algorithm.

Table 1. Sequence specification of domains in the design. Sequences are indicated in 5'→3' direction.

Domain	Sequence	Domain	Sequence
a	TCTCCC	h_y	GCACGCTCGAGCTCGTATCGCAGTA
b	GCCA	k_x	CTCTAATCAC
c	GCACACACTTC	k_y	CATCCCTATA
d	ACACCACTTC	l_x	AGACAAAAAA
e	GGGAGACCAA	l_y	ATTTTTTTCC
f	CGGCGG	m	TATGACTGCAA
g	CTGCC	x	AGACCGCTAAA
h_x	ATTAGTAGGT	y	ATACTGCTTTA

3.2   Experimental Manipulation of DNA

DNA oligomers were provided by Eurogentec (Belgium) on a $100\,\mu M$ synthesis scale, with a standard desalting procedure or a required denaturing polyacrylamide gel electrophoresis (PAGE) purification for oligomers longer than 50 nucleotides and/or any 3'/5' modification. Streptavidin coated gold nanoparticles of 5 and 10 nm diameter were supplied by Life Technologies (Alexa Fluor 488 streptavidin). Samples and stock solutions were stored at $-20°C$.

The DNA recorder was prepared by sequentially adding 200 nM of each brick with 240 min waiting time between additions. DNA samples were dissolved in a total volume of $20\,\mu L$ of nuclease free water and 50 mM potassium acetate, 20 mM tris-acetate, 10 mM magnesium acetate, pH 7.9 buffer at room temperature $(\tilde{2}5°C)$ and incubated for ten minutes if not otherwise specified. The mixture was shaken at 300 revolutions per minute in an Eppendorf Thermomixer Comfort set at 25°C.

Capillary electrophoresis has been performed using the Agilent Technology 2100 Bioanalyzer system with its DNA High Sensitivity Chip and adhered to manufacturer protocols.

Transmission electron microscopy (TEM) was performed with a Philips CM 100 Compustage (FEI) microscope and digital images were collected using an AMT CCD camera (Deben). A volume of $5\mu L$ sample was applied on glow discharge grids preliminary washed with 0.5 mM magnesium chloride to change the hydrophilic surface charge orientation.

4   Results

4.1   Single Brick Calibration

We performed capillary electrophoresis measurements of all individual bricks in order to determine the response of the Agilent 2100 Bioanalyzer High Sensitivity DNA Assay for our non-standard DNAs. All bricks where provided in 200 nM concentration. Electropherograms always detected a single clear peak per brick. Table 2 summarizes for each brick its known size, the measured migration time and fluorescence area under the peak, as well as the calculated size and molarity derived by the instrument software from comparison to the reference ladder. Averages and standard deviations have been calculated from at least three independent measurements.

The measurements successfully discriminate the migration times of almost all strands (disregarding *report* strands) with significant differences. Only *start* and *read* cannot be reliably differentiated.

Striking discrepancies between the known brick sizes and the sizes derived by the software from comparison to the ladder might be attributed to two reasons: firstly, short oligomers such as *start*, *read* and *report* are well below the detection limit of the high sensitivity kit, which can resolve dsDNA fragments between 50–7000 base pairs in length. Secondly, the reported deviations might lie in the fact that our bricks contain extensive secondary structures that might affect their motility in the gel matrix.

Table 2. Calibration results (given as averages and standard deviation) for all individual strands provided in 200 nM concentrations.

Brick	Size [nt]	Measured		Derived	
		Time [s]	Area [FU]	Size [bp]	Molarity [nM]
start (S)	27	45.22±0.92	94.6±61.23	51±7.6	34.80±15.92
push (P)	64	46.81±0.76	74.4±39.2	64±6.9	8.08±0.174
write-X (X)	98	53.27±0.34	55.93±39.65	128±3.78	5.961±0.473
write-Y (Y)	128	55.35±0.06	5.27±1.15	147±0.8	0.845±0.221
report-X (Rx)	22	44.81±0.81	248.5±60.57	47±6.4	78.25±16.81
report-Y (Ry)	22	45.18±1.02	241.3±84.49	47±11.3	86.44±12.77
read (R)	31	44.61±0.35	73.85±15.76	46±2.82	31.67±1.21
pop (Q)	64	47.89±0.28	28.13±25.4	74±3.4	6.602±6.78

A similar discrepancy is observed in the derived molarity values. This is partly due to the fact that molarity calculation is based on the base pair estimation and will thus suffer from the issues described before, partly because our bricks contain extensive ssDNA regions which interact differently with the fluorescent dye than dsDNA.

4.2   Recording Experiments

To probe the performance of the data recording (push) cycle, we performed experiments in which we sequentially recorded five signals (X, X, X, Y, X) onto the growing stack. We ran five parallel experiments and stopped them at different steps in the protocol. Gel-like images of the Bioanalyzer output are shown in Fig. 2.

For the first three recorded signals, addition of each write-X brick is accompanied by the appearance of a new clear peak in the spectrum: after addition of the first write-X brick this peak (start-push-write-X complex, or SPX) accounts for more than 58 % of the total fluorescence. Lane 2 shows the appearance of a second peak (SPXPX) that corresponds to the two signals. However, this second peak accounts for only about 22 % of the total fluorescence, whereas almost 40 % still correspond to the first signal (SPX). The situation repeats in the third lane, where the correct complex (SPXPXPX) accounts for slightly more than 17 % of the fluorescence, the second signal peak (SPXPX) for about 30 % and the first peak still for about 23 %.

The addition of write-Y in lane 4 leads to the appearance of several new peaks, which we identify as SPY, SPXPY, and SPXPXPY. A very faint peak at about 98 s migration time might correspond to the desired SPXPXPPXPY, but the signal is too weak to be properly identified by the analysis software. Lane 5 essentially shows the same peaks as lane 4, with peak sizes changing as expected: peaks from complexes ending in a write-Y brick become smaller, whereas the corresponding complexes with added write-X become proportionally larger.

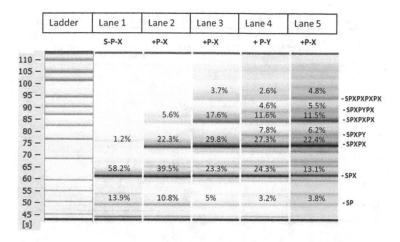

Fig. 2. Capillary electrophoresis of the recording process. Lane 1 = SPX; Lane2 = SPXPX; Lane 3 = SPXPXPX; Lane 4 = SPXPXPXPY; Lane 5 = SPXPXPXPYPX. Data obtained from five parallel experiments.

In all lanes faint higher peaks indicate that there is a very small potential for run-away processes to create complexes with more signals than the provided ones. Yet, in all cases, the fluorescence of all these longer bands combined does not exceed 10 % of the total.

4.3   Read Out Experiments

Next, we performed experiments to test the read-out (pop) cycle of the DNA stack. In this experiment, three signals (X, Y, X) where pushed onto the stack and subsequently removed by adding *read* (R) and *pop* (Q) bricks in molarities equal to the *start*, *push* and *write* bricks. Figure 3 shows the gel-like images of the experiment.

Lanes 1 through 3 reconfirm the working of the recording cycle with the same observations than for the experiment of the last section: each added *write* brick generates a new peak in the spectrum with very little evidence for run-away processes and persistence of peaks that indicate intermediate complexes.

Lane 4 shows the response of the device after provision of 200 nM *read* and *pop*, which is supposed to trigger one readout cycle: newly created *push-pop* as well as *read-write* complexes result in the appearance of three new peaks at around 47.42 (QP), 52.22 (RX), and 57.39 (RY) seconds. The *push-pop* complexes account for 38 % of the fluorescence, whereas *start-write-X* and *start-write-Y* account for 2.8 and 12 % respectively. Peaks associated with the different stack states SPXPYPY, SPYPY, SPXPY, and SPY decrease accordingly. The situation repeats in Lane 5 where the second readout cycle further increases *push-pop* and *read-write* peaks and simultaneously reduces intensities of the corresponding stack complexes. Noteworthily, after reading out the two recorded signals, 14.1 % of the fluorescence results from the *start-push* complex whereas

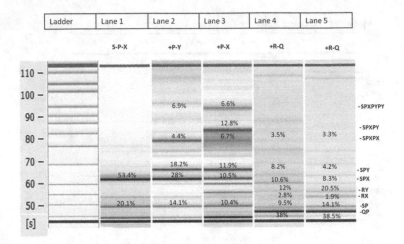

Fig. 3. Capillary electrophoresis of the recording and reading of three signals. Recording: Lane 1 = SPX; Lane 2 = SPXPY; Lane 3 = SPXPYPY. Reading: Lane 4 = SPXPYPY+RQ; Lane 5 = SPXPYPY+RQRQ.

peaks of stacks that still contain recorded information only register with 8, 4.2, 4.8 and 3.3 %.

4.4 Imaging

For additional confirmation of the recording, we imaged the assembled nanodevice using TEM. For this purpose, assembled stacks were mixed with *report* strands that, in turn, are decorated with 5 and 10 nm gold nanoparticles. *Report* bricks associate with their respective *write* bricks at any position in the assembled stack. Nanoparticles appear in TEM images as black dots that can be easily distinguished and classified.

Simple geometric considerations estimate an assembled structure where data hairpins are separated by about 15 nm with 247° twist. OxDNA simulations [17] (Fig. 4 left panel) indicate that the assembled stack does not necessarily extend straight forward but might instead contain a kink at each *signal-push* holiday junction. Figure 4 (right panel) shows TEM results from an experiment where five signals (X, Y, X, X, X) have been recorded. The image show a stack with just one extra *write-X* on the left side of the recorder, resulting in a stack with six signals (X, X, Y, X, X, X). The image shows a separation of 15–20 nm between the nanoparticles with a zig-zag configuration predicted by the simulations.

5 Discussion and Future Work

We have presented a design and experimental evidence for the working of an in-vitro signal recorder based on DNA strand assembly and displacement. The recorder implements a stack data structure with push and pop operations and allows for storing two signal types.

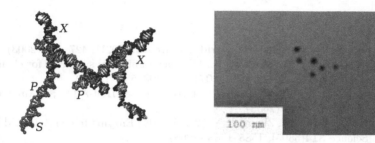

Fig. 4. Left: oxDNA simulation of a SPXPX complex. **Right:** Representative TEM image of a SPXPXPYPXPXPX complex.

Because we employ non-standard DNA strands, the electrophoresis analysis software does not correctly detect molecular concentrations, which prevents us to gain a precise quantitative picture of the involved processes. Nonetheless, capillary electrophoresis and TEM imaging indicate that the nanodevice is able to store at least three consecutive signals and does not suffer from problematic runaway processes.

However, after recording several signals, electrophoresis analysis indicates that the device is not only present in the desired final state, but also in several intermediate recording states. Because of the limits of experimental quantification, we can currently not offer a satisfying explanation for these intermediate peaks. This currently impacts the readout cycle, as the pop operation interacts with all present stacks and thus returns a superposition of recorded signals. While this is contrary to the intended working, we point out that such a superposition might also have advantages, as it might allow one to reverse engineer the composition *and order* of recorded information from a single electrophoresis read out.

We plan to improve experimental analysis methods using different capillary electrophoresis analysis kits (such as RNA assay kits) or molecular beacon experiments. Better experimental quantification will allow us to calibrate computational models that will in turn help us increase our understanding of the fidelity of the device.

Tantalizingly, as our design is based on ssDNA bricks, our entire data structure could – in principle – be expressed *in vivo* by a living cell as an RNA data structure and post-transcriptionally controlled. As we store data in a double-stranded fashion rather than in dangling single strands, an *in vivo* realization is likely to suffer less from enzymatic attack. Alternatively, the device could be used to programmatically and reversibly arrange matter such as liposomes [18,19] on the nanoscale. We are currently exploring routes to implement this.

Acknowledgments. This work has been supported by EPSRC grant agreements no EP/J004111/1, EP/J004111/2, EP/L001489/1, EP/L001489/2. We thank Chien-yi Chang, Christoph Flamm, Alessandro Ceccarelli, Omer Markovitch, and Ben Shirt-Ediss for helpful discussions.

References

1. Seeman, N.C.: DNA in a material world. Nature **421**(6921), 427–431 (2003)
2. Soloveichik, D., Seelig, G., Winfree, E.: DNA as a universal substrate for chemical kinetics. Proc. Nat. Acad. Sci. USA **107**(12), 5393–5398 (2010)
3. Stojanović, M.N., Stefanović, D.: Deoxyribozyme-Based Half-Adder. J. Am. Chem. Soc. **125**(22), 6673–6676 (2003)
4. Seelig, G., Soloveichik, D., Zhang, D.Y., Winfree, E.: Enzyme-free nucleic acid logic circuits. Science **314**(5805), 1585–1588 (2006)
5. Cardelli, L.: Strand algebras for DNA computing. Nat. Comput. **10**, 407–428 (2011)
6. Chen, Y., Dalchau, N., Srinivas, N., Phillips, A., Cardelli, L., Soloveichik, D., Seelig, G.: Programmable chemical controllers made from DNA. Nat. Nano. **8**(10), 755–762 (2013)
7. Qian, L., Winfree, E.: A simple DNA gate motif for synthesizing large-scale circuits. J. R. Soc. Interface **8**(62), 1281–1297 (2011)
8. Qian, L., Winfree, E.: Scaling up digital circuit computation with DNA strand displacement cascades. Science **332**(6034), 1196–201 (2011)
9. Li, W., Zhang, F., Yan, H., Liu, Y.: DNA based arithmetic function: a half adder based on DNA strand displacement. Nanoscale **8**(6), 3775–3784 (2016)
10. Liu, H., Wang, J., Song, S., Fan, C., Gothelf, K.V.: A DNA-based system for selecting and displaying the combined result of two input variables. Nature Comm. **6**, 10089 (2015)
11. MacDonald, J., Li, Y., Sutovic, M., Lederman, H., Pendri, K., Lu, W., Andrews, B.L., Stefanovic, D., Stojanovic, M.N.: Medium scale integration of molecular logic gates in an automaton. Nano Lett. **6**(11), 2598–2603 (2006)
12. Qian, L., Soloveichik, D., Winfree, E.: Efficient turing-universal computation with DNA polymers. In: Sakakibara, Y., Mi, Y. (eds.) DNA 16 2010. LNCS, vol. 6518, pp. 123–140. Springer, Heidelberg (2011)
13. Terrazas, G., Gheorghe, M., Kendall, G., Krasnogor, N.: Evolving tiles for automated self-assembly design. In: IEEE Congress on Evolutionary Computation, CEC 2007, pp. 2001–2008 (2007)
14. Siepmann, P., Martin, C.P., Vancea, I., Moriarty, P.J., Krasnogor, N.: A genetic algorithm approach to probing the evolution of self-organized nanostructured systems. Nano Lett. **7**(7), 1985–1990 (2007)
15. Woolley, R.A.J., Stirling, J., Radocea, A., Krasnogor, N., Moriarty, P.: Automated probe microscopy via evolutionary optimization at the atomic scale. Appl. Phys. Lett. **98**(25), 253104 (2011)
16. Lorenz, R., Bernhart, S.H., Höner zu Siederdissen, C., Tafer, H., Flamm, C., Stadler, P.F., Hofacker, I.L.: ViennaRNA Package 2.0. Algorithms. Mol. Biol. **6**(1), 26 (2011)
17. Doye, J.P.K., Ouldridge, T.E., Louis, A.A., Romano, F., Šulc, P., Matek, C., Snodin, B.E.K., Rovigatti, L., Schreck, J.S., Harrison, R.M., Smith, W.P.J.: Coarse-graining DNA for simulations of DNA nanotechnology. Phys. Chem. Chem. Phys. **15**(47), 20395 (2013)
18. Hadorn, M., Bnzli, E., Fellermann, H., Eggenberger Hotz, P., Hanczyc, M.: Specific and reversible DNA-directed self-assembly of emulsion droplets. Proc. Nat. Acad. Sci. USA **109**(47) (2012)
19. Fellermann, H., Cardelli, L.: Programmable chemistry in DNA addressable bioreactors. R. Soc. Interface **11**(99), 20130987 (2014)

Analysis of Boolean Logic Gates Logical Complexity for Use with Spiking Memristor Gates

Ella Gale[1,2](✉)

[1] University of Bath, Claverton Down, Somerset, Bath BA2 7AY, UK
em734@bath.ac.uk
[2] International Center for Unconventional Computing,
University of the West of England,
Coldharbour Lane, Frenchay, Bristol BS16 1QY, UK

Abstract. 2-Bit Boolean logical operations have been considered before, however, the focus has always been on the AND, OR, NOT, NAND and NOR gates that are of use in traditional electronics. The memristor tends to require implication and similar logics, which can be considered as sequential logics, especially when used with spiking memristor gates. Here we introduce the concept of logical efficiency based on how many differentiable operations exist in a truth table, and sequence sensitive gates (e.g. IMP) are found to have a higher logical efficiency. We propose an ideal gate which is both functionally complete and maximally logically efficient and demonstrate that it does not exist in 2-bit binary gates, but can exist in trinary. We propose that this novel theoretical approach will aid the building of neuromorphic computers that will be highly efficient, powerful and resilient.

Keywords: Memristor · Boolean logic · Trinary · Logic gates

1 Introduction

Theory and experiment can often be artificially divorced and often are to aim at a more specific audience. However, the motivation and engine of theoretical development is novel experimental results, often arising from novel technologies, that cause the theorist to ask new questions. The technology that inspires this work is the memristor, a brand new fundamental circuit element, and specifically using their spiking ability to perform logical operations. This invention [1] works by using the short-term memory of the memristor to store bits and perform computation. This invention raises significant theoretical questions: what is our 'conversion rate' between space (in terms of wires into a circuit element) and time (in terms of time-steps of computation); how do we quantify the complexity of a logical operation (in order to allow the comparison between memristor logic gates and transistor logic gates); what is the limit of complexity of a logical operation of a single memristor? To our knowledge (and best efforts of a literature

© Springer International Publishing Switzerland 2016
M. Amos and A. Condon (Eds.): UCNC 2016, LNCS 9726, pp. 99–115, 2016.
DOI: 10.1007/978-3-319-41312-9_9

review) these questions have not been considered before. In order to attempt to answer such questions, we examine the information content and complexity of Turing-complete (functionally complete) logic gate sets, adders and other computer components: specifically we find that a Turing complete set of logic gates requires a polarity change and the loss of information. We attempt to quantify the logical computation of logic gates by considering the percentage of ○ and |s in an operated on a stream of randomly-distributed 50 % ○ : | (we use ○ and | for logical 0 and logical 1, and use 0 and 1 for the numbers).

1.1 Memristors

Chua introduced the memristor concept in 1971 [2] as a device which related its internal state to the time-integral of current or voltage. The concept has been expanded and refined [3–5] and there is still some debate about what definition should be used to describe the memristor (see this recent review [6]). There are many different types of memristor, from the original titanium dioxide version [7], although there are many metal oxide memristors and recent work has expanded the range of memristor materials [6]. This work is general in scope, inspired by memristors that exhibit a spike when a voltage is applied or changed, and motivated by explaining the action of our devices [1]. Our memristors are made of a thin film titanium dioxide layer between aluminium electrodes [8,9], and their material and action has been reported elsewhere [9–14]. However, the general discussion of implication logic as utilised by memristors is relevant to non-spiking devices that use this logic (of which there are many and it is thought that physical action of memristors in general is IMP logic [15]).

The memristor memory is usually stored in ions, for example in the best-known version of the device [7], it is stored in oxygen vacancies, this is also the case in our devices [9,16]. Putting a voltage across the device causes the movement of ions which changes the resistance, leading to an altered current, specifically a current spike (there is far more detail available than this, see [6,17,18]).

1.2 Memristor Spiking Logic Gates

I have developed several 1-port logic gates using a single memristor. A voltage applied to a memristor will cause a current spike, if a second (or third) spike is input to the memristor within the 'short-term memory' time of the memristor [10,19] (defined as the time taken for a memristor to achieve its long-time resistance value, i.e. 'forget' the spike happened), the resulting current value is altered from what only one spike would give, and seems to follow implication logic. This interaction allows us to compute, with the proviso that input values are voltages and output values are currents, and thus would need to be converted to voltage values to allow chaining of gates. Using the spikes to compute in this way, we can make several two bit Boolean gates (AND, OR, XOR, NOT) [1] with one memristor. The memristor has only one wire in and one wire out, so the computation is a type of sequential logic and takes two time-steps. This type of invention motivates the question of how the 'space' of input and output wires of a standard gate is exchanged for the 'time' in terms of number of time-steps required to compute the same thing with a spiking memristor gate.

I also managed to make a type of full adder using a single memristor [11], three input time steps and two output time-steps, one output read (current measurement) at the time the third input spike is sent, and one input 'read' spike and current measurement; thus the full adder computes in 5 time-steps with 3 input spikes and a read spike (the read spike is always the same value), again with the proviso that circuitry to convert current to voltage is required to chain the outputs into inputs. This gate was also slightly different from the standard full adder. By measuring the negative voltage in within a range we get our carry bit (| if a current is measured in that range, $\bigcirc$ if it is not). By looking at the positive current values over a range we can get the arithmetical sum of the inputs, i.e., separate out 0, 1, 2, and 3, which can be converted into a standard summation bit, or could be used as is. Most interestingly, the current value of the read output bit gives us the order of the input bits, allowing us to separate out an $\{\bigcirc, \bigcirc, |\}$ from $\{\bigcirc, |, \bigcirc\}$ and $\{|, \bigcirc, \bigcirc\}$, and so on. This motivates the question of how do we measure the efficiency and circuit complexity of such a system and allow a fair comparison between it and a standard full adder, and it is this question that motivates this work.

1.3 Logic

To design a circuit, we need to consider circuit complexity.

As this is a paper about designing and instantiating logic gates, we shall briefly review computer logic (although the area is large) and how it has been implemented in memristors. In this paper, we use the Arabic numerals $\{1,2,3\}$ as a set of counting numbers capable of standard arithmetical operations and we use the following set of symbols $\{\bigcirc, |\}$ for logical values 0 and 1 in binary and $\{\bigcirc, |, ||\}$ 0,1,2 in trinary.

Philosophical Roots of IMP Logic. Bertrand Russell and Whitesides invented and developed implication logic in 1910 [20]. However, it was Shannon's master's thesis that associated Boolean algebra with a digital logic system [21] that almost all computers since have been based on (he built Boolean logic gates out of relays and switches). Material implication logic is the logical form of the philosophical statement "*if A then B*" (which has uses as the if/then conditional in many programming languages). In philosophy, if statement A is false, and statement B is false, we can say 'if A then B' is true, this is equivalent to saying that A and B are both false so the statement that $A \rightarrow B$ is true (in a logical sense given what we know from just those statements, of course, there may be no causation between the statements). Similarly, if A and B are both true, we could infer that $A \rightarrow B$. In both these cases we are inferring a positive correlation between these two statements (again logically, scientifically we would need to do more work to attempt to prove causation). If A is false and B is true, we can infer that A implies B, but the relation in this sense is a negative correlation. If A is true and B is false, we cannot infer that A implies B because B is not true, its value could be anything and could be related to anything, thus $A \rightarrow B$ would be false. This logical system is IMP in binary.

1.4   Analyses of Boolean Logic

Logic gates are usually worked with via their truth table – if you know the truth table of a gate, you can design with it, similarly to how if you know the V-I characteristics of a device you can use it in a circuit. Mathematically, the truth tables have been investigated as Boolean functions

Boolean logic has been analysed from a mathematical point of view, as Boolean functions [22]. Karnaugh maps [23], graphical version of Veitch charts [24], can be used (and often are) to find the best representation of a function with a Boolean truth table. The are 16 2-bit Boolean functions that have been classified by Simpson [25].

Emil Post [26] classified Boolean functions into four sets: Monotonic $(\wedge, \vee, \top, \bot)$ where $| \longrightarrow \bigcirc$ and we never have $\bigcirc \longrightarrow |$; self-dual, i.e. $\neg$ where the gate is equal to its own de Morgan dual; truth-preserving, such as $\wedge, \vee, \bot, \rightarrow \leftrightarrow$, where $|, | \longrightarrow |$; falsity preserving, such as $\wedge, \vee, \bot, \nrightarrow, \nleftrightarrow$, where $\bigcirc, \bigcirc \longrightarrow \bigcirc$.

Functional Completeness. In mathematics, a Sheffer function is a minimal Boolean operation that is functionally complete by itself, where functional completeness means that all other logic gates can be expressed with that operation alone (of the same bit order, i.e. a two bit Sheffer function can express all 2-bit Boolean functions). In dealing with the physical instantiation of these functions, a functionally complete logic gate can be used in a circuit to make every other type of Boolean function, although it need not be the most efficient or easy way to do this. In electronic engineering the set $\{\wedge, \vee, \neg\}$ is often taken as our working set, and is functionally complete, also the sets $\{\wedge \neg\}$ and $\{\vee \neg\}$ are functionally complete by themselves. From this reasoning, it is obvious that NAND (a.k.a. Sheffer Stroke), $\bar{\wedge}$ and NOR (a.k.a. Peirce stroke) $(\bar{\vee})$ gates are functionally complete by themselves.

1.5   Circuit Complexity

To decide how to design a circuit board, we need to be able to compare logically equivalent methods of performing an arbitrary logical function. There have been a few approaches to determining how 'complex' a circuit is. Circuit size complexity of a Boolean function is the minimal size of a circuit that can compute that function (in the abstract mathematical sense, how many logic gates required, in the concrete electronic engineering sense we would take into account the size of those components). Circuit depth complexity of a Boolean function is the minimal depth of a circuit, i.e. the maximum length of a path from input to output gate for the physical devices. Another approach is the graph of nodes where each node is a logic gate. Karnaugh maps are often used as a method of finding the best approach to build a logical system or express a logical function.

1.6   Logical Systems

There are several logical systems that can be used, binary, trinary and other higher order logics, multi-value logics (an interesting example of which has the four values True, False, Neither true or false, Both true and false, which has been used in Buddhist thought), non-monatonic logics. The only ones which need concern us here is binary and trinary. Binary logic operates on two values, true $\top$ and false $\bot$ usually designated as | and $\bigcirc$ (these assignations are entirely arbitrary and have more to do with mankind's preference for positive associations over negative) and is arithmetically equivalent to base 2. Trinary has three values, $\bigcirc, |, ||$, which can be viewed as logic done in base 3, but can be used as different logical meanings, such as: { true, irrelevant, false} or { true, null, false }. One of the early computers Setun used trinary logic, but most modern computers are based on binary.

1.7   How Logic Gates Have Been Instantiated with Memristors

Strukov et al. [15] used implication logic to design logic gates which required two memristors (IMP-FALSE ($\{\rightarrow, \bot\}$) logic is Turing complete, but somewhat unfamiliar to computer scientists). The most notable Boolean logic gates were simulated by Pershin and di Ventra [27] and required a memcapacitor, three or four memristive systems and a resistor. Before the gate was sent the two bits of data, a set of initialization pulses were required to be sent to put the gate into the correct state to give the correct answer. This system, however, is not true Boolean logic because these initialization pulses were different dependent on what the logic to follow would be. Thus the gate can not be considered to be operating only on the two bits of input data and is not a simple Boolean logic gate (it is a Turing machine doing a computation on several bits of data (Boolean input pulses and initialization pulses) which is capable of modelling a Boolean logic gate). Note also that this scheme was tested with memristor emulators, not real devices. There have been other more complex designs for memristor based Boolean logic gates, the simplest of which requires 11 circuit elements. [28] In this paper, we will demonstrate how to perform Boolean logic with a single memristor.

Interesting work involving designing memristor logic gates by Lehtonen and Laiho. In [29] they work with implication logic using a memristor reset as the false operation, they also suggest that 3 memrsitors are sufficient to compute any 2-bit in, 1-bit out Boolean function and state that: $2^2 \rightarrow 2^m$ need $m + 2$ working memristors, for example a full adder would require 10 memristors under this scheme as it is 2^{2^3}. In [30] they suggest using parallelism to avoid the sequential nature of memristors, and choose NcIMP as the best version of Implication logic for memristor cross-bars. Spiking logic gates [1] represent a novel way of computing using memristor spike addition.

2   Results

In order to compare the memristor logic gates to standard logic gates, we need a fair comparison of circuit complexity.

There are two approaches to do such a comparison based on current theory. The first is to use the area of the circuit board. In this sense the memristor logic gate scores very well as the memristor can be made very small and the switches required to convert the output of a full adder to input are smaller than a transistor. The area of a circuit board however is not the best comparison as the numbers will change depending on technological development in shrinking sizes of components, which does not seem the best way to compare the logical complexity of the operation. Standard approaches of counting the number of gates and length of the circuit bypasses this issue, however, in this scheme the memristor full adder seems to be amazing as it involves 1 memristor and a switching selector.

2.1   Energetics

When building a novel computer system, we concentrate on building either a universal gate (a single gate which can be used to create all Boolean functions) or a functionally complete set (a set of gates that is sufficient to create all Boolean functions). In unconventional computing, biological computing, chemical computing, and molecular electronics the states | and ○ have different energies (this is also the case in electronics where different voltages are used to represent different logical states). Much of the difficulty in creating a universal logic gate out of a new system is in creating a $\{○, ○\} \rightarrow |$ transition, as if the | state is higher in energy than the ○ state, we must input energy from somewhere to represent that state.

2.2   Reclassification of Binary Logic Gates

We shall assume that | state is higher in energy than ○ state (the entire argument still holds if the association of the energy levels with logic is switched). In this section, we shall use binary, as represented by the states ○ and |. The truth tables for all possible 2 input bit, 1 output bit gates, 2^{2^2}, is given in Table 1.

We can classify these gates based on the energy and efficiency of the gate, to allow us to answer the questions, what functionality can implication gates offer us and how can we compare our single memristor gates.

These gates have been classified before and have been separated out into 4 sets [26], monotonic, self-dual, truth-preserving and falsity preserving.

We compare 4 different sets based on the number of differentiable operations, i.e. how many of the 4 inputs could you identify if given only the output and the arithmetical sum.

Table 1. All 2-bit binary Boolean functions and their corresponding gate names (as used in this work). Note that cIMP and NcIMP are not standard names as there are no agreed upon names for these gates (people work with just their function number or truth table, if they work with them at all).

p q	1	2	3	4	5	6	7	8	9	10	11	12	13	14	15	16
○ ○	○	|	○	○	○	|	|	|	○	○	○	|	|	|	○	|
○ |	○	○	|	○	○	|	○	○	|	|	○	|	|	○	|	|
| ○	○	○	○	|	○	○	|	○	|	○	|	|	○	|	|	|
| |	○	○	○	○	|	○	○	|	○	|	|	○	|	|	|	|
Name	False	NOR	NcIMP	NIMP	AND	Not p	Not q	NXOR	XOR	q	p	NAND	IMP	cIMP	OR	True
Symbol	⊥	⊽	↚	↛	∧	¬p	¬q	↔	↮	q	p	⊼	→	←	∨	⊤
No.*	F_0	F_8	F_4	F_2	F_1	F_{12}	F_{10}	F_9	F_6	F_5	F_3	F_{14}	F_{13}	F_{11}	F_7	F_{15}

Existence Gates. There are two existence gates, $\{\top, \bot\}$. In standard electronics, true is equivalent to a short circuit and false to a open circuit. In our system, they represent a gate which fires out a | or a ○ regardless of the input, and so they react to the existence of an incoming logic signal, and not its value, in fact they are information destroying[1].

Half-Value Gates. There are four gates that, effectively, ignore half the input bits and are exactly equivalent to 1-bit in, 1-bit out logic gates, these are designated: $\{p, q, \neg p, \neg q\}$ after the 1-ports they represent. In physical devices, its easy to see how these 2-bit input gates result from failure of a more functional gate, for example by wire breaking.

Basic Gates (Arithmetical Gates). These are the standard gates that are most used in digital computing: $\{\wedge, \vee, \bar{\wedge}, \bar{\vee}, \not\leftrightarrow, \leftrightarrow\}$. The basic gates can be called arithmetical gates as they do not distinguish between $\{|, ○\}$ and $\{○, |\}$ (which arithmetically sum to the same value). These gates are 'self-sequence dual', see later.

Sequence Sensitive Gates. These are the more exotic and rarely used gates, based on Implication logic: $\{\rightarrow, \not\rightarrow, \leftarrow, \not\leftarrow\}$, which we have called $\rightarrow$ for Material Implication (IMP), the de Morgan Dual (i.e. negative) of IMP, $\not\rightarrow$, (NIMP), the reverse-time complement of $\rightarrow$ (cIMP) and the de Morgan Dual of cIMP which is $\not\leftarrow$ (NcIMP). Let's explain what we mean by 'reverse-time complement'.

In our system p and q the inputs have a related time-stamp to them. Input bit p is input at $t = 1\tau$, input bit q is input at $t = 2\tau$, so we find that $\{p(t_1), q(t_2)\} \neq \{p(t_2), q(t_1)\}$, i.e. the order that the bits are input has an effect. This is extra information compared to just the sum of these bits.

---

[1] An interesting fact about existence gates is that they are useless in standard electronics, in our scheme they allow a method of recording the presence or absence of a logical signal without knowing anything about the content, which has applications in cryptography, monitoring, meta-data tracking and hacking of such systems.

Table 2. Reverse time complementation of IMP give cIMP

p	q	IMP	q	p	cIMP	NIMP
○ ⟶ ○		$\mid$	○ ⟶ ○		$\mid$	○
○ ⟶ $\mid$		$\mid$	$\mid$ ⟵ ○		○	○
$\mid$ ⟵ ○		○	○ ⟶ $\mid$		$\mid$	$\mid$
$\mid$ ⟶ $\mid$		$\mid$	$\mid$ ⟶ $\mid$		$\mid$	○

We take the following direction as being the 'natural order of things': increasing in value or staying the same as time goes on, and if this is present, we output a $\mid$, if not, (i.e. things are decreasing) we output a ○. For the 2-bit binary gate, an example is: $\{○,○\} \longrightarrow \mid$, $\{\mid,\mid\} \longrightarrow \mid$ and $\{○,\mid\} \longrightarrow \mid$ whereas $\{\mid,○\} \longrightarrow ○$ (this rule is equivalent to monotonicity (I think)). This is the truth table for IMP logic. If we draw the arrow of time going in the direction we expect from this viewpoint, it looks as shown on the left hand side in Table 2. Reversing the order, so replacing $\{p(t_1), q(t_2)\}$ with $\{q(t_1), p(t_2)\}$, following the rule above to generate a new truth table we get the truth table for cIMP (the truth table for NIMP is shown as a comparison to demonstrate that this different from negation under de Morgan's law). And so, we refer to IMP and NIMP gates as being Time-conserving, and their time complements cIMP and NcIMP as being Time-reversing. N.B. I am not suggesting that these gates reverse time, merely that if the physical processes that give rise to the effect of, say, IMP were to be reversed, the truth-table would be cIMP.

Essentially, this is a measure of energy conservation. What is actually happening in our system can be represented as: $\{.pq.\}$ where '.' represents the system with no applied voltage; the first '.' the systems is usually zeroed, the second '.' the response of the system (which is a convolution of p, q and .) is measured. As our response is in the opposite direction to the applied voltage (due to 'bounce-back'), and the energy in the system decays with time (auto-destruction/short-term memory), the state $\{\mid(t_1), ○(t_2)\}$ has less energy at time $t = 3\tau$ than $\{○(t_1), \mid(t_2)\}$, so the responses at $t = 3$ (measured as a ○ for the first example, $\mid$ for the second) are a result of energy conservation.

It is interesting to ponder here if a cIMP gate could be created with a memristor[2]. For our devices using sequential logic we would need a system where $\{\mid, ○\}$ had more energy than $\{○\mid\}$ but that $\{○○\}$ and $\{\mid\mid\}$ still had more energy. It's hard to think what would make this work in this system, perhaps a dissipative media? However, [30] demonstrates a scheme based on a more conventional voltage drop simultaneous logic using a 'rectifying memristor model' which uses NcIMP (they call it 'converse non-implication') to implement Boolean functions in cellular neural/nanoscale network (CNN).

2.3 Logical Efficiency

We now go on to discuss the efficiency of these 16 2-bit logic gates to attempt to describe how functional each of them are, as shown in Table 3. We define

---

[2] Other than the trivial way of using a high voltage for ○ and a low voltage for $\mid$.

the number of inputs, N, to be the number of lines in the truth table, i.e. the number of different combinations we can input. Our first set, existence gates, can exist with an arbitrary number of inputs, for example, see the 1-bit $\top$ and $\bot$ gates in Table 4, and as these only react to the presence of an input, not its logical value, we say there are zero input values, only 1 distinguishable operation ($\{x\} \longrightarrow \{o\}$ where x is any input and o is the output value). The gate efficiency is defined as the number of distinguishable operations over the possible number of distinguishable operations (which is 4 for these gates as there 4 possible input combinations). Existence gates always have an efficiency of $^1/_N$. Half value gates ignore one of the inputs, so although there are 4 possible inputs, they only distinguish 2 of them, giving an efficiency of 50 % (hence the name half value gates). Logically these are equivalent to the 1-bit gates in Table 4, but in terms of circuit space they would take up a greater area (and this example demonstrates why we need a measure of logical complexity that is separate from current measures of area of silicon or number of transistors). Basic gates do not differentiate between the middle two inputs in the truth table and thus only distinguish 3 out of four operations. We can call them arithmetic gates as they successfully separate out the sums of the inputs into three groups i.e. if we arithmetically add the logical values for the four inputs we get: $\{0 + 0\} = 0$, $\{0 + 1\} = 1$, $\{1 + 0\} = 1$, $\{1 + 1\} = 2$ (where we have taken logical 1 (|) and logical 0 (◯) as one and zero). We can see that under the arithmetical addition operation the 4 inputs have only 3 distinguishable values. Finally sequence sensitive gates separate out the arithmetically equivalent $\{◯, |\}$ and $\{|, ◯\}$, allowing them maximum efficiency.

We should point out here that the separation is on distinguishable operations, not outputs. As we are using binary and these gates have only one output bit, we always have 2 sets of outputs, those equal to ◯ and those equal to |. By distinguishable operations we mean, if we know the arithmetical sum of our set and our logic gate outputs, can we identify which outputs matched which inputs? This might seem a slightly arbitrary approach, but, due to 'bounce-back' and the summation properties of our devices, we retain the information on the arithmetical sum as well as getting the logical output, so this is information available to us in the laboratory.

From these arguments it is clear that the sequence sensitive gates have a higher possible functionality than that basic gates and thus, I suggest, it is far more efficient to build memristor computers using IMP (or another sequence sensitive logic primitive) gates instead of using IMP gates to make basic gates. By using a sequence sensitive gate to express a basic gate we are projecting a 100 % efficient gate onto a 75 % gate, which will obviously cost size and energy for implementing it (of course, the argument can be made about the time and energy in redesigning the processor design). This also means that by switching from a basic design to sequence sensitive design we should be able to decrease the number of gates up to a maximum of 25 % with clever (and possibly arduous) design.

Table 3. The number of distinguishable operations

No. of inputs considered	No. of input values 'considered'	No. of distinguishable operations	Efficency
Existence gates	0 (presence of input)	1	25 %
Half value gates	1 (p or q)	2	50 %
Basic gates	2 (p and q)	3	75 %
Sequence-sensitive gates	2 + time value (order of p,q)	4	100 %

Table 4. 1-port logic gates (1 bit in, 1 bit out Boolean functions)

p	H_1	H_2	H_3	H_4
○	○	○	|	|
|	○	|	○	|
symbol	⊥	p	$\neg p$	⊤

2.4   An Aside on Ideal Gates and Functional Completeness

Are sequence-sensitive gates more useful than basic gates? Not necessarily. NAND and NOR gates are functionally complete, which means that they can be used to implement any Boolean function, so when making gates using a new technology, making a functionally complete gate is a good approach. None of the sequence sensitive gates are functionally complete. However, it is not necessary to fixate on Sheffer functions because functionally complete sets might be easier to fabricate involving sequence-sensitive gates, for example, Lehtonen et al. demonstrated that false could be applied to imp logic performing memristors (under standard voltage drop cross-bar array architecture) by reversing the voltage and zeroing the device [29, 30].

To be a functionally complete gate or set of gates, we require:

1. destruction: that the one of the gates is truth-destroying ($\{○, ○\} \longrightarrow |$)
2. and creation: one of the gates is falsity-destroying ($\{|, |\} \longrightarrow ○$), the gates do not need to separate out the arithmetically equal to 1 states (which raises the interesting question of whether it might be possible to define a different logic based on sequence as well as arithmetic).

Here I posit an 'ideal gate' would combine functional completeness with maximum logical efficiency. Thus, an ideal gate would be:

1. Functionally complete, i.e.:
   - Truth-destroying $\{|, |\} \longrightarrow ○$
   - Falsity-destroying $\{○, ○\} \longrightarrow |$
2. Maximum efficiency, i.e. can separate arithmetically equal parts of the truth table .

Effectively, we need to be able to identify each input sequence for each arithmetical output. with a memristor this would allow the differentiation of each input and does not destroy information (or rather it does, but we can recover the starting state in a way that you cannot recover from the NAND or NOR operations).

An ideal gate would be a good thing to make as it would combine the maximum functionality in a single gate, and, as I am implicitly assuming that all these gates are roughly the same size, it would allow the further shrinking and speeding up of computation, this is not unreasonable as we have demonstrated functionality up to a full adder (and not that that is the limit) with one memristor, so we don't need to add extra transistors.

Such a gate is impossible to make as a 2-bit in, 1 bit out gate using binary logic. The 2-bit gates that posses both properties in their truth table are $\neg p$ and $\neg q$ (gates 6 and 7), but as these work by effectively logically ignoring one of the inputs they are not ideal gates. The one-bit $\neg p$ and $\neg q$ are 100 % logically efficient gates, the 2-bit versions are only 50 % efficient, and this example demonstrates why we needed to develop the idea of logical efficiency rather than just looking for creation, destruction and logical separation of arithmetically-equal in a truth table (because throwing away one bit regardless of value is not efficient computation!).

Table 5. Relation between the number of ports, n, and number of Sheffer gates for binary and trinary logic. Of these Sheffer gates, some will be ideal gates, suggesting that devices with more ports are more likely to be ideal (although calculating the proportion has not been done in this work).

$n \longrightarrow$	0	1	2	3
No. of triary gates [31]	3	27	729	59,049
No of 3-ary Sheffer gates [31]	0	0	90	11,484
No. of binary gates	2	4	16	–
No. of 2-ary Sheffer gates	0	0	2	–

To create an ideal gate we either need to increase the number of output bits (it is possible to differentiate between the arithmetically equal states with a second output) or use trinary logic. One might think that we could make an ideal gate from a 2-bit in, 2-bit out binary gate, but this does not work as the only $\neg p$ and $\neg q$ satisfy the conditions of separating out $\{|, \bigcirc\}$ and $\{\bigcirc, |\}$ and truth- and falsity-destroying (using NAND and NOR as outputs does not separate the arithmetically equal to one states). This gate fits our definition of an ideal gate, but is effectively only a 2 bit NOT gate.

Perhaps because the ideal gate is more functional than the Sheffer gates, they are not found in 2-bit binary gates. It is interesting to have a brief aside here on the number of functionally complete gates found as we increase either the number of ports (n) or the modulus (k) of the k-ary logic (eg. $k = 3$ for trinary), see Table 5. For two inputs there are 90 Sheffer gates in trinary compared to 2 in binary, so there is a bigger combination space in which to find Sheffer gates. Interestingly, as the modulus of the arithmetic increases, the proportion of Sheffer gates of the total tends to $^1/e$ which is approximately 36.79 % [31]. Thus, it is expected that 2-bit trinary gates will have more than a couple of ideal gates.

As existence gates (also called constant gates in the literature) are often 'free' in circuit design, the number of 2 element sets, $\{x, y\}$, that are functionally complete and include an existence gate is a useful number to know. In trinary, there are 333 such sets compared to 4 in binary. As these binary gate sets[3] are all based on sequence sensitive gates, it shows that these gates are more functional than the basic gates (because they form a functionally complete set combined with a simpler gate).

For example the 3-bit trinary gate is ideal because it allows the separation of arithmetically equal states. Essentially, we need a larger output space than the largest number of arithmetically equivalent gates. We need to redefine the Truth-, Falsity- destroying criteria for trinary, depending on the meaning of the trinary values. If we choose || to mean irrelevant, then it makes sense to require:

$$\{\bigcirc, \bigcirc\} \longrightarrow |$$
$$\{|, |\} \longrightarrow \bigcirc$$
$$\{||, ||\} \longrightarrow ||, \tag{1}$$

then, we keep the form of truth- and falsity- destruction and a double 'irrelevant' value is still 'irrelevant' (as you'd expect from the logic reasoning, adding irrelevant values should not effect the outcome).

If we choose to take || to be a number (so we are doing computation in base 3 rather than base 2), then the following $\bigcirc$-, |-, ||-destroying rules make sense:

$$\{\bigcirc, \bigcirc\} \longrightarrow |$$
$$\{|, |\} \longrightarrow ||$$
$$\{||, ||\} \longrightarrow \bigcirc. \tag{2}$$

There are 16 ideal 2-bit in, 1-bit out trinary gates for each of the definitions above. These requirements were found from inspection of 2-bit binary gates and binary gate sets followed by induction to trinary. In 2-bit binary gates and gate sets, we require both truth-destroying (destruction) and falsity-destroying (creation) to be present in a gate or set of gates. However, in [31], the requirement that a function $f(x, x, x, ..., x) \neq x, \forall x \in \{1, 2, 3, ..., k-1\}$ was found to give a Sheffer function with a probability tending to $1/e$ (0.36) as $k \longrightarrow \infty$, i.e. so long as the homogeneous input lines (e.g. $[|, |]$) of the truth table are destroying (e.g. $[||, ||, ||] \longrightarrow \bigcirc$) the function is likely to be a Sheffer function.

Table 6 shows two examples of ideal trinary logic gates. Using the p and q as the input bits, then the output A separates arithmetically equal values

---

[3] $\{\rightarrow, \bot\}, \{\leftarrow, \bot\}, \{\nrightarrow, \top\}, \{\nleftarrow, \top\}$.

(this could be argued as a second bit of information, but, of course, it is one that we have using memristor spiking logic gates). Using p and q as input bits, and taking A and B as output bits we have a 2-bit input, 2-bit output gate, where each input value can be separated from the others (i.e. it is reversible logic).

Table 6. An example of a trinary ideal gate. Inputs are p and q, column $\sum$ is the arithmetical sum, A and B are outputs. The combination of p, q and A is the truth table of a 2-bit in, 1-bit out ideal gate. The combination of p, q, A and B is the truth table of a 2-bit in, 2-bit out ideal trinary logic gate that is reversable without the requirement of needing the arithmetical sum.

p	q	$\sum$	A	B
○	○	0	|	|
○	|	1	○	|
|	○	1	||	|
|	|	2	||	||
||	○	2	|	||
○	||	2	○	||
|	||	3	||	○
||	|	3	|	○
||	||	4	○	○

2.5 Logical Complexity of a Full Adder

A half adder is a 2-bit output basic gate, it is equivalent to an XOR and an AND gate.

Now we are in a position to analyse our full adder from the point of view of logical efficiency. The 2-bit full adder separates 8 3-bit inputs into 4 arithmetical groups. arbitrarily large numbers can be added by chaining full adders as the carry bit out to the carry bit (C) in. Using the same description as before, as standard full adder has $N = 8$ (2^3) possible inputs, and 4 distinguishable operations, giving us a logical efficiency of 50 %. Our spiking logic full adder allows the differentiation of all 8 operations, and gives us a logical efficiency of 100 %. Using standard circuit complexity measures of circuit depth complexity and circuit size complexity we get $1 +$ selection circuitry for our full adder and 10 for a standard transistor based full adder [32]. This is not a fair comparison, of course, because a standard full adder has multiple ports and all bits are received at the same time, in our full adder we have to take 2 time-steps to get the answer.

As an aside, this measure of logical efficiency means that the full adder is less logically efficient than a half adder. A half adder requires 2 input bits and 2 output bits ($B^2 \longrightarrow B^2$) and can separate out 4 inputs into 3 groups, giving a logical efficiency of 75 %. The full adder has to add an entire extra bit to count up to 3 and separate out 8 inputs into 4 groups. Of course, a single logic gate doing a full adder's truth table is better (as it involves 3 bits of input not $2 * 2 = 4$) and of course the full adder is more useful. However the half adder is 75 % efficient on 4 inputs, allowing it to separate out 3 different inputs, the

Table 7. Full adder truth table

A	B	C	Σ	C	Arithmetical Σ
○	○	○	○	○	0
|	○	○	|	○	1
○	|	○	|	○	1
○	○	|	|	○	1
|	|	○	○	|	2
|	○	|	○	|	2
○	|	|	○	|	2
|	|	|	|	|	3

full adder is 50 % efficient on 8 inputs which allow it to separate out 4 groups of inputs (Table 7).

Relatively simply, we can immediately write that for each input port removed from the gate, an extra input time-step must be added. Thus, we can replace circuit connections with extra time steps. Thus we arrive at an answer to the 'conversion rate' between space and time where we count space by the number of input wires and time by the time-step (in a spiking clocked system). It seems to be approximately 1:1 for the simple gates. In standard electronics a full adder involves 3 input wires (one time-step), in the memristor system, we use 1 input wire and 3 time-steps. Output in standard electronics is 2 output wires, in the memristor system we can either use 1 time output plus 1 read pulse. As the output pulse happens at the same time as the last input pulse, a 5 wire, 1 time-step standard electronics full adder is compared to a 2 wire, 4 time-step memristor full adder.

3   Conclusions

In this paper, we explained logic gates by counting the number of differentiable operations (as in, the number of operations we can usefully differentiate, not a numerical differentiation approach). This has practical uses. In this paper, Ideal logic gates have been invented and explained and it has been shown that they are impossible in binary but achievable in trinary. There we suggestions that memristors might be more naturally described in trinary than binary.

In this paper, I put forward a new way of classifying logic gates that takes into account the energetics of the devices and, I hope, will make it easier to design logic gates from nanoscale components by clarifying the properties required.

This paper also suggested a measure of efficiency to compare (computation) time and (circuit) space complexity, and this measure was used to compare the spiking memristor full adder with a standard full adder and put a number to that improvement.

Spiking existence gates fire when a signal reaches them, but they do not conserve the information of that signal, merely its existence. This could be useful for systems where you might want to know if a signal is passed without knowing what it is (for example for tech support tests on a confidential line).

As cIMP has applications in Bayesian reasoning in evolutionary computing. cIMP is equivalent to asking what is the likelihood of B given A, where the reverse time complement is due to us asking the question about an event in the past. I do not know if cIMPs can be built with spiking logic in memristors, but cIMP gates could act as natural iotas of evolutionary computing.

The spiking memristor gates are logically reversible, in that, we have the information required at the output to reconstruct the full set of inputs. As time is not reversible, the gates are not physically reversible, to get that we would need a gate where the time effectively ran backwards. And we have that! The time-complement gates do this. Thus, if we used an IMP gate to do a computation and then ran the output straight into a cIMP gate we would get input to the IMP as the output. This would allow us to build a hardware encryption box. If a signal were to be encrypted in a circuit built of IMP gates. However, if the output was fed into the mirror image circuit made with cIMPs, the original input sequence would be extracted (the NIMP and NcIMP pair would work the same way). This has obvious applications in encryption. For a binary IMPs and cIMPs the key might be hackable, but using a larger k-ary space arithmetic and perhaps changing the number of input bits (how many are included in refresh of the memristors short-term memory) occasionally would make the system less hackable. If the line was good at keeping the separation of the spikes in time, the refresh of the memristor's short-term memory could be included and changed on the fly.

References

1. Gale, E., de Lacy Costello, B., Adamatzky, A.: Boolean logic gates from a single memristor via low-level sequential logic. In: Mauri, G., Dennunzio, A., Manzoni, L., Porreca, A.E. (eds.) UCNC 2013. LNCS, vol. 7956, pp. 79–89. Springer, Heidelberg (2013)
2. Chua, L.O.: Memristor - the missing circuit element. IEEE Trans. Circuit Theory **18**, 507–519 (1971)
3. Di Ventra, M., Pershin, Y.V., Chua, L.O.: Putting memory into circuit elements: memristors, memcapacitors, and meminductors [point of view]. Proc. IEEE **97**(8), 1371–1372 (2009)
4. Chua, L.O., Kang, S.M.: Memristive devices and systems. Proc. IEEE **64**, 209–223 (1976)
5. Chua, L.: Resistance switching memories are memristors. Applied Physics A: Materials Science & Processing, pp. 765–782, 2011
6. Gale, E.: Memristors and ReRAM: materials, mechanisms and models (a review). Semicond. Sci. Technol. **29**, 104004 (2014)
7. Strukov, D.B., Snider, G.S., Stewart, D.R., Williams, R.S.: The missing memristor found. Nature **453**, 80–83 (2008)
8. Gergel-Hackett, N., Hamadani, B., Dunlap, B., Suehle, J., Richer, C., Hacker, C., Gundlach, D.: A flexible solution-processed memrister. IEEE Electr. Device Lett. **30**, 706–708 (2009)
9. Gale, E., Pearson, D., Kitson, S., Adamatzky, A., Costello, B.L.: The effect of changing electrode metal on solution-processed flexibletitanium dioxide memristors. Mater. Chem. Phy. **162**, 20–30 (2015)

10. Gale, E., de Lacy, B., Costello, A.A.: Observation, characterization and modeling of memristor current spikes. Appl. Math. Inf. Sci. **7**, 1395–1403 (2013)
11. Gale, E., de Lacy, B., Costello, A.A.: Is spiking logic the route to memristor-based computers? In: 2013 International Conference on Electronics, Circuits and Systems (ICECS), pp. 297–300, Abu Dhabi, UAE. IEEE, 8–11 December 2013
12. Gater, D., Iqbal, A., Davey, J., Gale, E.: Connecting spiking neurons to a spiking memristor network changes the memristor dynamics. In: 2013 International Conference on Electronics, Circuits and Systems (ICECS), pp. 534–537, Abu Dhabi, UAE. IEEE, 8–11 December 2013
13. Gambuzza, L.V., et al.: Int. J. Bifurcation Chaos **25**, 1550101 (2015) [9 pages]. http://dx.doi.org/10.1142/S0218127415501011
14. Gale, E., de Costello, B.L., Adamatzky, A.: Emergent spiking in non-ideal memristor networks. Microelectron. J. **45**, 1401–1415 (2014)
15. Borghetti, J., Snider, G.D., Kuekes, P.J., Joshua Yang, J., Stewart, D.R., Stanley Williams, R.: 'Memristive' switches enable 'stateful' logic operations via material implication. Nature **464**, 873–876 (2010)
16. Gale, E., Mayne, R., Adamatzky, A., de Costello, B.L.: Drop-coated titanium dioxide memristors. Mater. Chem. Phy. **143**, 524–529 (2014)
17. Sawa, A.: Resistive switching in transition metal oxides. Mater. Today **11**, 28–36 (2008)
18. Waser, R., Aono, M.: Nanoionics-based resistive switching memories. Nat. Mater. **6**, 833–840 (2007)
19. Gale, E., de Lacy, B., Costello, V.E., Adamatzky, A.: The short-term memory (d.c. response) of the memristor demonstrates the causes of the memristor frequency effect. In: Proceedings of CASFEST 2014, June 2014
20. Whitehead, A.N., Russell, B.: Principia Mathematica. In: Marchant Books, vol. 1, pp. 394–508 (1910)
21. Shannon, C.E.: Trans. AIEE. A symbolic analysis of relay and switching circuits **57**, 713–723 (1938)
22. Comtet, L.: Boolean algebra generated by a system of subsets. In: Reidel, D. (ed.) Advanced Combinatorics: The Art of Finite and Infinite Expansions, pp. 185–189, Dordrecht (1974)
23. Karnaugh, M.: The map method for synthesis of combinational logic circuits. Trans. Am. Inst. Electr. Eng. part I **72**, 593–599 (1953)
24. Veitch, E.W.: Chart method for simplifying truth functions. In: Transactions of the 1952 ACM Annual Meeting, ACM Annual Conference/Annual Meeting, pp. 127–133 (1952)
25. Simpson, R.E.: Introductory Electronics for Scientists and Engineers. Allyn and Bacon, Boston (1987)
26. Post, E.L.: Introduction to a general theory of elementary propositions. Am. J. Math. **43**, 167–168 (1921)
27. Pershin, Y.V., Ventra, M.D.: Neuromorphic, digital and quantum computation with memory circuit elements. Proc. IEEE **100**, 2071–2081 (2012)
28. Pino, R.E., Bohl, J.W.: Self-reconfigurable memristor-based analog resonant computer. US Patent, pages US 8,274,312 B2 (2012)
29. Lehtonen, E., Laiho, M.: Stateful implication logic with memristors. In: IEEE/ACM International Symposium on Nanoscale Architectures, NANOARCH 2009, pp. 33–36, July 2009
30. Lehtonen, E., Poikonen, J.H., Laiho, M.: Applications and limitations of memristive implication logic. In: 13th International Workshop on Cellular Nanoscale Networks and Their Applications (CNNA), pp. 1–6, August 2012

31. Stojmenovi, I.: On sheffer symmetric functions in three-valued logic. Discrete Appl. Math. **22**(3), 267–274 (1989)
32. Lin, J.-F., Hwang, Y.-T., Sheu, M.-H., Ho, C.-C.: A novel high-speed and energy efficient 10-transistor full adder design. IEEE Trans. Circ. Syst. I Regular Papers **54**(5), 1050–1059 (2007)

Language Recognition Power and Succinctness of Affine Automata

Marcos Villagra[1](✉) and Abuzer Yakaryılmaz[2](✉)

[1] Universidad Nacional de Asunción
NIDTEC, Campus Universitario, San Lorenzo C.P. 2619, Paraguay
mvillagra@pol.una.py
[2] National Laboratory for Scientific Computing,
Petrópolis, RJ 25651-075, Brazil
abuzer@lncc.br

Abstract. In this work we study a non-linear generalization based on affine transformations of probabilistic and quantum automata proposed recently by Díaz-Caro and Yakaryılmaz [6] referred as affine automata. First, we present efficient simulations of probabilistic and quantum automata by means of affine automata which allows us to characterize the class of exclusive stochastic languages. Then, we initiate a study on the succintness of affine automata. In particular, we show that an infinite family of unary regular languages can be recognized by 2-state affine automata, whereas the number of states of any quantum and probabilistic automata cannot be bounded. Finally, we present the characterization of all (regular) unary languages recognized by two-state affine automata.

Keywords: Probabilistic automata · Quantum automata · Affine automata · State complexity · Stochastic language · Bounded-error · One-sided error

1 Introduction

1.1 Background

Probabilistic and quantum computing are popular computation models with a very rich literature. Quantum computation, in particular, apparently violates the so-called *strong Church-Turing thesis*, which states that all reasonable models of computation can be efficiently simulated by a probabilistic universal Turing machine. Evidence comes from the efficient solution to certain problems believed to be computationally hard, like factoring large composite numbers. Much research is devoted to pinpoint the exact source of this computational power of quantum computers.

The omitted proofs can be found in [22].

A. Yakaryılmaz—Yakaryılmaz was partially supported by CAPES with grant 88881.030338/2013-01 and some parts of this work was done while he was visiting Universidad Nacional de Asunción in September 2015.

© Springer International Publishing Switzerland 2016
M. Amos and A. Condon (Eds.): UCNC 2016, LNCS 9726, pp. 116–129, 2016.
DOI: 10.1007/978-3-319-41312-9_10

In this paper, we continue the work initiated in [6] on a quantum-like classical computational model based on affine transformations. In particular, we make emphasis in finite-state automata, which is arguably the most simple computation model. Affine automata are finite-state machines whose transition operators are affine operators, hence the name.

There are several sources that apparently gives power to quantum computers, like quantum parallelism and entanglement. Several researchers may agree that quantum interference (using negative amplitudes), however, seems to be the key component. Therefore, the reason to study affine automata is to simplify the study of quantum interference in the context of a simple classical computation model.

Probabilistic automata are computation models whose transitions are governed by stochastic operators preserving the ℓ_1-norm of a normalized vector with entries in the continuous set of real numbers $[0, 1]$. Similarly, the transitions in a quantum automaton are governed by unitary operators preserving the ℓ_2-norm of a normalized vector with entries over the complex numbers $\mathbb{C}$. The only restriction that affine transformations impose over finite-state machines is the preservation of barycenters of vectors with entries over the real numbers $\mathbb{R}$, or equivalently, preservation of the sum of all entries in the state vector. It is clear that any affine operator defined on non-negative real numbers is a stochastic operator.

Since affine transformations are linear, the evolution of an affine automaton is linear. Nonlinearity comes from a measurement-like operator (which we call weighting operator) that is applied at the end of every computation to determine the probability of observing an inner-state of the machine. We refer the reader to [6] for the detailed explanations and discussions. A continuation of this paper appeared in [5].

1.2 Contributions

In this work we present the following results on affine automata language classes. First, in Sect. 4 we show how to simulate a probabilistic automaton using an affine automaton (Theorem 1). Then we use that simulation to show that any rational exclusive stochastic language can be recognized by positive one-sided bounded-error affine automata (Theorem 2). This fact immediately implies a characterization of the language recognition power of nondeterministic quantum automata by one-sided bounded-error affine automata. In Sect. 5 we show how to simulate an n-state quantum automaton exactly by an $(n^2 + 1)$-state affine automaton (Theorem 4). In Sect. 6 we study the state complexity (succintness) of affine automata. First, we show that the so-called unary counting problem can be computed by some bounded-error affine automata with constant state complexity (Theorem 5), whereas any bounded-error quantum automaton requires at least a logarithmic number of states. Second, we show the existence of a promise language that is solved exactly by an affine automaton with constant state complexity (Theorem 7), whereas any probabilistic automaton requires exponential state complexity. Finally, in Sect. 7 we give a complete characterization of all (regular) unary languages recognized by two-state affine automata (Theorem 8).

Affine transformations are arguably simpler to understand compared to unitary operators. Therefore, the characterizations given in terms of affine automata of quantum language classes present a simpler setting where to study and research the power of interference.

2   Preliminaries

We assume the reader is familiar with the common notation used in automata theory. For details on the models of probabilistic and quantum automata, we recommend references [4,15,19].

Let Σ be a finite alphabet, not containing ¢ and $ called the left and right end-markers, respectively. The set of all the strings of finite length over Σ is denoted Σ^*. We define $\tilde{\Sigma} = \Sigma \cup \{¢, \$\}$ and $\tilde{w} = ¢w\$$ for any string $w \in \Sigma^*$. For any given string $w \in \Sigma^*$, $|w|$ denotes its length, $|w|_\sigma$ is the number of occurrences of the symbol σ, and w_j is the j-th symbol of w.

A *probabilistic finite automaton* (or PFA) [16] is a 5-tuple $P = (E, \Sigma, \{A_\sigma \mid \sigma \in \tilde{\Sigma}\}, e_s, E_a)$, where $E = \{e_1, \ldots, e_n\}$ is a finite set of inner states for some $n \in \mathbb{Z}^+$, $e_s \in E$ is the starting inner state, $E_a \subseteq E$ is a set of accept inner states, and A_σ is the stochastic transition matrix for the symbol $\sigma \in \tilde{\Sigma}$. Any input $w \in \Sigma^*$ is always given in the form $\tilde{w} = ¢w\$$ and it is scanned by P from left to right, symbol by symbol.[1] After scanning the j-th symbol, the configuration state of P is $v_j = A_{\tilde{w}_j} v_{j-1} = A_{\tilde{w}_j} A_{\tilde{w}_{j-1}} \cdots A_{\tilde{w}_1} v_0$, where $1 \leq j \leq |\tilde{w}|$ and v_0 is the initial state vector. The final configuration state is denoted $v_f = v_{|\tilde{w}|}$. The acceptance probability of P on w is given by $f_P(w) = \sum_{e_k \in E_a} v_f[k]$, where $v_f[k]$ is the k-th entry of the vector v_f.

A *quantum finite automaton* (or QFA) [4] is a 5-tuple $M = (Q, \Sigma, \{\mathcal{E}_\sigma \mid \sigma \in \tilde{\Sigma}\}, q_s, Q_a)$, where $Q = \{q_1, \ldots, q_n\}$ is a finite set of inner states for some $n \in \mathbb{Z}^+$, $\mathcal{E}_\sigma$ is a transition superoperator[2] for a symbol $\sigma \in \Sigma$, the inner state q_s is the initial state, and $Q_a \subseteq Q$ is a set of accept states. For any given input $w \in \Sigma^*$, the computation of M on w is given by $\rho_j = \mathcal{E}_{\tilde{w}_j}(\rho_{j-1})$, where $\rho_0 = |q_s\rangle\langle q_s|$ and $1 \leq j \leq |\tilde{w}|$. The final state is denoted $\rho_f = \rho_{|\tilde{w}|}$. The accept probability of M on w is given by $f_M(w) = \sum_{q_j \in Q_a} \rho_f[j,j]$, where $\rho_f[j,j]$ is the j-th diagonal entry of ρ. The most restricted model of QFA currently known is the so-called *Moore-Crutchfield QFA* (or MCQFA) [14]. An MCQFA is a 5-tuple $M = (Q, \Sigma, \{U_\sigma \mid \sigma \in \tilde{\Sigma}\}, q_s, Q_a)$, where all components are defined exactly in the same way as for QFAs except that U_σ is a unitary transition operator for a symbol $\sigma \in \Sigma$ acting on $span\{|q\rangle \mid q \in Q\}$. Physically, M corresponds to a closed-system based on pure states.[3] For any given input $w \in \Sigma^*$, the machine

---

[1] This way of scanning an input tape is sometimes referred to as "strict realtime.".

[2] A superoperator or quantum operator is a positive-semidefinite operation that maps density matrices to density matrices [4,19].

[3] Pures states are vectors in a complex Hilbert space normalized with respect to the ℓ_2-norm.

M is initialized in the quantum state $|v_0\rangle = |q_s\rangle$. Each step of a computation is given by $|v_j\rangle = U_{\tilde{w}_j}|v_{j-1}\rangle$, where $1 \leq j \leq |\tilde{w}|$. The final quantum state is denoted $|v_f\rangle = |v_{|\tilde{w}|}\rangle$. The accept probability of M on w is $f_M(w) = \sum_{q_j \in Q_a} |\langle q_j|v_f\rangle|^2$. Note that the inner product $\langle q_j|v_f\rangle$ gives the amplitude of q_j in $|v_f\rangle$.

If we restrict the entries in the transitions matrices of a PFA to zeros and ones we obtain a *deterministic finite automaton* (or DFA). A DFA is always in a single inner state during the computation and the input is accepted if only if the computation ends in an accept state. A language is said to be recognized by a DFA if and only if any member of the language is accepted by the DFA. Any language recognized by a DFA is called a *regular language* [17] and the class of regular languages is denoted REG.

Let $\lambda \in [0, 1)$ be a real number. A language L is said to be recognized by a PFA P with *cutpoint* λ if and only if $L = \{w \in \Sigma^* \mid f_P(w) > \lambda\}$. Any language recognized by a PFA with a cutpoint is called a *stochastic language* [16] and the class of stochastic languages is denoted SL, which is a superset of REG. As a special case, if $\lambda = 0$, the PFA is also called a *nondeterministic finite automaton* (or NFA). Any language recognized by an NFA is also a regular language.

A language L is said to be recognized by P with *isolated cutpoint* λ if and only if there exists a positive real number δ such that $f_P(w) \geq \lambda + \delta$ for any $w \in L$ and $f_P(w) \leq \lambda - \delta$ for any $w \notin L$. When the cutpoint is required to be isolated, PFAs are not more powerful than DFAs; that is, any language recognized by a PFA with isolated cutpoint is regular [16].

Language recognition with isolated cutpoint can also be formulated as recognition with bounded error. Let $\epsilon \in [0, \frac{1}{2})$. A language L is said to be recognized by a PFA P with error bound ϵ if and only if $f_P(w) \geq 1 - \epsilon$ for any $w \in L$ and $f_P(w) \leq \epsilon$ for any $w \notin L$.

As a further restriction, if $f_P(w) = 1$ for any $w \in L$, then we say that P recognizes L with *negative one-sided bounded error*; if $f_P(w) = 0$ for any $w \notin L$, then we say that P recognizes L with *positive one-sided bounded error*. If the error bound is not specified, then we say that L is recognized by P with *[negative/positive one-sided] bounded error*.

A language L is an *exclusive stochastic language* [15] if and only if there exists a PFA P and a cutpoint $\lambda \in [0, 1]$ such that $L = \{w \in \Sigma^* \mid f_P(w) \neq \lambda\}$. The class of exclusive stochastic languages is denoted by $\mathsf{SL}^{\neq}$. Its complement class is denoted by $\mathsf{SL}^{=}$ (that is $L \in \mathsf{SL}^{\neq}$ iff $\overline{L} \in \mathsf{SL}^{=}$). Note that for any language in $\mathsf{SL}^{\neq}$ we can choose as cutpoint any value between 0 and 1, but not 0 or 1, because in that case we can only recognize regular languages. Also notice that both $\mathsf{SL}^{\neq}$ and $\mathsf{SL}^{=}$ are supersets of REG (it is still open whether REG is a proper subset of $\mathsf{SL}^{\neq} \cap \mathsf{SL}^{=}$).

In the case of QFAs, they recognize all and only regular languages with bounded-error [12] and stochastic languages with cutpoint [24,26]. The class of languages recognized by nondeterministic QFAs, however, is identical to $\mathsf{SL}^{\neq}$.

For any language class C, we use C_{X} to denote the subclass of C when all transitions of the corresponding model are restricted to $\mathbb{X}$.

3   Affine Finite Automaton

In this section we define our model of finite-state machine based on affine transformations. We refer to [6] for the basics of affine systems. An *affine finite-state automaton*, or simply AfA, is a 5-tuple

$$M = (E, \Sigma, \{A_\sigma \mid \sigma \in \widetilde{\Sigma}\}, e_s, E_a),$$

where all the components are the same as in the definition of a PFA except that A_σ is an affine transformation matrix (each column sum is 1). Note that each configuration state of M is a column vector on $\mathbb{R}$ satisfying that the summation of entries is always 1. On input $w \in \Sigma^*$, let v_f be the final configuration state after scanning the right end-marker \$. Define the *accept probability* of M as

$$f_M(w) = \sum_{e_k \in E_a} \frac{|v_f[k]|}{|v_f|} \in [0,1], \tag{1}$$

where each value contributes with its absolute value. More specifically, when M is in the final state v_f, this vector is normalized with respect to the ℓ_1-norm obtaining a new vector v_f'; thus, in order to obtain the accept probability we project the vector v_f' on the subspace spanned by the accept inner states E_a of M and then taking the ℓ_1-norm again, that is, the summation of the absolute value of each entry.

Language recognition for M is defined in the same way. Any language recognized by an AfA with cutpoint is called an *affine language*. The class of affine languages is denoted AfL. Any language recognized by an AfA with cutpoint 0 (called nondeterministic AfA or NAfA for short) is called a *nondeterministic affine language*. The corresponding class is denoted NAfL. A language is called an *exclusive affine language* if and only if there exists an AfA M and a cutpoint $\lambda \in [0,1]$ such that $L = \{w \in \Sigma^* \mid f_M(w) \neq \lambda\}$. The class of exclusive affine languages is denoted by AfL$^{\neq}$ and its complement class is denoted AfL$^=$. Any language recognized by an AfA with bounded error is called an *bounded affine language*. The corresponding class is denoted BAfL. If the error is positive one-sided (all non-members are accepted with value 0), then the corresponding language class is denoted BAfL^0, whereas for negative one-sided error (all members are accepted with value 1) the corresponding language class is denoted BAfL^1. Note that if $L \in$ BAfL^0, then $\overline{L} \in$ BAfL^1, and vice versa. Any language recognized by an AfA with zero-error is called *exact affine language* and its corresponding language class is EAfL.

4   Simulation of Rational PFAs

In this section we present a simulation of PFAs by AfAs. Since 1-state PFAs are trivial, we focus on PFAs with two more states.

Theorem 1. *Any language L recognized by an n-state rational PFA with cutpoint $\frac{1}{2}$ can be recognized by an $(n+1)$-state integer AfA with cutpoint $\frac{1}{2}$.*

Proof. Let $P = (E, \Sigma, \{A_\sigma \mid \sigma \in \widetilde{\Sigma}\}, e_s, E_s)$ be an n-state PFA defined with only rational numbers with $n > 1$. With the help of end-markers, we can assume with no loss of generality that the initial state $e_s = e_1$ and $E_a = \{e_1\}$. Moreover, for any given $w \in \Sigma^*$, we can assume with no loss of generality that the final state vector of M is always

$$\begin{pmatrix} f_P(w) \\ 1 - f_P(w) \\ 0 \\ \vdots \\ 0 \end{pmatrix}.$$

Using P as defined above, we construct an AfA $MP = (E \cup \{e_{n+1}\}, \Sigma, \{B_\sigma \mid \sigma \in \widetilde{\Sigma}\}, e_1, \{e_1\})$, where $n = |E|$. Let d be the smallest positive integer such that for each $\sigma \in \Sigma$ the entries of the matrix dA_σ are integers. If v_0 is the initial state of P, for any string w, we have that

$$\left(dA_{\tilde{w}_{|\tilde{w}|}}\right)\left(dA_{\tilde{w}_{|\tilde{w}|-1}}\right) \cdots \left(dA_{\tilde{w}_1}\right) v_0 = d^{|\tilde{w}|} \begin{pmatrix} f_P(w) \\ 1 - f_P(w) \\ 0 \\ \vdots \\ 0 \end{pmatrix} \in \mathbb{Z}^n.$$

Define a new matrix A'_σ for each $\sigma \in \widetilde{\Sigma}$ as

$$A'_\sigma = \left(\begin{array}{c|c} dA_\sigma & 0 \\ \hline \overline{1} & 1 \end{array}\right),$$

where $\overline{1}$ is a row vector that makes the summation of each column under dA_σ equal to 1. Then, for a given string w, we have that

$$v'_f = A'_{\tilde{w}_{|\tilde{w}|}} A'_{\tilde{w}_{|\tilde{w}|-1}} \cdots A'_{\tilde{w}_1} \begin{pmatrix} v_0 \\ 0 \end{pmatrix} = \begin{pmatrix} d^{|\tilde{w}|} f_P(w) \\ d^{|\tilde{w}|} (1 - f_P(w)) \\ 0 \\ \vdots \\ 0 \\ 1 - d^{|\tilde{w}|} \end{pmatrix} \in \mathbb{Z}^{n+1}.$$

Using the vector v'_f, we can subtract the second entry from the first one and then sum everything else on the second entry by using an extra affine operator $A''_{\tilde{w}_{|\tilde{w}|}}$ obtaining

$$v''_f = A''_{\tilde{w}|\tilde{w}|} v'_f = \begin{pmatrix} d^{|\tilde{w}|}(2f_P(w) - 1) \\ 1 - d^{|\tilde{w}|}(2f_P(w) - 1) \\ 0 \\ \vdots \\ 0 \end{pmatrix} \in \mathbb{Z}^{n+1}.$$

Here the entries of $A''_{\tilde{w}|\tilde{w}|}$ are as follows:

$$A''_{\tilde{w}|\tilde{w}|} = \begin{pmatrix} 1 & -1 & 0 & \cdots & 0 \\ 0 & 2 & 1 & \cdots & 1 \\ \hline & & \mathbf{0} & & \end{pmatrix},$$

where $\mathbf{0}$ is a $(n-1, n+1)$-dimensional zero matrix. The vector v''_f is our desired final state for machine MP. Thus, for each $\sigma \in \Sigma \cup \{\mathtt{\cent}\}$, we set $B_\sigma = A'_\sigma$, and, for the last operator we set $B_\$ = A''_\$ A'_\$$. The initial vector of MP is $u_0 = \begin{pmatrix} v_0 \\ 0 \end{pmatrix}$. Then, $\forall w \in \Sigma^*$, $f_P(w) > \frac{1}{2} \leftrightarrow f_{MP}(w) > \frac{1}{2}$.   □

The simulation in Theorem 1 is helpful for recognizing rational exclusive stochastic languages with bounded-error.

Theorem 2. $\mathsf{SL}^{\neq}_{\mathbb{Q}} \subseteq \mathsf{BAfL}^0_{\mathbb{Z}}$.

The following corollary is obtained immediately from Theorem 2.

Corollary 1. $\mathsf{SL}^{=}_{\mathbb{Q}} \subseteq \mathsf{BAfL}^1_{\mathbb{Z}}$.

It was shown in [6] that $\mathsf{SL}^{\neq} = \mathsf{NAfL} = \mathsf{NQAL}$, and therefore, our new result is stronger (bounded-error) but for a restricted case (using only rational numbers). One may immediately ask whether $\mathsf{BAfL}^0_{\mathbb{Q}} \subseteq \mathsf{SL}^{\neq}_{\mathbb{Q}}$. This follows from the simulation of a NAfA by a NQFA given in [6], and a simulation of a NQFA by a PFA with exclusive cutpoint (see [25]). Note that all the intermediate machines can use only rational transitions. Moreover, we can give a direct simulation of a NAfA by a PFA by using Turakainen's techniques [21].

Corollary 2. $\mathsf{BAfL}^0_{\mathbb{Z}} = \mathsf{BAfL}^0_{\mathbb{Q}} = \mathsf{SL}^{\neq}_{\mathbb{Q}}$ and $\mathsf{BAfL}^1_{\mathbb{Z}} = \mathsf{BAfL}^1_{\mathbb{Q}} = \mathsf{SL}^{=}_{\mathbb{Q}}$.

The class $\mathsf{SL}^{\neq}_{\mathbb{Q}}$ is important because, as pointed in [23], it contains many well-known nonregular languages like $\mathtt{UPAL} = \{a^n b^n \mid n > 0\}$, $\mathtt{PAL} = \{w \in \Sigma^* \mid w = w^r\}$, $\mathtt{SQUARE} = \{a^n b^{n^2} \mid n > 0\}$, $\mathtt{POWER} = \{a^n b^{2^n} \mid n > 0\}$, etc. Interestingly, any language in $\mathsf{SL}^{\neq}_{\mathbb{Q}}$ ($\mathsf{SL}^{=}_{\mathbb{Q}}$) can also be recognized by two-way QFAs with positive (one-sided) bounded-error. Therefore, it is reasonable to compare AfAs with two-way QFAs.

We can provide logarithmic-space bounds for one-sided bounded-error affine languages. We know that $\mathsf{SL}^{\neq}_{\mathbb{Q}} \cup \mathsf{SL}^{=}_{\mathbb{Q}}$ is in the deterministic logarithmic space class L [13] and $\mathtt{PAL}$ cannot be recognized by a probabilistic Turing machine in sublogarithmic space [7]. Hence, we can immediately obtain the following result.

Corollary 3. $\mathsf{BAfL}_\mathbb{Q}^0 \cup \mathsf{BAfL}_\mathbb{Q}^1 \subseteq \mathsf{L}$ *and* $\mathsf{BAfL}_\mathbb{Q}^0 \cup \mathsf{BAfL}_\mathbb{Q}^1 \not\subseteq \mathsf{BSpace}(o(\log n))$.

The language $\mathtt{EQNEQ} = \{aw_1 \cup bw_2 \in \{a, b\}^* \mid w_1 \in \mathtt{EQ} \text{ and } w_2 \in \mathtt{NEQ}\}$ is not in $\mathsf{SL}^{\neq} \cup \mathsf{SL}^{=}$, where $\mathtt{EQ} = \{w \in \{a, b\}^* \mid |w|_a = |w|_b\}$ and $\mathtt{NEQ}$ is the complement of $\mathtt{EQ}$ [25]. We know that $\mathtt{EQ}$ can be recognized by an AfA with bounded-error, and hence, it is not hard to design an AfA recognizing $\mathtt{EQNEQ}$ with bounded-error; the error, however, must be two-sided since it is not in $\mathsf{SL}^{\neq} \cup \mathsf{SL}^{=}$.

Theorem 3. $\mathsf{BAfL}_\mathbb{Q}^0 \cup \mathsf{BAfL}_\mathbb{Q}^1 \subsetneq \mathsf{BAfL}_\mathbb{Q}$.

5 Exact Simulation of QFAs

In this section, we present an exact simulation of QFAs by AfAs. We start with the exact simulation of MCQFAs due to its simplicity.

Lemma 1. *For a given MCQFA M with n inner states defined over $\mathbb{R}^n$, there exists an AfA MM with $(n^2 + 1)$ inner states that exactly simulates M.*

Proof. Let $M = (Q, \Sigma, \{U_\sigma \mid \sigma \in \widetilde{\Sigma}\}, q_s, Q_a)$ be an n-state MCQFA and $|v_0\rangle = |q_s\rangle$ be the initial quantum state. All transitions of M use only real numbers. For any given input $w \in \Sigma^*$, the final quantum state is $|v_f\rangle$ is

$$|v_f\rangle = U_{\tilde{w}_{|\tilde{w}|}} U_{\tilde{w}_{|\tilde{w}|-1}} \cdots U_{\tilde{w}_1} |v_0\rangle.$$

In order to turn amplitudes into probabilities of observing the basis states from the final vector, we can tensor $|v_f\rangle$ with itself [14]. Thus,

$$|v_f\rangle \otimes |v_f\rangle = (U_{\tilde{w}_{|\tilde{w}|}} \otimes U_{\tilde{w}_{|\tilde{w}|}})(U_{\tilde{w}_{|\tilde{w}|-1}} \otimes U_{\tilde{w}_{|\tilde{w}|-1}}) \cdots (U_{\tilde{w}_1} \otimes U_{\tilde{w}_1})(|v_0\rangle \otimes |v_0\rangle).$$

We construct an AfA MM that simulates the computation of M. The set of inner states is $Q \times Q \cup \{q_{n^2+1}\}$ and the initial state is (q_s, q_s). We assume with no loss of generality that there is only one accept state (q_1, q_1). For any symbol $\sigma \in \Sigma \cup \{\mathphantom{}\!\!\text{¢}\}$, the transition affine matrix A_σ is defined as

$$A_\sigma = \left(\begin{array}{c|c} U_\sigma \otimes U_\sigma & 0 \\ \hline \overline{1} & 1 \end{array} \right),$$

where $\overline{1}$ is a row vector that makes the summation of each column under $U_\sigma \otimes U_\sigma$ equal to 1. The affine transformation $A_\$$ is composed by two affine operators

$$A_\$ = A_\$' \left(\begin{array}{c|c} U_\sigma \otimes U_\sigma & 0 \\ \hline \overline{1} & 1 \end{array} \right),$$

where $A_\$'$ is an affine operator to be specified later. Then, on input w, the final affine state is

$$u_f = A_\$' \left(\begin{array}{c} v_f \otimes v_f \\ \hline \overline{1} \end{array} \right),$$

where $\overline{1}$ is equal to 1 minus the summation of the rest of the entries in u_f. The accept value of M on w can now be calculated from the values of $v_f \otimes v_f$, that is, the summation of entries corresponding to (q_j, q_j) for all $q_j \in Q_a$. Similar to the simulation in the previous section, we define $A'_\$$ as an operation that computes the summation over all entries corresponding to each accepting state of the form (q_j, q_j) and copies the result to the first entry of u_f; all remaining values are added and copied to the second entry of u_f. (The first and second rows of $A'_\$$ are 0–1 vectors and all the other rows are by zero vectors.) Thus, our final state is $u_f = (f_M(w), 1 - f_M(w), 0, \ldots, 0)^T$. Finally, we have that $f_{MM}(w)$ equals $f_M(w)$ and the number of inner states of MM is $n^2 + 1$.   □

It is known that the computation of any n-state QFA M (defined with complex numbers) can be simulated by an n^2-state *general finite-state automaton* G such that $f_M(w) = f_G(w)$ for any $w \in \Sigma^*$ [26]. Then, by adding one more state, we can design an AfA MM such that $f_M(w) = f_{MM}(w)$ for any $w \in \Sigma^*$. Hence, the following result immediately follows.

Theorem 4. *For a given QFA M with n inner states, there exists an AfA MM with $(n^2 + 1)$ inner states that exactly simulates M.*

By using this theorem, we inherit the superiority results of QFAs over PFAs [4] as the superiority results of AfAs over PFAs. The only issue we should be careful about is the quadratic increase in the number of states, which could be significant depending on the context.

The simulation techniques given here can be applied to different cases. For example, an affine circuit can be defined similarly to a quantum circuit, using affine operators instead of unitary operators. Then, using the above simulation(s), it follows that any quantum circuit of width $d(n)$ and length $s(n)$ can be simulated exactly by an affine circuit of width $d^2(n) + 1$ and length $s(n)$, where n is the parameter of the input length. Therefore, we can say that the class BQP is a subset of bounded-error affine polynomial-time defined with circuits. Moreover, PSPACE is a trivial upper bound for these polynomial-time circuits.

6   Succinctness of Affine Computation

6.1   Bounded-Error

For any prime number p, the language $\text{MOD}_p = \{a^{jp} \mid j \geq 0\}$, over the unary alphabet $\{a\}$, can be recognized by a bounded-error MCQFA with $O(\log(p))$ inner states; any bounded-error PFA, however, requires at least p states [2]. The MCQFA algorithm for MOD_p is indeed composed by $O(\log(p))$ copies of 2-state MCQFAs. Since we can simulate these 2-state MCQFAs exactly by 5-state AfAs, it follows that MOD_p can be recognized by bounded-error AfAs with $O(\log(p))$ inner states.

The language $\text{COUNT}_n = \{a^n\}$ for any $n > 0$, also known as the (unary) *counting problem*, can be solved by bounded-error AfAs with a constant number of states; moreover, any DFA requires n states [11], which implies that any bounded-error QFAs must have at least $\Omega(\sqrt{\log(n)})$ states [4].

Theorem 5. *The language* COUNT$_n$ *can be recognized by a 2-state AfA with negative one-sided bounded-error.*

Using a few copies of the AfA of Theorem 5, the error can be made arbitrarily close to 0 with a number of inner states that depends only on the error bound.

6.2 Zero-Error

For any $k > 0$, MOD2^k = (0MOD2^k, 1MOD2^k) is a promise problem,[4] where 0MOD2^k = $\{a^{j2^k} \mid j \equiv 0 \mod 2\}$ and 1MOD2^k = $\{a^{j2^k} \mid j \equiv 1 \mod 2\}$.

It is known that MOD2^k can be solved exactly by a 2-state MCQFA [3]. Any bounded-error PFA, however, requires at least 2^{k+1} states [18]. Due to Lemma 1, we can obtain the following result.

Theorem 6. *The promise problem* MOD2^k *can be solved by a 5-state AfA exactly.*

In consequence, zero-error AfAs are also interesting like MCQFAs. Now we consider the promise problem MOD4^k = (0MOD4^k, 1MOD4^k) where 0MOD4^k = $\{a^{j \cdot 2^k} \mid j \equiv 0 \mod 4\}$ and 1MOD4^k = $\{a^{j \cdot 2^k} \mid j \equiv 1 \mod 4\}$.

Theorem 7. *The promise problem* MOD4^k *can be solved exactly by a 3-state AfA.*

Using the techniques given in [3,18], we can show that any bounded-error PFA (and some other classical automata models [9]) requires at least 2^{k+1} states to solve MOD4^k.

In summary, we can say that MOD2^k (and so MOD4^k) is a classically expensive promise problem, but inexpensive for quantum and affine automata. As further examples, in the same line of research, a classically expensive generalized version of MOD2^k was defined in [10], in which was shown that the same expensive language can be solved by 3-state MCQFAs exactly; furthermore, a classically expensive function version of MOD2^k was defined in [1], which was shown to be solved by width-2 quantum OBDDs exactly. Trivially, all quantum results for these families of promise problems are inherited for affine models.

7 Unary Languages Recognized by Affine Automata with Two Inner States

All of our results of the previous sections, excepting the succintness results of Sect. 6, were obtained for languages defined over generic alphabets. Hence, using the superiority result of QFAs over PFAs given in [8], it immediately follows that AfAs computing unary languages are more powerful than unary PFAs with bounded-error on promise problems.

In this section, we give a complete characterization of the unary languages recognized by 2-state AfAs with cutpoint. It is known that 2-state unary PFAs

---

[4] A promise problem L = (L$_{yes}$, L$_{no}$) is solved by a machine M, or M *solves* L, if for all $w \in$ L$_{yes}$, M accepts w, and for all $w \in$ L$_{no}$, M rejects w.

can recognize only a few regular languages, whereas 2-state unary QFAs (with transitions defined over $\mathbb{R}$) can recognize uncountable many languages [15,20]. Here we obtain an analogous result to PFAs with the difference that AfAs can recognize more regular languages.

Consider the following unary regular languages over $\Sigma = \{a\}$; the empty language $\varnothing$, $\text{E} = \{a\}^*$, $\text{LESS}_n = \{a^i \mid i \leq n\}$ for $n \geq 0$, and $\text{EVEN} = (aa)^*$.

The complete list of languages recognized by 2-state unary PFAs with cutpoint are E, LESS_n, $\text{LESS}_n \cap \text{EVEN}$, $\text{LESS}_n \cap \overline{\text{EVEN}}$, $\overline{\text{LESS}_n} \cap \text{EVEN}$, $\overline{\text{LESS}_n} \cap \overline{\text{EVEN}}$, and the complement of each of these languages, with $n \geq 0$ [20].

The main result of this section is the following. Let $\text{INTERVAL}_{k,l} = \{a^i \mid k \leq i \leq l\}$ for $1 \leq k < l$.

Theorem 8. *The only unary regular languages recognized by AfAs with 2 inner states are the languages recognized by 2-state unary PFAs with cutpoint and additionally* $\text{INTERVAL}_{k,l} \cap \text{EVEN}$, $\text{INTERVAL}_{k,l} \cap \overline{\text{EVEN}}$, $\overline{\text{INTERVAL}_{k,l}} \cap \text{EVEN}$, *and* $\overline{\text{INTERVAL}_{k,l}} \cap \overline{\text{EVEN}}$.

The remaining of this section is devoted to the proof of Theorem 8. To that end, first we will consider the computation of a 2-state unary AfA M, which is inspired by a 2-state unary PFA of [20]. Let $\{e_1, e_2\}$ be the only inner states of M. With no loss of generality, we assume that the initial and only accepting state is e_1. The affine transformations for symbols a and $\$$ are

$$A_a = \begin{pmatrix} 1-q & p \\ q & 1-p \end{pmatrix} \text{ and} \tag{2}$$

$$A_\$ = \begin{pmatrix} f_1 & f_2 \\ 1-f_1 & 1-f_2 \end{pmatrix}, \tag{3}$$

respectively, for some real numbers p, q, f_1 and f_2.

Let $v_f = \begin{pmatrix} x \\ 1-x \end{pmatrix}$ be the final configuration vector of string a^j ($j \geq 0$). The accept probability of M on a^j is $f_M(a^j) = \dfrac{-x}{1-2x} = \dfrac{1}{2} + \dfrac{1}{4x-2}$ when $x < 0$ and $x > 1$, and $f_M(a^j) = x$ when $0 \leq x \leq 1$.

Lemma 2. *If $p = q = 0$ in Eq.(2), then E and $\varnothing$ can be recognized by AfAs with 2 states.*

Proof. It is clear that if $p = q = 0$, then A_a is the identity, and hence f_M is a constant function on Σ^*. Thus, M can recognize E and $\varnothing$. □

For the remaining of this section, we assume that at least one of p or q is non-zero.

Lemma 3. *There exists $p \in \mathbb{R}$ satisfying $p + q = 0$ in Eq.(2) such that M recognizes LESS_n.*

Corollary 4. *There exists $p \in \mathbb{R}$ satisfying $p + q = 0$ in Eq.(2) such that M recognizes $\overline{\text{LESS}_n}$.*

Lemma 4. *There exists $p \in \mathbb{R}$ satisfying $p + q = 0$ such that M recognizes* INTERVAL$_{k,l}$ *with cutpoint $3/4$.*

Corollary 5. *The language* $\overline{\text{INTERVAL}_{k,l}}$ *can be recognized by a 2-state AfA with cutpoint $\frac{3}{4}$.*

From Lemma 4 and Corollary 5 we conclude that AfAs with two inner states can recognize more languages than PFAs with two inner states. Moreover, for the case of $p + q = 0$, there are no more regular unary languages recognized by AfAs with two states (see [22]).

Lemma 5. *There exists $p, q \in \mathbb{R}$ satisfying $p + q \neq 0$ such that M recognizes all languages recognized by 2-state unary PFAs with cutpoint and the languages* INTERVAL$_{k,l} \cap$ EVEN, INTERVAL$_{k,l} \cap \overline{\text{EVEN}}$, $\overline{\text{INTERVAL}_{k,l}} \cap$ EVEN, *and* $\overline{\text{INTERVAL}_{k,l}} \cap$ $\overline{\text{EVEN}}$.

With Lemma 5 we conclude the proof of Theorem 8.

8   Concluding Remarks

Affine computation and affine finite automata were introduced in [6] with a few initial results. For example, it was proved that AfAs can recognize more languages than PFAs and QFAs in the bounded and unbounded error modes, the exclusive affine languages form a superset of the exclusive quantum and stochastic languages, and nondeterministic AfAs and QFAs are both equivalent to the class of exclusive stochastic languages.

In this paper, we continued to investigate AfAs and obtained some new and complementary results. We presented efficient simulations of PFAs and QFAs by AfAs. In addition, we characterized the class of languages recognized by positive and negative one-sided bounded-error AfAs using rational transitions, which turn out to be equal to the union of rational exclusive and co-exclusive stochastic languages; this latter result improved the proof of equivalence between nondeterministic AfAs and QFAs. We also initiated the study of the state complexity of AfAs and showed that they can be more succint than PFAs and QFAs. Finally, we presented a complete characterization of 2-state unary AfAs, showing at the same time that AfAs can recognize more languages than 2-state unary PFAs but still only regular languages.

In a recent and related work on AfAs [5], some further results on state complexity are presented. It is proven in [5] that AfAs can separate any pair of strings with zero-error using only two states, and can separate efficiently any pair of disjoint finite sets of words with one-sided bounded-error.

We close this paper with a few open problems that we consider challenging.

1. It is conjectured in [6] that affine and quantum computation can be incomparable. The simulation results in this paper give the feeling that quantum models can be simulated by their affine counterparts but it might require a quadratic increase in memory. It is interesting to study the relations, particularly in the bounded-error setting, between quantum and affine language classes.

2. Currently we are not aware of any non-trivial upper bound for BAfL$_Q$. Using the techniques of [13] it might be possible to prove an upper bound of logarithmic space.
3. Considering that AfAs completely capture the power of NQFAs, it is interesting to investigate lower bound techniques that can exploit the simpler structure of affine transformations (compared to unitary and positive-semidefinite operators).

Acknowledgements. We thank the anonymous referees for their helpful comments.

References

1. Ablayev, F., Gainutdinova, A., Khadiev, K., Yakaryılmaz, A.: Very narrow quantum OBDDs and width hierarchies for classical OBDDs. In: Jürgensen, H., Karhumäki, J., Okhotin, A. (eds.) DCFS 2014. LNCS, vol. 8614, pp. 53–64. Springer, Heidelberg (2014)
2. Ambainis, A., Freivalds, R.: 1-way quantum finite automata: strengths, weaknesses and generalizations. In: FOCS 1998, pp. 332–341 (1998). arXiv:9802062
3. Ambainis, A., Yakaryılmaz, A.: Superiority of exact quantum automata for promise problems. Inf. Process. Lett. **112**(7), 289–291 (2012)
4. Ambainis, A., Yakaryılmaz, A.: Automata and quantum computing. Technical report 1507.01988, arXiv (2015)
5. Belovs, A., Montoya, J.A., Yakaryılmaz, A.: Can one quantum bit separate any pair of words with zero-error? Technical report 1602.07967, arXiv (2016)
6. Díaz-Caro, A., Yakaryılmaz, A.: Affine computation and affine automaton. In: Kulikov, A.S., Woeginger, G.J. (eds.) CSR 2016. LNCS, vol. 9691, pp. 146–160. Springer, Heidelberg (2016). doi:10.1007/978-3-319-34171-2_11
7. Freivalds, R., Karpinski, M.: Lower space bounds for randomized computation. In: ICALP 1994, pp. 580–592 (1994)
8. Gainutdinova, A., Yakaryılmaz, A.: Unary probabilistic and quantum automata on promise problems. In: Potapov, I. (ed.) DLT 2015. LNCS, vol. 9168, pp. 252–263. Springer, Heidelberg (2015)
9. Geffert, V., Yakaryılmaz, A.: Classical automata on promise problems. Discrete Math. Theor. Comput. Sci. **17**(2), 157–180 (2015)
10. Gruska, J., Qiu, D., Zheng, S.: Potential of quantum finite automata with exact acceptance. Int. J. Found. Comput. Sci. **26**(3), 381–398 (2015)
11. Kupferman, O., Ta-Shma, A., Vardi, M.Y.: Counting with automata. Short paper presented at the 15th Annual IEEE Symposium on Logic in Computer Science (LICS 2000) (1999)
12. Li, L., Qiu, D., Zou, X., Li, L., Wu, L., Mateus, P.: Characterizations of one-way general quantum finite automata. Theor. Comput. Sci. **419**, 73–91 (2012)
13. Macarie, I.I.: Space-efficient deterministic simulation of probabilistic automata. SIAM J. Comput. **27**(2), 448–465 (1998)
14. Moore, C., Crutchfield, J.P.: Quantum automata and quantum grammars. Theor. Comput. Sci. **237**(1–2), 275–306 (2000)
15. Paz, A.: Introduction to Probabilistic Automata. Academic Press, New York (1971)
16. Rabin, M.O.: Probabilistic automata. Inf. Control **6**, 230–243 (1963)

17. Rabin, M., Scott, D.: Finite automata and their decision problems. IBM J. Res. Dev. **3**, 114–125 (1959)
18. Rashid, J., Yakaryılmaz, A.: Implications of quantum automata for contextuality. In: Holzer, M., Kutrib, M. (eds.) CIAA 2014. LNCS, vol. 8587, pp. 318–331. Springer, Heidelberg (2014)
19. Say, A.C.C., Yakaryılmaz, A.: Quantum finite automata: a modern introduction. In: Calude, C.S., Freivalds, R., Kazuo, I. (eds.) Gruska Festschrift. LNCS, vol. 8808, pp. 208–222. Springer, Heidelberg (2014)
20. Shur, A.M., Yakaryılmaz, A.: More on quantum, stochastic, and pseudo stochastic languages with few states. Nat. Comput. **15**(1), 129–141 (2016)
21. Turakainenn, P.: Word-functions of stochastic and pseudo stochastic automata. Ann. Acad. Scientiarum Fennicae, Ser. A. I Math. **1**, 27–37 (1975)
22. Villagra, M., Yakaryılmaz, A.: Language recognition power and succintness of affine automata. Technical report 1602.05432, arXiv (2016)
23. Yakaryılmaz, A., Say, A.C.C.: Succinctness of two-way probabilistic and quantum finite automata. Discrete Math. Theor. Comput. Sci. **12**(2), 19–40 (2010)
24. Yakaryılmaz, A., Say, A.C.C.: Languages recognized with unbounded error by quantum finite automata. In: Frid, A., Morozov, A., Rybalchenko, A., Wagner, K.W. (eds.) CSR 2009. LNCS, vol. 5675, pp. 356–367. Springer, Heidelberg (2009)
25. Yakaryılmaz, A., Say, A.C.C.: Languages recognized by nondeterministic quantum finite automata. Quantum Inf. Comput. **10**(9&10), 747–770 (2010)
26. Yakaryılmaz, A., Say, A.C.C.: Unbounded-error quantum computation with small space bounds. Inf. Comput. **279**(6), 873–892 (2011)

Training a Carbon-Nanotube/Liquid Crystal Data Classifier Using Evolutionary Algorithms

Eléonore Vissol-Gaudin[(✉)], Apostolos Kotsialos[(✉)], M. Kieran Massey, Dagou A. Zeze, Chris Pearson, Chris Groves, and Michael C. Petty

School of Engineering and Computing Sciences, Durham University, Durham, UK
{eleonore.vissol-gaudin,apostolos.kotsialos,m.k.massey,d.a.zeze,
christopher.pearson,chris.groves,m.c.petty}@durham.ac.uk

Abstract. Evolution-in-Materio uses evolutionary algorithms (EA) to exploit the physical properties of unconfigured, physically rich materials, in effect transforming them into information processors. The potential of this technique for machine learning problems is explored here. Results are obtained from a mixture of single walled carbon nanotubes and liquid crystals (SWCNT/LC). The complex nature of the voltage/current relationship of this material presents a potential for adaptation. Here, it is used as a computational medium evolved by two derivative-free, population-based stochastic search algorithms, particle swarm optimisation (PSO) and differential evolution (DE). The computational problem considered is data classification. A custom made electronic motherboard for interacting with the material has been developed, which allows the application of control signals on the material body. Starting with a simple binary classification problem of separable data, the material is trained with an error minimisation objective for both algorithms. Subsequently, the solution, defined as the combination of the material itself and optimal inputs, is verified and results are reported. The evolution process based on EAs has the capacity to evolve the material to a state where data classification can be performed. PSO outperforms DE in terms of results' reproducibility due to the smoother, as opposed to more noisy, inputs applied on the material.

1 Introduction

Unconventional computing aims at investigating methods for designing systems able to perform a computation in different ways than the current paradigm. One such direction of research is evolution in materio (EIM) [10], which is concerned with computing performed directly by the materials. EIM focuses on the underlying properties of the materials aiming at exploring and exploiting them in such a way so that they are brought to a computation inducing state. Contrary to traditional computing with metal-oxide-silicon-field-effect-transistor (MOSFET) technology, where everything is designed, produced and programmed very carefully, EIM uses a bottom up approach where computation is performed by the material without having explicit knowledge of its internal properties.

© Springer International Publishing Switzerland 2016
M. Amos and A. Condon (Eds.): UCNC 2016, LNCS 9726, pp. 130–141, 2016.
DOI: 10.1007/978-3-319-41312-9_11

The idea of EIM can be found in early work of Pask [17] concerned with growing an electrochemical ear. In more recent work [22], observations were made when evolutionary algorithms were used for designing electrical circuits on field-programmable-gate-arrays (FPGAs). The resulting circuit topologies were influenced by the material of the board used. Because of feedback provided by the iterative nature of stochastic optimisation interacting with the material, identified solutions were based on the specific FPGA's properties that were unaccounted for during the board's design. EIM replaced the FPGAs with material systems favouring exploitation of all physical properties by a search algorithm [11].

EIM has a broad scope, which can be delineated along four dimensions: (a) the type of material used, (b) the physical property manipulated for obtaining a computation, (c) the computation problem addressed and (d) the evolutionary algorithm used for solving the corresponding training problem.

Different materials have been used, including biological ones like slime moulds [6], bacterial consortia [1] and cells (neurons) [19]. In [20] it is argued that inorganic materials make a better medium for unconventional computing exploration. Nano-particles were used in [2] for developing a reconfigurable Boolean logic network. In [4,5] liquid crystals (LC) panels were used for evolving logic gates, a tone discriminator and a robot controller. Single walled carbon nanotubes (SWCNT) based materials have shown the potential to solve variety of computational problems [7,9,12–15,23].

Candidate computational problems include Boolean function calculation, finding a minimum, evolving a controller, obtaining a tone discriminator, developing a neuron and data clustering problems. A more comprehensive review of potential problems can be found in [16]. Here, a simple binary data classification problem is considered.

Because of the complexity of the material EIM generally employs population based derivative free stochastic methods. Here a Particle Swarm Optimisation (PSO) algorithm as described in [8] is used.

2   Hardware Architecture and the SWCNT/LC Material

Figure 1 illustrates the concept of EIM. An optimisation algorithm selects a set of incident signals applied on to the material (configuration voltages in our case) changing in effect its physical properties. During training, the state the material is brought to by application of the configuration voltages is tested against a number of known input/output pairs of a correct computation. The material's response is recorded for each of those test inputs and a global error function is evaluated. Using the error function as part of a fitness function allows a swarm intelligence algorithm to explore the search space.

In our implementation, the signals sent are constant voltage charges applied by an *mbed* micro-controller and the outputs are direct current measurements. The voltages are sent to the SWCNT/LC compound via the motherboard through digital-to-analogue converters (DACs). These are connected to a glass slide where the electrodes are etched as seen on the right hand side of Fig. 1. There are sixteen connections on the micro-electrode, but only twelve of them are used due to hardware constraints. Ten connections are used for sending inputs and another two for collecting the output measurements used for transforming the material's response to a computation.

The nanotubes used were obtained from Carbon Nanotechnologies 101 Inc. (Houston, TX, USA). They are single walled carbon (SWCNT) both semiconducting and conducting; they also contain less than 15 % impurity according to vendor specifications. LCs were obtained from Merck Japan. Their purpose is to provide a fluid medium in which the SWCNT can move in response to the applied electric field enabling the nanotubes to form reconfigurable and variable complex electrical networks. As is shown in [23] SWCNTs tend to bundle under an applied electric field, establishing a percolation path between electrodes. The greater length of these bundles or "ropes" with respect to the dimensions of LC molecules suggests that they are not highly influenced by movement of the latter. This adds an extra dimension to the problem compared to previous experiments, where SWCNT were mixed with a solid polymer [7,9] and the resulting material system was in solid state, as opposed to the liquid state of the material used here.

The SWCNT/LC blend used in these experiments are of 0.05 wt % which has been chosen empirically. It was drop-deposited within a nylon washer (5 mm internal diameter). The washer was glued to a glass microscope slide upon which an array of gold electrodes had previously been deposited using etch-back photolithography. The electrode array contacts are 50 μm with 100 μm pitch.

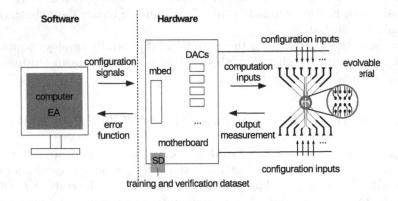

Fig. 1. EiM concept and electrode array (50 μm contacts, 100 μm pitch)

3   The Classification Problem

The computing problem considered here is that of data classification. Two different two-dimensional (2D) datasets are used for two problems of the same nature. A typical training and verification approach is followed for assessing the material's capability to act as a classifier. Figure 2 depicts the training datasets for the two problems. In both cases, two classes are formed, each covering a square area. In the first case the data are highly separable and don't overlap, resulting to the separable classes (SC) problem. In the second case, there is some small overlap where a pair of data can belong to any of the two, resulting to the merged classes (MC) problem. Training aims at evolving the material so that it is brought into a state such that when randomly selected input pairs are given as input, it can infer the class they belong to. The size of the training dataset for the SC and MC problems $K_t = 800$ pairs and the verification datasets' size is $K_v = 4,000$ pairs.

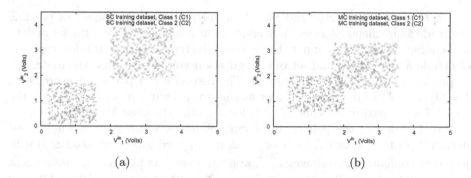

Fig. 2. Training datasets. (a) SC problem. (b) MC problem.

SC and MC are simple binary classification problems and a comparison scheme can result to the correct classification. However, the EIM approach taken here is not equipped intrinsically with such a capability. The material is trained by forcing it to change its shape and adapt its electrical properties so that an incident signal, in the form (V_1, V_2), results to an output that can be interpreted as a classification of that input. There is no explicit design of memory storage or bit comparison or a mechanism for numerical operations. It is just the material's shape and form that is evolved towards a state that produces the desired outcome.

4   Training Problem Formulation

The material training is formulated as an optimisation problem tailored for the evolvable material board. The classification task is about determining the class a pair of data $\mathbf{V}^{in} = (V_1^{in}, V_2^{in})$ belongs to. Hence, two of the ten available electrodes are reserved as data input connections. The inputs come in the form of voltage pulses of amplitude V_1^{in} and V_2^{in} (Volts). The remaining eight connections are used for applying configuration voltages to the material. They are realised as voltage pulses of amplitude $V_j \in [V_{\min}, V_{\max}], j = 1, \ldots, 8$ (Volts). In order to evaluate a potential set of configuration voltages V_j, first the electrodes where each of the V_j is applied is decided. These voltages are then applied and the corresponding electrodes are kept charged while K_t known pairs of training inputs are send to the two electrodes selected for receiving the data inputs.

Two output connections are used for measuring the material response when it is constantly charged with the configuration voltages V_j and a pair of data $\mathbf{V}^{in}$ is send as input. Although the output locations are fixed because of hardware constraints, the connections where the inputs are going to be applied are variable and are part of the optimisation problem's vector of decision variables $\mathbf{x}$. The optimisation problem's vector of decision variables is defined as

$$\mathbf{x} = [V_1 \ldots V_8 \; R \; p]^T . \tag{1}$$

where R is a scaling factor and $p \in \mathbb{N}$ an index running on the set of possible electrode assignments. An electrode assignment is a mapping from the set of data and configuration voltage inputs to the set of the ten electrodes. It is for a specific electrode assignment p and set of configuration voltages V_j, that the material's response to an input $\mathbf{V}^{in}$ is recorded. The response is a pair of measurements $\mathbf{I} = (I_1, I_2)$ (A) of the direct current at the two output locations, which are the basis of a comparison scheme using R for deciding the class $\mathbf{V}^{in}$ belongs to.

Let $\mathbf{I}^{(k)}$ denote the pair of direct current measurements taken when input data $\mathbf{V}^{in}(k)$ from class C_i, $i = 1$ or $i = 2$, are applied *while* the material is subjected to configuration voltages $V_j^{(k)}$, applied according to electrode assignment number $p^{(k)}$ using scaling factor $R^{(k)}$. Also, let $C(\mathbf{V}^{in}(k))$ denote $\mathbf{V}^{in}(k)$'s real class and $C_M(\mathbf{V}^{in}(k), \mathbf{x})$ the material's assessment of it calculated according to the following rule.

$$C_M(\mathbf{V}^{in}(k), \mathbf{x}) = \begin{cases} C_1 \text{ if } I_1(k) > RI_2(k) \\ C_2 \text{ if } I_1(k) \leq RI_2(k). \end{cases} \tag{2}$$

For every training pair of data $\mathbf{V}^{in}(k)$, $k = 1, \ldots, K_t$ the error from translating the material response according to rule (2) is

$$\epsilon_\mathbf{x}(k) = \begin{cases} 0 \text{ if } \quad\quad C_M(\mathbf{V}^{in}(k), \mathbf{x}) = C(\mathbf{V}^{in}(k)) \\ 1 \text{ otherwise.} \end{cases} \tag{3}$$

The mean total error is given by

$$\Phi_e(\mathbf{x}) = \frac{1}{K_t} \sum_{k=1}^{K_t} \epsilon_\mathbf{x}(k). \tag{4}$$

Two penalty terms are added to (4), H and U. $H(\mathbf{x})$ penalises solutions with high configuration voltages and is given by

$$H(\mathbf{x}) = \frac{\sum_{j=1}^{8} V_j^2}{8V_{max}^2}. \tag{5}$$

The rationale behind this penalisation is that incremental and generally low levels of configuration voltages are preferable. Solutions where high voltages are applied can destroy possible material structures favourable to the problem formed gradually during evolution. On the other hand, solutions that render the material unresponsive need to be avoided. A measure of such unresponsiveness is calculated at the end of each search iteration ι, where a sample equal to the population size S of error function evaluations is available. Let $\sigma_{o,\iota}^2$ denote the variance of $\Phi(\mathbf{x})$ and $\sigma_{V,\iota}^2$ the variance of $\sum_{j=1}^{8} V_j^2$ at iteration ι. A value of $\sigma_{o,\iota}^2$ close to zero indicates a non-responsive material and the penalty term takes the form

$$U_\iota = \left(1 - \frac{\sigma_{o,\iota}^2}{\sigma_{V,\iota}^2}\right)^2. \tag{6}$$

Hence, the total objective function $\Phi_s(\mathbf{x})$ for an arbitrary individual s at iteration ι is given by

$$\Phi_s(\mathbf{x}) = \Phi_e(\mathbf{x}) + H(\mathbf{x}) + U_\iota. \tag{7}$$

U_ι aims at leading the optimisation away from material states where the same response is given for different inputs.

The optimisation to be solved is that of minimising (7) for a population of size S, subject to voltage bound constraints $V_j \in [V_{\min}, V_{\max}]$, $R > 0$, electrode assignment p and classification rule (2). $V_{\min} = 0$ Volts and for the SC problem $V_{\max} = 4$ Volts whereas for the MC $V_{\max} = 7$ Volts.

Two different evolutionary optimisation algorithms are used for solving this problem, differential evolution (DE) [21] and particle swarm optimisation (PSO) [3]. A constricted version of PSO with parameters taken from [8] is implemented. The DE algorithm implementation uses the parameters suggested in [18]. A population size of $S = 8$ is used for DE and $S = 10$ for PSO.

5   Results and Discussion

Training is performed by the DE and PSO algorithms solving the optimisation problem described in Sect. 4 using the K_t pairs of data for problems SC and MC. Termination criterion is either a maximum number of optimisation iterations defined by previous experiments, a lack of significant reduction for a number of iterations or a minimal value of the error function Φ_e. A baseline experiment is first run for each problem. Before any test was performed, the two optimisation algorithms were run without material between the electrodes to establish the effect of hardware on the optimisation procedure. Tests with LCs only were also performed as another baseline, showing that it is changes in the conduction path established by the SWCNTs that allow a computation. For each test, comprising training and verification, a new, thus un-configured, sample of SWCNT/LC was used. As the vector of decision variable is initialised randomly, the first iteration of each test is considered a baseline of the material's computational capabilities before training. Convergence profiles for the DE algorithm applied to the SC and MC data are shown in Fig. 3(a) and (b), respectively.

For the three runs, the training error averaged over the values achieved by the eight individuals of the population at iteration ι is shown along with the

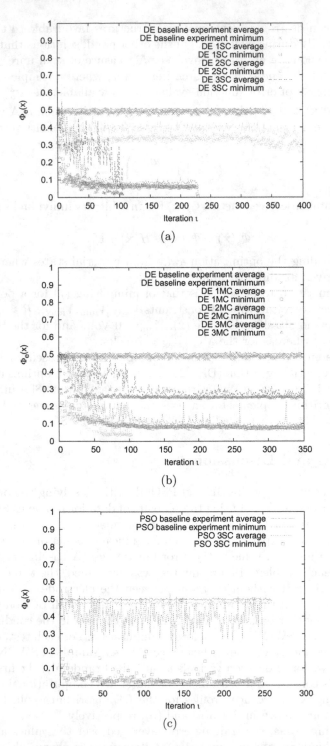

Fig. 3. Convergence profile for different runs. (a) All runs of DE for the SC problem. (b) All runs of DE for the MC problem. (c) Third run of PSO for the SC problem.

best value achieved in that iteration (not the best up to iteration ι). It can be seen that the DE algorithm trains the material and the average error follows the trend of the best result per iteration. This is not the case of the PSO algorithm, shown in Fig. 3(c) (a single run is presented for the sake of clarity). The average error per iteration is much higher than the best achieved, although a positive correlation between the two is evident. The material is also evolved, but the PSO tends to explore more the search space. In both cases, during training the material morphology changes in order to provide a response that leads to a correct classification. However, the emphasis on exploitation displayed by DE tends to produce solutions that are either very good or very bad and thus inconstitant from test to test.

Once training is terminated, verification is performed on the trained material by applying back the optimal configuration voltages and sending as input K_v verification data pairs different from the K_t pairs used in training. The same verification experiment is repeated ten times and each time the mean error (4) is calculated and recorded. Since the optimum may have been achieved several iterations before the algorithm's termination, the optimal solution will not have the same effect because the material would have undergone a number of non-reversible changes by that time. Hence, in order to achieve good verification results, structures inside the material need to be built that favour an error minimising response. It is the gradual evolution performed on the material that builds these structures of SWCNT conductive networks.

Table 1 provides the training Φ_e^* error, the best verification error $\Phi_{e,v}^*$ from the ten experiments conducted using the optimal solution, the worst verification error $\Phi_{e,v}^w$, and the mean verification error $\overline{\Phi}_{e,v}$ for three runs of PSO and DE for the SC problem. It can be seen that the PSO algorithm outperforms the DE with respect to consistency between tests comprising both training and verification. In terms of training error, the second experiment of DE resulted to a material with over 25 % error, which is too large. On the contrary, all PSO experiments resulted to a Φ_e^* less than 2 %. Figure 3 shows evolution of the objective function for SC baseline tests, with LC only or no material at all. In both cases Φ_e^* remains around 50 % which is also the case for $\Phi_{e,v}^*$.

Table 1. Problem SC training and verification errors for experiments using PSO and DE.

Experiment	$\Phi_e^*(\%)$	$\Phi_{e,v}^*(\%)$	$\Phi_{e,v}^w(\%)$	$\overline{\Phi}_{e,v}(\%)$
PSO 1SC	1.3	1.675	2.5	2.0375
PSO 2SC	1.6	2.125	3.2	2.6175
PSO 3SC	1.3	1.975	2.5	2.25
DE 1SC	0.7	1.05	1.625	1.3975
DE 2SC	25.9	29.475	35.625	33.808
DE 3SC	1.6	1.625	2.55	2.185

The solution degradation on the verification data is on average lower for the three PSO runs. The difference on the average error value does not grow above 1.2 % in the worst case. This indicates that the material has a consistent behaviour by the end of the search and internal structures built are not completely destroyed by the evolution process.

Table 2 provides the training and verification errors for the MC problem. Because this is a more difficult problem due to the small overlap of the data a bias of about 3 % error is created. This is consistent with the training error, since the best PSO and DE values of Φ_e are larger by 4.5 % and 2.7 %, respectively. Once again, DE achieves better training error but tends to be inconsistent between tests. The PSO solutions generalise slightly better and the verification errors are very similar to the training. Hence, the PSO algorithm yields better solutions. As in the case of SC, Fig. 3 shows that the objective function for all MC baseline tests remains around 50 %. In addition, the best verification error $\Phi_{e,v}^*$ is also around 50 % for both PSO and DE.

Table 2. Problem MC training and verification errors for experiments using PSO and DE.

Experiment	$\Phi_e^*(\%)$	$\Phi_{e,v}^*(\%)$	$\Phi_{e,v}^w(\%)$	$\overline{\Phi}_{e,v}\ (\%)$
PSO 1MC	7.1	8.625	9.975	8.924
PSO 2MC	5.8	6.6	7.025	7.815
PSO 3MC	7.5	7.4	8.075	7.6275
DE 1MC	6.8	7.575	8.6	8.285
DE 2MC	3.4	4.375	5.2	4.5
DE 3MC	24.2	15.925	26.725	26.485

In the absence of analytical models of the material's dynamics, it is difficult to provide a rigorous explanation as to why PSO is more consistent than DE. A distinctive difference between the two is the form of the configuration voltages' trajectories over iterations as they are exploring the search space. Figure 4 depicts the trajectories of sample configuration voltages *averaged per iteration* for the PSO and DE algorithms. It can be seen that the search performed by DE is more noisy. On the other hand, PSO's exploration of the search space is much smoother. DE sends signals to the material that are noisy even when it aims to exploit a minimum. Hence, a conjecture about PSO algorithm's better performance is that the smoother trajectories of configuration inputs build more stable structures inside the material reinforcing at the same time responses minimising the classification error. The noisy configuration voltages applied by DE make the formation of such stable structures more difficult. This conjecture needs to be supported by more experiments and evidence, such as image analysis of the material before and after training.

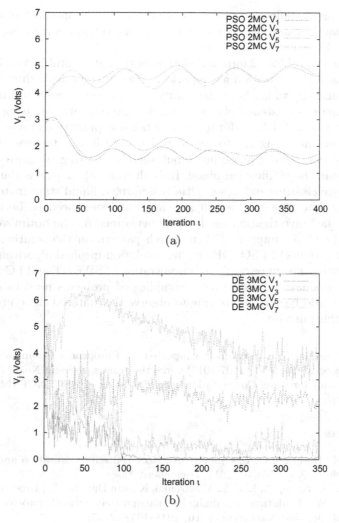

Fig. 4. Average configuration voltages per iteration for (a) PSO and (b) DE.

6   Conclusions

This paper has presented the results of an investigation on evolution in materio for a new type of material, a mixture of single walled carbon nanotubes and liquid crystals. It is in liquid form and the nanotubes inside it form conductive networks. Under the influence of different levels of voltage applied at various locations of its body, different networks are formed. The material is placed on a glass slide with electrodes etched on it and a custom made board based on the *mbed* micro-controller is used for evolving it as a data classifier.

Two simple classification problems are considered in an effort to evolve the material towards a state where measurements of electrical current can be interpreted following a pre-specified rule.

The training problem is formulated as an optimisation problem and results of both training and verification are reported. Two different algorithms have been used, PSO and DE which have the ability to converge to good solutions. PSO displays a more consistent behavior always converging to low error solutions which generalise well. DE performs more detailed exploitation of a solution and generally sends noisy signals to the material. PSO has a stronger exploration element and sends much smoother input signals resulting to more consistent performance in the verification phase. In both cases, the result is the evolution of an analogue classifier out of an initially unformed liquid state material.

This is a new area of research and a lot of issues need to be addressed. A more detailed investigation needs to be performed on the optimisation algorithms used and the impact of their search pattern on the solutions' quality. More recent variants of PSO, DE or other evolution-inspired algorithms need to be implemented. The impact of the concentration of SWCNT and LC in the mix needs to be evaluated. Finally, more complicated problems need to be considered and it would be very interesting to observe the material structure patterns formed for this purpose.

Acknowledgment. The research is supported by European's Community Seventh Framework programme (FP7/2007-2013) under the grant agreement No. 317662 (NAno Scale Engineering for Novel Computation using Evolution - NASCENCE (http://www.nascence.eu)).

References

1. Amos, M., Hodgson, D.A., Gibbons, A.: Bacterial self-organisation and computation. eprint arXiv:q-bio/0512017, December 2005
2. Bose, S., Lawrence, C., Liu, Z., Makarenko, K., van Damme, R., Broersma, H., van der Wiel, W.: Evolution of a designless nanoparticle network into reconfigurable boolean logic. Nat. Nanotechnol. **10**, 1048–1052 (2015)
3. Eberhart, R., Kennedy, J.: A new optimizer using particle swarm theory. In: Proceedings of the 6th International Symposium on Micro Machine and Human Science, New York, NY, vol. 1, pp. 39–43 (1995)
4. Harding, S., Miller, J.: Evolution in materio: a tone discriminator in liquid crystal. In: Congress on Evolutionary Computation, CEC 2004, vol. 2, pp. 1800–1807. IEEE (2004)
5. Harding, S., Miller, J.: Evolution in materio: evolving logic gates in liquid crystal. In: Proceedings of European Conference on Artificial Life (ECAL 2005), Workshop on Unconventional Computing: From Cellular Automata to Wetware, pp. 133–149 (2005)
6. Jones, J., Whiting, J., Adamatzky, A.: Quantitative transformation for implementation of adder circuits in physical systems. Biosystems **134**, 16–23 (2015)
7. Kotsialos, A., Massey, M.K., Qaiser, F., Zeze, D.A., Pearson, C., Petty, M.C.: Logic gate and circuit training on randomly dispersed carbon nanotubes. Int. J. Unconventional Comput. **10**(5–6), 473–497 (2014)

8. Laskari, E., Parsopoulos, K., Vrahatis, M.: Particle swarm optimization for integer programming. In: WCCI, pp. 1582–1587. IEEE (2002)
9. Massey, M.K., Kotsialos, A., Qaiser, F., Zeze, D.A., Pearson, C., Volpati, D., Bowen, L., Petty, M.C.: Computing with carbon nanotubes: optimization of threshold logic gates using disordered nanotube/polymer composites. J. Appl. Phys. 117(13), 134903 (2015)
10. Meyers, R.: Encyclopedia of Complexity and Systems Science. Springer, New York (2009)
11. Miller, J., Downing, K.: Evolution in materio: looking beyond the silicon box. In: Proceedings of the NASA/DoD Conference on Evolvable Hardware, pp. 167–176. IEEE (2002)
12. Miller, J., Mohid, M.: Function optimization using cartesian genetic programming. In: Proceedings of the 15th Annual Conference Companion on Genetic and Evolutionary Computation, pp. 147–148. ACM (2013)
13. Mohid, M., Miller, J., Harding, S., Tufte, G., Lykkebø, O.R., Massey, M.K., Petty, M.C.: Evolution-in-materio: a frequency classifier using materials. In: 2014 IEEE International Conference on Evolvable Systems (ICES), pp. 46–53. IEEE (2014)
14. Mohid, M., Miller, J., Harding, S., Tufte, G., Lykkebø, O., Massey, M.K., Petty, M.C.: Evolution-in-materio: solving bin packing problems using materials. In: 2014 IEEE International Conference on Evolvable Systems (ICES), pp. 38–45. IEEE (2014)
15. Mohid, M., Miller, J.F., Harding, S.L., Tufte, G., Lykkebø, O.R., Massey, M.K., Petty, M.C.: Evolution-in-materio: solving machine learning classification problems using materials. In: Bartz-Beielstein, T., Branke, J., Filipič, B., Smith, J. (eds.) PPSN 2014. LNCS, vol. 8672, pp. 721–730. Springer, Heidelberg (2014)
16. NASCENCE project (ICT 317662): Report on suitable computational tasks of various difficulties (2013) deliverable D4.2
17. Pask, G.: Physical analogues to the growth of a concept. In: Mechanization of Thought Processes, Symposium, vol. 10, pp. 765–794 (1958)
18. Pedersen, M.: Good parameters for differential evolution. Technical report, Hvass Computer Science Laboratories (2010)
19. Prasad, S., Yang, M., Zhang, X., Ozkan, C., Ozkan, M.: Electric field assisted patterning of neuronal networks for the study of brain functions. Biomed. Microdevices 5(2), 125–137 (2003)
20. Stepney, S.: The neglected pillar of material computation. Phys. D 237(9), 1157–1164 (2008)
21. Storn, R., Price, K.: Differential evolution-a simple and efficient heuristic for global optimization over continuous spaces. J. Global Optim. 11(4), 341–359 (1997)
22. Thompson, A.: An evolved circuit, intrinsic in silicon, entwined with physics. In: Higuchi, T., Iwata, M., Weixin, L. (eds.) ICES 1996. LNCS, vol. 1259, pp. 390–405. Springer, Heidelberg (1997)
23. Volpati, D., Massey, M.K., Johnson, D., Kotsialos, A., Qaiser, F., Pearson, C., Coleman, K., Tiburzi, G., Zeze, D.A., Petty, M.C.: Exploring the alignment of carbon nanotubes dispersed in a liquid crystal matrix using coplanar electrodes. J. Appl. Phys. 117(12), 125303 (2015)

Towards Quantitative Verification
of Reaction Systems

Artur Męski[1]([⊠]), Maciej Koutny[2], and Wojciech Penczek[1,3]

[1] Institute of Computer Science, PAS, Jana Kazimierza 5, 01-248 Warsaw, Poland
{meski,penczek}@ipipan.waw.pl
[2] School of Computing Science, Newcastle University, Newcastle upon Tyne, UK
maciej.koutny@ncl.ac.uk
[3] University of Natural Sciences and Humanities, ICS, Siedlce, Poland

Abstract. Reaction systems are a formal model for computational processes inspired by the functioning of the living cell. The key feature of this model is that its behaviour is determined by the interactions of biochemical reactions of the living cell, and these interactions are based on the mechanisms of facilitation and inhibition. The formal treatment of reaction systems is qualitative as there is no direct representation of the number of molecules involved in biochemical reactions.

This paper introduces reaction systems with discrete concentrations which are an extension of reaction systems allowing for quantitative modelling. We demonstrate that although reaction systems with discrete concentrations are semantically equivalent to the original qualitative reaction systems, they provide much more succinct representations in terms of the number of molecules being used. We then define the problem of reachability for reaction systems with discrete concentrations, and provide its suitable encoding in SMT, together with a verification method (bounded model checking) for reachability properties. Experimental results show that verifying reaction systems with discrete concentrations instead of the corresponding reaction systems is more efficient.

1 Introduction

Reaction systems (see, e.g., [5,7,8]) are a formal model for processes inspired by the functioning of living cells. The key feature of this model is that the functioning of the living cell is determined by the interactions of biochemical reactions, and these interactions are based on the mechanisms of facilitation and inhibition: the (products of the) reactions may facilitate or inhibit each other. Reaction system related research topics have been motivated by biological issues or by a need to understand computations/processes underlying the dynamic behaviour of reaction systems.

Following their introduction, a number of extensions of reaction systems were studied, e.g., reaction systems with time [9] and quantum and probabilistic reaction systems [13]. Mathematical properties of reaction systems were investigated

© Springer International Publishing Switzerland 2016
M. Amos and A. Condon (Eds.): UCNC 2016, LNCS 9726, pp. 142–154, 2016.
DOI: 10.1007/978-3-319-41312-9_12

in, e.g., [10–12,17–20]. Examples of application of reaction systems to modelling of systems include, e.g., [3,6]. Recently, there has been an increasing interest in verification of reaction systems as described in, e.g., [1,2,15].

The formal treatment of basic reaction systems is qualitative as no direct representation of the number of molecules involved in biochemical reactions. This paper introduces reaction systems with discrete concentrations which are an extension of reaction systems allowing for quantitative modelling. We demonstrate that although reaction systems with discrete concentrations are semantically equivalent to the original qualitative reaction systems, they provide much more succinct representations in terms of the number of molecules being used.

There exist also other approaches that allow for modelling of complex dependencies of concentration levels and their changes, e.g. chemical reaction networks theory based on [14]. The formalism of reaction systems is much simpler and the processes of reaction systems depend on interactions with the environment.

We define the problem of state reachability for reaction systems with discrete concentrations, and provide its suitable encoding in SMT, together with a verification method (bounded model checking) for reachability properties. Experimental results show that verifying reaction systems with discrete concentrations instead of the corresponding reaction systems is more efficient.

2   Preliminaries

A *reaction system* is a pair $rs = (S, A)$, where S is a finite *background* set and A is a set of *reactions* over the background set. Each reaction in A is a triple $b = (R, I, P)$ such that R, I, P are nonempty subsets of S with $R \cap I = \emptyset$. The sets R, I, and P are respectively denoted by R_b, I_b, and P_b and called the *reactant*, *inhibitor*, and *product set* of reaction b.

A reaction $b \in A$ is *enabled* by $T \subseteq S$, denoted $en_b(T)$, if $R_b \subseteq T$ and $I_b \cap T = \emptyset$. The *result* of b on T is given by $res_b(T) = P_b$ if $en_b(T)$, and by $res_b(T) = \emptyset$ otherwise. Then the *result* of A on T is $res_A(T) = \bigcup \{res_b(T) \mid b \in A\} = \bigcup \{P_b \mid b \in A \text{ and } en_b(T)\}$.

Intuitively, T represents a state of a biochemical system being modelled by listing all present biochemical entities. A reaction b is enabled by T and can take place if all its reactants are present and none of its inhibitors is present in T.

Example 1. Let $(S, A) = (\{1, 2, 3, 4\}, \{a_1, a_2, a_3, a_4\})$ be a reaction system, where:
$$a_1 = (\{1, 4\}, \{2\}, \{1, 2\}) \quad a_2 = (\{2\}, \{3\}, \{1, 3, 4\})$$
$$a_3 = (\{1, 3\}, \{2\}, \{1, 2\}) \quad a_4 = (\{3\}, \{2\}, \{1\})$$

In state $T = \{1, 3, 4\}$ reactions a_1, a_3, and a_4 are enabled, while a_2 is not. Hence $res_A(T) = res_{a_1}(T) \cup res_{a_3}(T) \cup res_{a_4}(T) = \{1, 2\} \cup \{1, 2\} \cup \{1\} = \{1, 2\}$.   □

Entities in reaction systems are *non-permanent*, i.e., if entity x is present in the successor state T' of a current state T then it must have been produced (sustained) by a reaction enabled by T (thus $x \in res_A(T)$). Also, there are no conflicts between reactions enabled by T. Therefore there is no counting in reaction systems, and so it is a qualitative model. This follows from the level of abstraction adopted for the basic model. However, in the broad framework of reaction systems (see, e.g., [7]) one considers models with aspects of counting.

A reaction system is a finite system in the sense that the size of each state is a priori limited (by the size of the background set), and the state transformations it describes are deterministic since there are no conflicts between enabled reactions. This changes once we decided to take account of the external environment which is necessary to reflect the fact that the living cell is an open system. Such an environment can be represented by a context automaton.

A *context automaton* over a finite set Ct, is a triple $ca = (Q, q_0, R)$, where Q is a finite set of *states*, $q_0 \in Q$ is the *initial state*, and $R \subseteq Q \times Ct \times Q$ is a *transition relation* labelled with elements of Ct.

A *context restricted reaction system* is a pair $crrs = (rs, ca)$ such that $rs = (S, A)$ is a reaction system, and $ca = (Q, q_0, R)$ is a *context automaton* over 2^S. The dynamic behaviour of $crrs$ is then captured by the state sequences of its interactive processes. An *interactive process* in $crrs$ is $\pi = (\zeta, \gamma, \delta)$, where:

- $\zeta = (z_0, z_1, \ldots, z_n)$, $\gamma = (C_0, C_1, \ldots, C_n)$, and $\delta = (D_0, D_1, \ldots, D_n)$
- $z_0, z_1, \ldots, z_n \in Q$ with $z_0 = q_0$
- $C_0, C_1, \ldots, C_n, D_0, D_1, \ldots, D_n \subseteq S$ with $D_0 = \emptyset$
- $(z_i, C_i, z_{i+1}) \in R$, for every $i \in \{0, \ldots, n-1\}$
- $D_i = res_A(D_{i-1} \cup C_{i-1})$, for every $i \in \{1, \ldots, n\}$.

Then the *state sequence* of π is $\tau = (W_0, \ldots, W_n) = (C_0 \cup D_0, \ldots, C_n \cup D_n)$.

Intuitively, the state sequence of π captures the observed behaviour of $crrs$ by recording the successive states of the evolution of the reaction system rs in the environment represented by the context automaton ca.

3   Reaction Systems with Discrete Concentrations

The enabling of some of biochemical reactions encountered in practical applications depends not only on the availability of the necessary reactants and the absence of inhibitors, but also on their concentration levels. To address this aspect in biochemical modelling, we will now introduce an extension of the basic reaction systems supporting an explicit representation of the discrete concentration levels of entities. The resulting model uses bags of entities, but otherwise it retains key features of the original framework. The main new idea that the k-th level of concentration of an entity x is represented by a bag containing k copies of x.

In what follows, a *bag* over a set X is any mapping $\mathbf{b} : X \to \{0, 1, \ldots\}$, and the *empty* bag $\emptyset_X$ is one which always returns 0. We denote this by $\mathbf{b} \in \mathcal{B}(X)$, where $\mathcal{B}(X)$ is the set of all bags over X. For a set $\mathbf{B}$ of bags over X, $\mathbb{M}(\mathbf{B})$ is the bag over X such that $\mathbb{M}(\mathbf{B})(x) = \max(\{0\} \cup \{\mathbf{b}(x) \mid \mathbf{b} \in \mathbf{B}\})$, for every $x \in X$. For two bags, $\mathbf{b}$ and $\mathbf{b}'$, we denote $\mathbf{b} \leq \mathbf{b}'$ if $\mathbf{b}(x) \leq \mathbf{b}'(x)$, for every $x \in X$. The *carrier* of a bag $\mathbf{b}$ is the set $carr(\mathbf{b}) = \{x \in X \mid \mathbf{b}(x) > 0\}$.

A *reaction system with discrete concentrations* is a pair $rsc = (S, A)$, where S is a finite *background* set and A is a nonempty <u>finite</u> set of *c-reactions* over the background set. Each c-reaction in A is a triple $a = (\mathbf{r}, \mathbf{i}, \mathbf{p})$ such that $\mathbf{r}$, $\mathbf{i}$, $\mathbf{p}$ are bags over S with $\mathbf{r}(e) < \mathbf{i}(e)$, for every $e \in carr(\mathbf{i})$. The sets $\mathbf{r}$, $\mathbf{i}$, and $\mathbf{p}$ are respectively denoted by $\mathbf{r}_a$, $\mathbf{i}_a$, and $\mathbf{p}_a$ and called the *reactant, inhibitor*, and *product concentration levels* of c-reaction a. We would like to stress that an entity e is an inhibitor of a whenever $e \in carr(\mathbf{i}_a)$.

A c-reaction $a \in A$ is *enabled* by $\mathbf{t} \in \mathcal{B}(S)$, denoted $en_a(\mathbf{t})$, if $\mathbf{r}_a \leq \mathbf{t}$ and $\mathbf{t}(e) < \mathbf{i}_a(e)$, for every $e \in carr(\mathbf{i}_a)$. The *result* of a on $\mathbf{t}$ is given by $res_a(\mathbf{t}) = \mathbf{p}_a$ if $en_a(\mathbf{t})$, and by $res_a(\mathbf{t}) = \emptyset_S$ otherwise. Then the *result* of A on $\mathbf{t}$ is $res_A(\mathbf{t}) = \mathbb{M}\{res_a(\mathbf{t}) \mid a \in A\} = \mathbb{M}\{\mathbf{p}_a \mid a \in A \text{ and } en_a(\mathbf{t})\}$.

In the above, $\mathbf{t}$ is a *state* of a biochemical system being modelled such that, for each entity $e \in S$, $\mathbf{t}(e)$ is the *concentration level* of e (e.g., $\mathbf{t}(e) = 0$ indicates that e is not present in the current state, and $\mathbf{t}(e) = 1$ indicates that e is present at its lowest concentration level). A c-reaction a is enabled by $\mathbf{t}$ and can take place if the current concentration levels of all its reactants are at least as high as those specified by $\mathbf{r}_a$, and the current concentration levels of all its inhibitors (i.e., entities in the carrier of $\mathbf{i}_a$) are below the thresholds specified by $\mathbf{i}_a$.

A *context restricted reaction system with discrete concentrations* is a pair $crrsc = (rsc, ca)$ such that $rsc = (S, A)$ is a reaction system with discrete concentrations, and $ca = (Q, q_0, R)$ is a *context automaton* over $\mathcal{B}(S)$. The dynamic behaviour of $crrsc$ is then captured by the state sequences of its interactive processes. An *interactive process* in $crrsc$ is $\pi = (\zeta, \gamma, \delta)$, where:

- $\zeta = (z_0, z_1, \ldots, z_n)$, $\gamma = (\mathbf{c}_0, \mathbf{c}_1, \ldots, \mathbf{c}_n)$, and $\delta = (\mathbf{d}_0, \mathbf{d}_1, \ldots, \mathbf{d}_n)$
- $z_0, z_1, \ldots, z_n \in Q$ with $z_0 = q_0$
- $\mathbf{c}_0, \mathbf{c}_1, \ldots, \mathbf{c}_n, \mathbf{d}_0, \mathbf{d}_1, \ldots, \mathbf{d}_n \in \mathcal{B}(S)$ with $\mathbf{d}_0 = \emptyset_{\mathcal{B}(S)}$
- $(z_i, \mathbf{c}_i, z_{i+1}) \in R$, for every $i \in \{0, \ldots, n-1\}$
- $\mathbf{d}_i = res_A(\mathbb{M}\{\mathbf{d}_{i-1}, \mathbf{c}_{i-1}\})$, for every $i \in \{1, \ldots, n\}$.

Then the *state sequence* of π is $\tau = (\mathbf{w}_0, \ldots, \mathbf{w}_n) = (\mathbb{M}\{\mathbf{c}_0, \mathbf{d}_0\}, \ldots, \mathbb{M}\{\mathbf{c}_n, \mathbf{d}_n\})$.

A context restricted reaction system with discrete concentrations $crrsc = (rsc, ca)$ is a finite state system since it comprises finitely many c-reactions and finitely many bags labelling the arcs of its context automaton. More precisely, let $\#_{crrsc}(e)$ be the maximum integer assigned to $e \in S$ in all the bags of entities occurring in both rsc and ca. Then, $\mathbf{w}(e) \leq \#_{crrsc}(e)$, for all $e \in S$ and all states occurring in the state sequences of the interactive processes in $crrsc$. (Note that this bound can be improved by ignoring the reactant and inhibitor bags in c-reactions.) Moreover, the behaviour of $crrsc$ can be simulated by a suitable context restricted reaction system.

To construct such a system, for every $\mathbf{t} \in \mathcal{B}(S)$, we define two <u>sets</u> of entities, $\Gamma(\mathbf{t}) = \{e.i \mid e \in S \wedge \mathbf{t}(e) = i > 0\}$ and $\Gamma_{all}(\mathbf{t}) = \{e.i \mid e \in S \wedge 1 \leq i \leq \mathbf{t}(e)\}$. The $e.i$'s will be entities of the system we are going to construct. Note that $\Gamma_{all}(\mathbf{t})$ is a *downward-closed* set in the sense that if $e.i \in \Gamma_{all}(\mathbf{t})$ and $i > 1$, then $e.1, \ldots, e.(i-1) \in \Gamma_{all}(\mathbf{t})$. In fact, Γ_{all} is a bijection from $\mathcal{B}(S)$ to all the downward-closed sets, and its inverse Γ_{all}^{-1} is given by $\Gamma_{all}^{-1}(Z)(e) = \max\{\{0\} \cup \{i \mid e.i \in Z\}$, for every $e \in S$. In what follows, Γ_{all} and Γ_{all}^{-1} will be applied component-wise to sequences of respectively bags and downward-closed sets. For such $crrsc$, we define the corresponding context restricted reaction system as $\Theta(crrsc) = (rs, ca) = ((S', A'), (Q, q_0, R'))$, where: $S' = \{e.i \mid e \in S \text{ and } 1 \leq i \leq \#_{crrsc}(e)\}$, $A' = \{(\Gamma(\mathbf{r}), \Gamma(\mathbf{i}), \Gamma_{all}(\mathbf{p})) \mid (\mathbf{r}, \mathbf{i}, \mathbf{p}) \in A\}$, and $R' = \{(z, \Gamma_{all}(\mathbf{c}), z') \mid (z, \mathbf{c}, z') \in R\}$. It is straightforward to see that $\Theta(crrsc)$ is well-defined.

As to the complexity of the translation, the number of reactions, states and arrows remains the same. Moreover, the representations of reaction and inhibitors are of the same order. What changes is the size of the background set, in the worst case by the factor $\max\{\#_{crrsc}(e) \mid e \in S\}$ as well as the representations of products and contexts (again by the same factor).

We will now investigate a very close correspondence between $\Theta(crrsc)$ and $crrsc$. First, we observe that, by the definitions of A' and R', all sets of entities occurring in the interactive processes of $\Theta(crrsc)$ are downward-closed. Then we obtain that all interactive processes of $crrsc$ can be simulated by $\Theta(crrsc)$.

Theorem 1. *If $\pi = (\zeta, \gamma, \delta)$ is an interactive process in $crrsc$, then $\pi' = (\zeta, \Gamma_{all}(\gamma), \Gamma_{all}(\delta))$ is an interactive process in $\Theta(crrsc)$.*

Proof. It suffices to show for $\mathbf{w}$ in the state sequence of π, $\Gamma_{all}(res_A(\mathbf{w})) = res_{A'}(\Gamma_{all}(\mathbf{w}))$. Suppose $a = (\mathbf{r}, \mathbf{i}, \mathbf{p}) \in A$ and $a' = (\Gamma(\mathbf{r}), \Gamma(\mathbf{i}), \Gamma_{all}(\mathbf{p})) \in A'$. We first observe that a is enabled in $\mathbf{w}$ (i.e., $\mathbf{r} \leq \mathbf{w}$ and $\mathbf{w}(e) < \mathbf{i}(e)$, for all $e \in carr(\mathbf{i})$) iff a' is enabled in $\Gamma_{all}(\mathbf{w})$ (i.e., $\Gamma(\mathbf{r}) \subseteq \Gamma_{all}(\mathbf{w})$ and $\Gamma(\mathbf{i}) \cap \Gamma_{all}(\mathbf{w}) = \emptyset$). Moreover, it is easy to check that $\Gamma_{all}(res_a(\mathbf{w})) = res_{a'}(\Gamma_{all}(\mathbf{w}))$. $\square$

Moreover, all interactive processes of $\Theta(crrsc)$ simulate those of $crrsc$.

Theorem 2. *If $\pi = (\zeta, \gamma, \delta)$ is an interactive process in $\Theta(crrsc)$, then $\pi' = (\zeta, \Gamma_{all}^{-1}(\gamma), \Gamma_{all}^{-1}(\delta))$ is an interactive process in $crrsc$.*

Proof. Similar to the proof of Theorem 1. $\square$

We have therefore obtained a one-to-one correspondence between the interactive processes of $\Theta(crrsc)$ and $crrsc$.

Remark 1. From the point of view of enabling c-reactions, not all concentration levels are important and, consequently, they do not need to be represented in the states of $\Theta(crrsc)$. To achieve the desired effect, all one needs to do is re-define Γ_{all}, in the following way: $\Gamma'_{all}(\mathbf{t}) = \Gamma(\mathbf{t}) \cup (\Gamma_{all}(\mathbf{t}) \cap \bigcup_{a \in A} \Gamma(\mathbf{r}_a) \cup \Gamma(\mathbf{i}_a))$.

Note that syntactically crrs are a subclass of crrsc, such that all the concentration levels in crrsc are limited to the value of at most one, that is, for any $\mathbf{t} \in \mathcal{B}(S)$ and for any $e \in carr(\mathbf{t})$ we have $\mathbf{t}(e) = 1$. Therefore, in the remainder of this paper we use crrs and crrsc interchangeably, depending on the concentration levels required.

4   Reachability Testing

In this section we define the reachability problem for $crrsc$ and provide its translation into a satisfiability modulo theory (SMT) with integer arithmetic.

Let $n \geq 0$ be an integer. A result $\mathbf{d} \in \mathcal{B}(S)$ is n-reachable in $crrsc$ if there exists an interactive process $\pi = (\zeta, \gamma, \delta)$ in $crrsc$ such that $\delta = (\mathbf{d}_0, \mathbf{d}_1, \dots, \mathbf{d}_n)$ and $\mathbf{d}_n = \mathbf{d}$. We say that $\mathbf{d}$ is $reachable$ in $crrsc$ if there is $n \geq 0$ such that $\mathbf{d}$ is n-reachable in $crrsc$.

Theorem 3. *The reachability problem for $crrsc$ ($crrs$) is* NP-*hard.*

Proof. We show a reduction of 3-SAT to reachability in crrs. The proof is similar to that in [15] for rsCTL model checking. Let $PV = \{x_1, x_2, \dots, x_n\}$ be a set of propositional variables and $\beta(x_1, x_2, \dots, x_n)$ be a boolean formula in 3-CNF. We define the set of the negated propositional variables $\overline{PV} = \{\bar{x} \mid x \in PV\}$ and assume $\beta = c_1 \wedge c_2 \wedge \cdots \wedge c_m$, where $c_i = (l_{i,1} \vee l_{i,2} \vee l_{i,3})$ with $l_{i,j} \in (PV \cup \overline{PV})$, for $1 \leq i \leq m$ and $1 \leq j \leq 3$. Moreover, for a clause c we define the set $vars(c) = \{1 \leq k \leq n \mid x_k \in PV \text{ is in } c\}$ and the set $\overline{vars}(c) = \{1 \leq k \leq n \mid \bar{x}_k \in \overline{PV} \text{ is in } c\}$. Next, we define the crrs which we use for the translation.

Let $\mathcal{V} = \{p_1, \bar{p}_1, \dots, p_n, \bar{p}_n\}$ be the set of entities representing the propositional variables and their negations, and $\mathcal{C} = \{\hat{c}_1, \hat{c}_2, \dots, \hat{c}_m\}$ be the set of the entities that correspond to the clauses. The entity t is used to indicate that under the considered valuation the formula β is true. The entity h is used as the inhibitor of the reactions where no inhibitors are needed for the translation to work. This guarantees that the inhibitor set is non-empty. The background set is $S = \mathcal{V} \cup \mathcal{C} \cup \{t, h\}$, and we define the following sets of reactions:

- $P_i = \{(\{p_i\}, \{h\}, \{p_i\}), (\{\bar{p}_i\}, \{h\}, \{\bar{p}_i\})\}$ for $1 \leq i \leq n$
- $L_i = \{(\{p_k\}, \{\bar{p}_k\}, \{\hat{c}_i\}) \mid k \in vars(i)\} \cup \{(\{\bar{p}_k\}, \{p_k\}, \{\hat{c}_i\}) \mid k \in \overline{vars}(i)\}$ for $1 \leq i \leq m$
- $F = \{(\{\hat{c}_i\}, \{h\}, \{\hat{c}_i\}) \mid 1 \leq i \leq m\} \cup \{(\{\hat{c}_1, \hat{c}_2, \dots, \hat{c}_m\}, \{h\}, \{t\})\}$.

The set P_i contains the reactions responsible for preserving the valuations of the variables along the execution sequences. The reactions of L_i produce entities that indicate whether a single clause is satisfied, whereas the reactions of F that the entity t indicating that all the clauses are satisfied is produced. The set of all the reactions of the crrs is defined as $A = \bigcup_{i=1}^{n} P_i \cup \bigcup_{i=1}^{n} L_i \cup F$. Next, we define the context automaton $ca = (Q, q_0, R)$ where $Q = \{1, \dots, n+2\}$, $q_0 = 1$, and $R = \{(i, \{p_i\}, i+1) \mid 1 \leq i \leq n\} \cup \{(i, \{\bar{p}_i\}, i+1) \mid 1 \leq i \leq n\} \cup \{(i+1, \emptyset, i+2)\}$. Then, $rs = (S, A)$ and $crrs = (rs, ca)$. Any path from 1 to $n+1$ in ca corresponds to a valuation of the variables, where a choice of an edge from i to $i+1$ (for $1 \leq i \leq n$) represents a choice of the valuation of x_i (true for p_i, false for $\bar{p}_i$). When a chosen valuation satisfies a clause c_j (for $1 \leq j \leq m$), then $\hat{c}_j$ is produced, and when $\hat{c}_j$ for all $1 \leq j \leq m$ are produced, then t is produced (in ca this is allowed by the step from $n+1$ to $n+2$). Finally, β is satisfiable if D such that $t \in D$ is reachable in $crrs$. $\qquad\square$

In this paper we focus on the approach of bounded model checking [4], i.e., we test the reachability for all the interactive processes of a given length, and increase the length until the reachability is proved. In what follows we show how n-reachability problem can be encoded by an SMT formula. Due to lack of space, our presentation is quite dense, but it contains the complete encoding.

Let $crrsc = ((S, A), (Q, q_0, R))$ and $\pi = (\zeta, \gamma, \delta)$ be an interactive process in $crrsc$, where $\zeta = (z_0, z_1, \ldots, z_n)$, $\gamma = (\mathbf{c}_0, \mathbf{c}_1, \ldots, \mathbf{c}_n)$, and $\delta = (\mathbf{d}_0, \mathbf{d}_1, \ldots, \mathbf{d}_n)$. Then, the i-th step of π is defined as $\pi_i = (z_i, c_i, d_i)$, where $0 \leq i \leq n$. To encode all the steps of π we introduce the following sets of positive integer variables used in the encoding: $\mathbf{P} = \bigcup_{i=0}^{n} \{\mathbf{p}_{i,1}, \ldots, \mathbf{p}_{i,n}\}$, $\mathbf{P}^{\mathcal{E}} = \bigcup_{i=0}^{n} \{\mathbf{p}_{i,1}^{\mathcal{E}}, \ldots, \mathbf{p}_{i,n}^{\mathcal{E}}\}$, and $\mathbf{Q} = \{\mathbf{q}_0, \ldots, \mathbf{q}_n\}$. Then, π_i is encoded as $s_i = (\mathbf{q}_i, \overline{\mathbf{p}}_i^{\mathcal{E}}, \overline{\mathbf{p}}_i)$, where $\mathbf{q}_i$ encodes the state z_i of the context automaton, $\overline{\mathbf{p}}_i^{\mathcal{E}} = (\mathbf{p}_{i,1}^{\mathcal{E}}, \ldots, \mathbf{p}_{i,n}^{\mathcal{E}})$ encodes the context set c_i, and $\overline{\mathbf{p}}_i = (\mathbf{p}_{i,1}, \ldots, \mathbf{p}_{i,n})$ encodes the result d_i. With $\overline{\mathbf{p}}_i^{\mathcal{E}}[j]$ and $\overline{\mathbf{p}}_i[j]$ we denote, respectively, $\mathbf{p}_{i,j}$ and $\mathbf{p}_{i,j}^{\mathcal{E}}$.

The entities of S are denoted by $e_1, \ldots, e_k$, where $k = |S|$. For π_i we define the following functions that map background set entities to the corresponding variables of the encoding: for all $0 \leq i \leq n$ we define $\mathbf{t}_i : S \to \mathbf{P}_i$ and $\mathbf{t}_i^{\mathcal{E}} : S \to \mathbf{P}_i^{\mathcal{E}}$ such that $\mathbf{t}_i(e_j) = \mathbf{p}_{i,j}$, $\mathbf{t}_i^{\mathcal{E}}(e_j) = \mathbf{p}_{i,j}^{\mathcal{E}}$ for all $1 \leq j \leq k$. The function $\mathbf{e} : Q \to \{0, \ldots, |Q| - 1\}$ maps states of the context automaton to the corresponding natural values used in the encoding. The set of the reactions that produce $e \in S$ is defined as $Prod(e) = \{a \in A \mid \mathbf{p}_a(e) > 0\}$.

To define the SMT encoding of the reachability problem for crrsc we need auxiliary functions that correspond to elements of the encoding.

Result: $\mathsf{Res}_{\mathbf{d}_i}(\overline{\mathbf{p}}_i) = \bigwedge_{e \in S}(\mathbf{t}_i(e) = \mathbf{d}_i(e))$ encodes a result $\mathbf{d}_i \in \mathcal{B}(S)$ as the conjunction of the variables with the corresponding concentration levels.

Context: $\mathsf{Ct}_{\mathbf{c}_i}(\overline{\mathbf{p}}_i^{\mathcal{E}}) = \bigwedge_{e \in S}(\mathbf{t}_i^{\mathcal{E}}(e) = \mathbf{c}_i(e))$ encodes a bag $\mathbf{c}_i \in \mathcal{B}(S)$ of context entities.

Enabledness: $\mathsf{En}_a(\overline{\mathbf{p}}_i, \overline{\mathbf{p}}_i^{\mathcal{E}}) = \bigwedge_{e \in S}(\mathbf{t}_i(e) \geq \mathbf{r}_a(e) \vee \mathbf{t}_i^{\mathcal{E}}(e) \geq \mathbf{r}_a(e)) \wedge \bigwedge_{e \in S}(\mathbf{t}_i(e) < \mathbf{i}_a(e) \wedge \mathbf{t}_i^{\mathcal{E}}(e) < \mathbf{i}(e))$ encodes the enabledness of a reaction a.

Entity Concentration: Let f_1, f_2, f_3 be expressions over $\mathbf{P} \cup \mathbf{P}^{\mathcal{E}}$, then we introduce the *if-then-else* operator: $f_1 \to f_2 \mid f_3 = (f_1 \wedge f_2) \vee (\neg f_1 \wedge f_3)$. Let $e \in S$, then $Prod^{sorted}(e) = (a_1, a_2, \ldots, a_m)$ is an ordered list of the reactions producing e, where $m = |Prod(e)|$ and $\mathbf{p}_{a_j} \leq \mathbf{p}_{a_{j+1}}$ for all $1 \leq j < m$. The produced concentration level for entity e and reaction a_j, $1 \leq j \leq m$, is encoded as: $\mathsf{C}_e^j(\overline{\mathbf{p}}_i, \overline{\mathbf{p}}_i^{\mathcal{E}}, \overline{\mathbf{p}}_{i+1}) = \mathsf{En}_{a_j}(\overline{\mathbf{p}}_i, \overline{\mathbf{p}}_i^{\mathcal{E}}) \to \mathbf{t}_{i+1}(e) = \mathbf{p}_{a_j} \mid \mathsf{C}_e^{j+1}(\overline{\mathbf{p}}_i, \overline{\mathbf{p}}_i^{\mathcal{E}}, \overline{\mathbf{p}}_{i+1})$ if $j < m$, and $\mathsf{En}_{a_j}(\overline{\mathbf{p}}_i, \overline{\mathbf{p}}_i^{\mathcal{E}}) \wedge \mathbf{t}_{i+1}(e) = \mathbf{p}_{a_j}$ if $j = m$. Finally, we define the complete entity concentration encoding for all the reactions. If $m = 0$, then $\mathsf{C}_e(\overline{\mathbf{p}}_i, \overline{\mathbf{p}}_i^{\mathcal{E}}, \overline{\mathbf{p}}_{i+1}) = (\mathbf{t}_{i+1}(e) = 0)$, otherwise $\mathsf{C}_e(\overline{\mathbf{p}}_i, \overline{\mathbf{p}}_i^{\mathcal{E}}, \overline{\mathbf{p}}_{i+1}) = \mathsf{C}_e^1(\overline{\mathbf{p}}_i, \overline{\mathbf{p}}_i^{\mathcal{E}}, \overline{\mathbf{p}}_{i+1}) \vee ((\bigwedge_{a \in Prod(e)} \neg \mathsf{En}_a(\overline{\mathbf{p}}_i, \overline{\mathbf{p}}_i^{\mathcal{E}})) \wedge \mathbf{t}_{i+1}(e) = 0)$.

Transitions of Context Automaton: The encoding of the transition relation of the context automaton is a disjunction of the encodings for each transition: $\mathsf{Tr}_{ca}(\mathbf{q}_i, \overline{\mathbf{p}}_i^{\mathcal{E}}, \mathbf{q}_{i+1}) = \bigvee_{(q, c, q') \in R}(\mathbf{q} = \mathbf{e}(q) \wedge \mathsf{Ct}_{\mathbf{c}}(\overline{\mathbf{p}}_i^{\mathcal{E}}) \wedge \mathbf{q}_{i+1} = \mathbf{e}_{i+1}(q'))$.

Step of Interactive Process: We build a conjunction of the produced concentration levels for all entities and the transition relation for the context automaton: $\mathsf{St}(\overline{\mathbf{p}}_i, \overline{\mathbf{p}}_i^{\mathcal{E}}, \overline{\mathbf{p}}_{i+1}, \mathsf{q}_i, \mathsf{q}_{i+1}) = (\bigwedge_{e \in S} \mathsf{C}_e(\overline{\mathbf{p}}_i, \overline{\mathbf{p}}_i^{\mathcal{E}}, \overline{\mathbf{p}}_{i+1})) \wedge \mathsf{Tr}_{ca}(\mathsf{q}_i, \overline{\mathbf{p}}_i^{\mathcal{E}}, \mathsf{q}_{i+1})$.

Interactive Process: To encode n steps of π we define the following formula:
$[\![\pi]\!]_n = \mathsf{Res}_{\emptyset_S}(\overline{\mathbf{p}}_0) \wedge \mathsf{e}(z_0) \wedge \bigwedge_{i=0}^{n-1} \mathsf{St}(\overline{\mathbf{p}}_i, \overline{\mathbf{p}}_i^{\mathcal{E}}, \overline{\mathbf{p}}_{i+1}, \mathsf{q}_i, \mathsf{q}_{i+1})$.

To perform the n-reachability test of $\mathbf{d} \in \mathcal{B}(S)$ in π we test the satisfiability of the formula $[\![\pi]\!]_n \wedge \bigvee_{i=0}^{n} \mathsf{Res}_{\mathbf{d}}(\overline{\mathbf{p}}_i)$. Note that the n-reachability can also be defined for a pair $\rho = (\mathbf{x}, \mathbf{y})$ where $\mathbf{x}, \mathbf{y} \in \mathcal{B}(S)$. Then, ρ is n-reachable if there exists an interactive process $\pi = (\zeta, \gamma, \delta)$ in $crrsc$ such that $\delta = (\mathbf{d}_0, \mathbf{d}_1, \ldots, \mathbf{d}_n)$, and $\mathbf{x} \leq \mathbf{d}_n$, $\mathbf{d}_n(e) < \mathbf{y}(e)$, for every $e \in carr(\mathbf{y})$. In this case, the reachability test for ρ is encoded as $[\![\pi]\!]_n \wedge \bigvee_{i=0}^{n} \bigwedge_{e \in S}(\mathsf{t}_i(e) \geq \mathbf{x}(e) \wedge \mathsf{t}_i(e) < \mathbf{y}(e))$.

5   Experimental Results

In this section we present the results of an experimental evaluation of the translation presented in Sect. 4. We compare the implementation for crrsc with an implementation for crrs by verifying the properties of the crrs obtained by applying the translation defined in Sect. 3 to crrsc.

To provide a fair comparison, both the verification tools were implemented in Python using similar techniques and use Z3 [16] for SMT solving. The implementation for crrs is based on the encoding from Sect. 4 which is optimised for crrs by using boolean variables instead of integer variables. The translation into SMT for crrs corresponds to the translation for crrsc – it is assumed that all concentration levels are equal to 1 when an entity is present, and equal to 0 otherwise. We also implement an incremental approach to SMT-solving, i.e., in a single SMT instance we increase the length of the encoded interactive processes by unrolling their encoding until the reachability is proved, instead of creating separate instances for each length tested.

When dealing with concentration levels we often need to perform incrementation and decrementation operations. For this we need additional notation (below we use the notation $e \mapsto i$ to indicate the multiplicity of an entity e in a bag of entities, e.g., $\{e \mapsto 1, f \mapsto 2\}$ is a bag with one copy of e, two copies of f, and nothing else).

Incrementation and Decrementation Operations: With $\uparrow_e^g$ and $\downarrow_e^g$ we denote the set of reactions encoding the operation of, respectively, incrementation and decrementation of concentration levels of $e \in S$ when $g \in S$ is present with a non-zero concentration. With M_e we denote the maximal allowed value of e. Then $\uparrow_e^g = \{(\{e \mapsto i, g \mapsto 1\}, \emptyset_S, \{e \mapsto i+1\}) \mid 1 \leq i < M_e\}$ and $\downarrow_e^g = \{(\{e \mapsto i, g \mapsto 1\}, \emptyset_S, \{e \mapsto i-1\}) \mid 2 < i \leq M_e\}$.

Permanency: $\Diamond_e^{\mathbf{i}} = \{(\{e \mapsto i\}, \mathbf{i}, \{e \mapsto i\}) \mid 1 \leq i \leq M_e\}$ is a set of reactions ensuring permanency of $e \in S$ which can be inhibited by $\mathbf{i} \in \mathcal{B}(S)$.

We exploit the notation to use $\uparrow_e^g$, $\downarrow_e^g$, and $\Diamond_e^{\mathbf{i}}$ in place of regular reactions ignoring that they are in fact sets of reactions. In the implementation for crrsc we introduce an optimisation where these reactions are encoded as *macro-reactions*, that is, as simple operations on integer variables that increment, decrement, or retain the value of the variable encoding concentration of e. Moreover, those macro-reactions are allowed only when no ordinary reaction is enabled.

5.1 Eukaryotic Heat Shock Response

Firstly, we test our implementation using the qualitative model of the eukaryotic heat shock response (HSR) introduced in [3]. HSR is an internal repair mechanism triggered when a cell is subjected to an environmental stressor – increased temperature that is not ideal for its functioning. A temperature exceeding the ideal temperature causes the proteins ($prot$) of a cell to misfold (mfp), which in turn may cause its malfunctioning. To facilitate refolding of the proteins, heat shock response proteins (hsp) are produced, which are molecular chaperones for the misfolded proteins. The production of hsp is initiated by heat shock factors (hsf) which are, dimerised (hsf_2), and then trimerised (hsf_3). Next, hsf_3 activates hsp production by binding to the heat shock element (hse) which is the promoter-site of the gene encoding the heat shock proteins.

Table 1. Entities used in the heat shock response model.

Entity	Description	Entity	Description
hsp	heat shock protein	$hsf_3{:}hse$	hsf_3 bound with hse
hsf	heat shock factor	$hsp{:}mfp$	hsp bound with mfp
hsf_2	dimerised heat shock factor	$hsp{:}hsf$	complex consisting of hsp and hsf
hsf_3	trimerised heat shock factor	$temp$	temperature value
hse	heat shock element	$cool$	decreases the temperature
mfp	misfolded protein	$heat$	increases the temperature
$prot$	protein		

The original model of [3] used *stress* and *nostress* entities to distinguish between the presence and absence of the heat shock. We assume here that the heat shock appears at (and above) the temperature of $42\,°C$, and this is modelled using the *temp* entity. All the entities except *temp* remain at the concentration level of 1. We assume that the maximal value of the temperature modelled using the entity *temp* is 50.

The background set S for the rsc modelling HSR consists of the entities in Table 1. The set A_{ord} comprises the reactions in Table 2. We also define the set of reactions dealing with temperature $A_{temp} = \uparrow^{heat}_{temp} \cup \downarrow^{cool}_{temp} \cup \diamond^{\mathbf{i}}_{temp}$, where $\mathbf{i} = \{heat \mapsto 1, cool \mapsto 1\}$. The rsc for HSR is defined as $rsc_{\text{HSR}} = (S, A_{ord} \cup A_{temp})$.

To define a crrrs for rsc_{HSR} we use the context automaton $ca_{\text{HSR}} = (Q, q_0, R)$ where $Q = \{0, 1\}$, $q_0 = 0$ and $R = \{(0, \{hsf \mapsto 1, prot \mapsto 1, hse \mapsto 1, temp \mapsto 35\}, 1), (1, \{cool \mapsto 1\}, 1), (1, \{heat \mapsto 1\}, 1), (1, \emptyset_S, 1)\}$. Then, the crrsc for rsc_{HSR}

Table 2. Reactions of the heat shock response model (curly brackets are omitted).

Reactants	Inhibitors	Products
$hsf \mapsto 1$	$hsp \mapsto 1$	$hsf_3 \mapsto 1$
$hsf \mapsto 1, hsp \mapsto 1, mfp \mapsto 1$	$\emptyset_S$	$hsf_3 \mapsto 1$
$hsf_3 \mapsto 1$	$hsp \mapsto 1, hse \mapsto 1$	$hsf \mapsto 1$
$hsp \mapsto 1, hsf_3 \mapsto 1, mfp \mapsto 1$	$hse \mapsto 1$	$hsf \mapsto 1$
$hsf_3 \mapsto 1, hse \mapsto 1$	$hsp \mapsto 1$	$hsf_3{:}hse \mapsto 1$
$hsp \mapsto 1, hsf_3 \mapsto 1, mfp \mapsto 1, hse \mapsto 1$	$\emptyset_S$	$hsf_3{:}hse \mapsto 1$
$hse \mapsto 1$	$hsf_3 \mapsto 1$	$hse \mapsto 1$
$hsp \mapsto 1, hsf_3 \mapsto 1, hse \mapsto 1$	$mfp \mapsto 1$	$hse \mapsto 1$
$hsf_3{:}hse \mapsto 1$	$hsp \mapsto 1$	$hsp \mapsto 1, hsf_3{:}hse \mapsto 1$
$hsp, mfp, hsf_3{:}hse \mapsto 1$	$\emptyset_S$	$hsp \mapsto 1, hsf_3{:}hse \mapsto 1$
$hsf \mapsto 1, hsp \mapsto 1$	$mfp \mapsto 1$	$hsp{:}hsf \mapsto 1$
$hsp{:}hsf \mapsto 1, temp \mapsto 42$	$\emptyset_S$	$hsf \mapsto 1, hsp \mapsto 1$
$hsp{:}hsf \mapsto 1$	$temp \mapsto 42$	$hsp{:}hsf \mapsto 1$
$hsp \mapsto 1, hsf_3 \mapsto 1$	$mfp \mapsto 1$	$hsp{:}hsf \mapsto 1$
$hsp \mapsto 1, hsf_3{:}hse \mapsto 1$	$mfp \mapsto 1$	$hse \mapsto 1, hsp{:}hsf \mapsto 1$
$temp \mapsto 42, prot \mapsto 1$	$\emptyset_S$	$mfp \mapsto 1, prot \mapsto 1$
$prot \mapsto 1$	$temp \mapsto 42$	$prot \mapsto 1$
$hsp \mapsto 1, mfp \mapsto 1$	$\emptyset_S$	$hsp{:}mfp \mapsto 1$
$mfp \mapsto 1$	$hsp \mapsto 1$	$mfp \mapsto 1$
$hsp{:}mfp \mapsto 1$	$\emptyset_S$	$hsp \mapsto 1, prot \mapsto 1$

is defined as $crrsc_{\mathrm{HSR}} = (rsc_{\mathrm{HSR}}, ca_{\mathrm{HSR}})$. The context set specified in ca_{HSR} for the transition from 0 (the initial state) corresponds to the initial context set used in [3] as the minimal set of entities needed in HSR, together with the *temp* entity indicating a temperature that does not cause the heat shock.

We test the efficiency of our implementation by verifying the reachability of the following results of $crrsc_{\mathrm{HSR}}$: $\rho_1 = (\mathbf{x}_1, \mathbf{y}_1)$ where $\mathbf{x}_1 = \{hsp{:}hsf \mapsto 1, hse \mapsto 1, prot \mapsto 1\}$, $\mathbf{y}_1 = \{temp \mapsto 42\}$. and $\rho_2 = (\mathbf{x}_2, \mathbf{y}_2)$ where $\mathbf{x}_2 = \{mfp \mapsto 1\}$, $\mathbf{y}_2 = \emptyset_S$. Reachability of ρ_1 proves that it is possible to enter the state where HSR may become stable, while reachability of ρ_2 proves that it is possible for the proteins to eventually misfold. The verification results[1] are summarised in Table 3. In terms of n-reachability, ρ_1 is proved for $n = 4$, while ρ_2 for $n = 9$. There is no noticeable improvement in memory consumption for the verification of crrsc over crrs. However, there is a significant difference in the execution times in favour of crrsc, e.g., for ρ_1 the verification for crrsc is 49.48 times faster.

---

[1] The experimental results were obtained using a system equipped with 3.7 GHz Intel Xeon E5 processor and 12 GB of memory, running Mac OS X 10.11.3.

Table 3. Results for the heat shock response model.

	ρ_1		ρ_2	
	time [s]	memory [MB]	time [s]	memory [MB]
crrs	17.32	25.08	38.78	28.38
crrsc	**0.35**	**24.87**	**0.93**	**24.99**
improvement	49.48×	1.01×	41.69×	1.13×

5.2 Scalable Chain

Here we introduce an abstract system that executes reactions incrementing concentration levels of m molecules up to a maximal concentration level k. The background set is defined as the set of the molecules combined with entities used in the context sets: $S = \{e_1, e_2, \ldots, e_m, inc, dec\}$. The inc and dec entities cause, respectively, incrementation or decrementation of concentration levels. We define the following sets of reactions: $\mathcal{P} = \{(\{e_i \mapsto k\}, \emptyset_S, \{e_{i+1} \mapsto 1\}) \mid 1 \leq i < m\}$, $\mathcal{O} = \{ \uparrow_{e_i}^{inc}, \downarrow_{e_i}^{dec} \mid 1 \leq i \leq m\}$, $\mathcal{F} = \{(\{e_m \mapsto k\}, \{dec \mapsto 1\}, \{e_m \mapsto k\})\}$. The reactions of $\mathcal{P}$ take care of the production of the subsequent molecules, while their concentration levels are changed by the reactions of $\mathcal{O}$. The reaction of $\mathcal{F}$ ensures persistency of the "final" molecule e_m when it reaches the concentration of k, unless dec is present. The rsc for the scalable chain system is defined as $rsc_{\mathrm{SC}} = (S, \mathcal{P} \cup \mathcal{O} \cup \mathcal{F})$. Next, we define the context automaton $ca_{\mathrm{SC}} = (Q, q_0, R)$ where $Q = \{0, 1\}$, $q_0 = 0$, and the set R consists of the following transitions: $(0, \{e_1 \mapsto 1, inc \mapsto 1\}, 1)$, $(1, \{inc \mapsto 1\}, 1)$, $(1, \{dec \mapsto 1\}, 1)$. Finally, we define $crrsc_{\mathrm{SC}} = (rsc_{\mathrm{SC}}, ca_{\mathrm{SC}})$. Time and memory consumption results are presented in Figs. 1 and 2. The verified reachability property is proved for $n = m \cdot k - 1$. In most cases there is an observable advantage of the implementation for crrsc when the value of k is relatively large compared to m, e.g., for $m = 8$ and $k = 20$ the results for crrsc are 5.6 times better. For $m = 10$ and $k = 14$ the verification of crrs proved to be 1.6 times more efficient as it only consumed 1334 s,

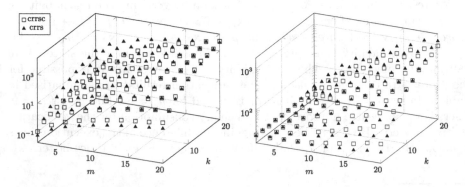

Fig. 1. Time (in seconds)   **Fig. 2.** Memory (in MB)

compared to 2155 s for crrsc. However, for $m = 20$ and $k = 16$ crrs was only 1.2 times better. We attribute this inconsequence to the heuristics of the SMT-solver used. The crrsc implementation appears to be more memory-efficient when dealing with larger concentration level values. It appears that when the verified system is highly-dependent on a large domain of concentration levels, then the crrsc will most likely be more suitable.

6   Concluding Remarks

In this paper, we introduced reaction systems with discrete concentrations which support quantitative modelling. Although the formalism is not more expressive than the standard reaction systems, the experimental results we obtained demonstrate that expressing concentration levels in an explicit way allows for some improvements in the efficiency of verification, and opens up possibilities for introducing different optimisations.

In our future work we plan to extend this approach to provide a comprehensive framework for verifying quantitative properties of reaction systems.

Acknowledgements. The study is cofounded by the European Union from resources of the European Social Fund. Project PO KL "Information technologies: Research and their interdisciplinary applications", Agreement UDA-POKL.04.01.01-00-051/10-00.

References

1. Azimi, S., Gratie, C., Ivanov, S., Manzoni, L., Petre, I., Porreca, A.E.: Complexity of model checking for reaction systems. Technical report. 1122, TUCS (2014)
2. Azimi, S., Gratie, C., Ivanov, S., Petre, I.: Dependency graphs and mass conservation in reaction systems. Technical report. 1123, TUCS (2014)
3. Azimi, S., Iancu, B., Petre, I.: Reaction system models for the heat shock response. Fundam. Inf. **131**(3–4), 299–312 (2014)
4. Biere, A., Cimatti, A., Clarke, E., Zhu, Y.: Symbolic model checking without BDDs. In: Cleaveland, W.R. (ed.) TACAS 1999. LNCS, vol. 1579, pp. 193–207. Springer, Heidelberg (1999)
5. Brijder, R., Ehrenfeucht, A., Main, M.G., Rozenberg, G.: A tour of reaction systems. Int. J. Found. Comput. Sci. **22**(7), 1499–1517 (2011)
6. Corolli, L., Maj, C., Marini, F., Besozzi, D., Mauri, G.: An excursion in reaction systems: from computer science to biology. Theoret. Comput. Sci. **454**, 95–108 (2012)
7. Ehrenfeucht, A., Kleijn, J., Koutny, M., Rozenberg, G.: Reaction systems: a natural computing approach to the functioning of living cells. A Computable Universe, Understanding and Exploring Nature as Computation, pp. 189–208 (2012)
8. Ehrenfeucht, A., Rozenberg, G.: Reaction systems. Fundamenta Informaticae **75**(1–4), 263–280 (2007)
9. Ehrenfeucht, A., Rozenberg, G.: Introducing time in reaction systems. Theoret. Comput. Sci. **410**(4–5), 310–322 (2009)

10. Formenti, E., Manzoni, L., Porreca, A.E.: Cycles and global attractors of reaction systems. In: Jürgensen, H., Karhumäki, J., Okhotin, A. (eds.) DCFS 2014. LNCS, vol. 8614, pp. 114–125. Springer, Heidelberg (2014)

11. Formenti, E., Manzoni, L., Porreca, A.E.: Fixed points and attractors of reaction systems. In: Beckmann, A., Csuhaj-Varjú, E., Meer, K. (eds.) CiE 2014. LNCS, vol. 8493, pp. 194–203. Springer, Heidelberg (2014)

12. Formenti, E., Manzoni, L., Porreca, A.E.: On the complexity of occurrence and convergence problems in reaction systems. Nat. Comput., 1–7 (2014)

13. Hirvensalo, M.: On probabilistic and quantum reaction systems. Theor. Comput. Sci. **429**(C), 134–143 (2012)

14. Horn, F., Jackson, R.: General mass action kinetics. Arch. Ration. Mech. Anal. **47**(2), 81–116 (1972)

15. Męski, A., Penczek, W., Rozenberg, G.: Model checking temporal properties of reaction systems. Inf. Sci. **313**, 22–42 (2015)

16. de Moura, L., Bjørner, N.S.: Z3: an efficient SMT solver. In: Ramakrishnan, C.R., Rehof, J. (eds.) TACAS 2008. LNCS, vol. 4963, pp. 337–340. Springer, Heidelberg (2008)

17. Salomaa, A.: Functions and sequences generated by reaction systems. Theoret. Comput. Sci. **466**, 87–96 (2012)

18. Salomaa, A.: On state sequences defined by reaction systems. In: Constable, R.L., Silva, A. (eds.) Logic and Program Semantics, Kozen Festschrift. LNCS, vol. 7230, pp. 271–282. Springer, Heidelberg (2012)

19. Salomaa, A.: Functional constructions between reaction systems and propositional logic. Int. J. Found. Comput. Sci. **24**(1), 147–160 (2013)

20. Salomaa, A.: Minimal and almost minimal reaction systems. Nat. Comput. **12**(3), 369–376 (2013)

Traversal Languages Capturing Isomorphism Classes of Sierpiński Gaskets

Nataša Jonoska, Milé Krajčevski, and Gregory McColm[⊠]

Department of Mathematics and Statistics,
University of South Florida, Tampa, FL 33620, USA
{jonoska,mile}@mail.usf.edu, mccolm@usf.edu

Abstract. We consider recursive structural assembly using regular d-dimensional simplexes such that a structure at every level is obtained by joining $d+1$ structures from a previous level. The resulting structures are similar to the Sierpiński gasket. We use intersection graphs and index sequences to describe these structures. We observe that for each $d > 1$ there are uncountably many isomorphism classes of these structures. Traversal languages that consist of labels of walks that start at a given vertex can be associated with these structures, and we find that these traversal languages capture the isomorphism classes of the structures.

1 Introduction

Diverse molecular self-assembly techniques have been used to construct various nanostructures ranging from arrays of shapes [7,16,20] to complex crystallographic structures [21,22]. Recent experimental developments [15] allowing "signals" to pass along building blocks have introduced techniques in DNA self-assembly that provide a better control during the assembly. Such signals allow structural recursive assembly of complexes, level by level, building "supertiles" geometrically similar to the "tiles" that comprise them [11]. At each level, the signaling mechanism guides each of the components to assume its respective role in the assembly of the next "supertile". Theoretical methods characterizing structures built at the nano level are still being developed. A study to describe crystallographic structures through formal languages obtained by traversing the structures was initiated in [12]. With this paper we consider formal language characterizations of aperiodic structures that are recursively built by d-dimensional simplexes (equilateral triangles in dimension two, such as the tensegrity triangle [14,22], tetrahedrons in dimension three [2], etc.). We assume that at each level a new "supertile" is obtained from $d+1$ components obtained at the previous level such that each of the $d+1$ components assumes its role in the assembly at one of the $d+1$ corners of the larger component (e.g., Fig. 1 for dimension 2).

Originally popularized as a fractal, discrete versions of the Sierpiński gasket have been used to model games (particularly the Tower of Hanoi game with n disks and 3 pegs [8,9]), VLSI architecture (as "recursively scalable", [19]), and have been used even in 3D printing. Finite graphs similar to the Sierpiński gasket,

© Springer International Publishing Switzerland 2016
M. Amos and A. Condon (Eds.): UCNC 2016, LNCS 9726, pp. 155–167, 2016.
DOI: 10.1007/978-3-319-41312-9_13

also known as Schrier graphs, are associated with a class of automata groups acting on words of length n [5,18]. In this article, we consider the Sierpiński gasket as a model of hierarchical structures that may, or may not, cover the entire space they inhabit.

Like many aperiodic tilings, the Sierpiński gasket may be generated by (self-similar) substitution. In this context, one begins with a single "tile", which appears within a "supertile" of tiles, then that supertile appears within a higher level supertile, and so on. In this paper we study the intersection graphs obtained by such a step-by-step construction and use index sequences [6, Chap. 10], also known as addressing systems [3,4], as an encoding system on the graph. For example, the 2-dimensional Sierpiński gasket, and associated intersection graph, is generated using an index sequence of 0 s, 1 s and 2 s (Fig. 1). Theorem 10.5.10 in [6] asserts that in substitution systems such as Penrose, tilings with two tiles having the same index sequences are isomorphic (i.e., their intersection graphs are isomorphic). This is confirmed for a large class of tilings ([1], [17, §2.5]), but it is false in general, in particular when the substitutions do not uniquely determine the entire tiling [17].

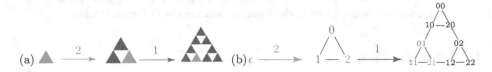

Fig. 1. (a) Given an index sequence 21..., if a tile assumes role 2, it appears in a supertile in the 2nd (lower right) corner. This new (super)tile assumes role 1 so it is part of an assembly in the 1st (lower left) corner of a new supertile etc. (b) The adjacency graphs of these complexes and the corresponding vertex labels (Color figure online).

Here we generalize finite Sierpiński gaskets to a class of unbounded structures, generated by a substitution which does not uniquely determine the structures, but are locally indistinguishable from the standard cone-shaped gasket. There are uncountably many isomorphism classes of these structures in each dimension $d > 1$, and by developing an analogue to 10.5.10 in [6], we show that the isomorphism classes correspond to their index sequences. We fix the isomorphism types in terms of "traversal languages" encoding classes of walks on these structures.

In [12,13] it is described how a "traversal language" consisting of labels of walks could capture the isomorphism class of a periodic structure. On the other side, decidability of some topological properties of fractal objects have been studied with multi-tape automata in [10]. In this note, we demonstrate how traversal languages capture the isomorphism classes of the Sierpiński gaskets. These languages consist of labels of walks that can be taken on the structures and are intimately connected to the index sequences used to generate those structures. Due to the uncountably many isomorphism classes of these structures, we conclude that almost all of these languages are not RE.

Notation and basic concepts

We use Σ to denote a finite alphabet and Σ^* for the set of all words over the alphabet Σ. For a word $w = w_1 w_2 \cdots w_n$, the word $w^R = w_n \cdots w_2 w_1$ is the *reverse* of w. The length of w is $|w| = n$. The empty word is denoted with ϵ and has length $|\epsilon| = 0$. Σ^n indicates the set of all words over Σ with length n and Σ^ω the set of all sequences $f : \mathbb{N} \rightarrow \Sigma$. A permutation $\gamma : \Sigma \rightarrow \Sigma$ naturally extends to a morphism $\gamma : \Sigma^* \rightarrow \Sigma^*$ with $\gamma(i_1 \cdots i_s) = \gamma(i_1) \cdots \gamma(i_s)$ and similarly to $\gamma : \Sigma^\omega \rightarrow \Sigma^\omega$. A *graph* is a pair $G = (V, E)$ where E consists of two element subsets of V. For an edge $e = \{u, v\}$ we say that u is adjacent to v and e is incident to u and v. The number of edges incident to a vertex v is the *degree* of v. A *graph homomorphism* is a map π from vertices of a graph $G = (V, E)$ to vertices of a graph $H = (V', E')$ such that for any edge $e = \{u, v\}$ in G we have $\pi(e) \in V' \cup E'$. This homomorphism is said to be *strict* if for all $e' = \{u', v'\} \in E'$, there are $u \in \pi^{-1}(u')$, $v \in \pi^{-1}(v')$ such that $\{u, v\} \in E$. A graph homomorphism is an *embedding* if it is injective and it is an *isomorphism* if it is bijective. If G is isomorphic to H we write $G \cong H$.

2   Sierpiński Structures

The Sierpiński gasket (like other self-similar fractal-like structures) is usually a "downwards construction" defined by contracting and translating affine maps applied to a two dimensional (triangular) region in the plane. In this paper we consider recursively built structures by assembling their components into larger self-similar components. We assume that the unit component is available in arbitrarily large number of copies and the process of building larger structures can continue indefinitely. Our example is the recursively built-up Sierpiński gasket.

2.1   Sierpiński Structures as Graphs

We define the Sierpiński gasket for arbitrary dimension $d > 1$, but our examples are for $d = 2$. Let $d > 1$ be an integer and $\Sigma = \Sigma_d = \{0, 1, 2, \ldots, d\}$. We adjust the definition from [8].

Definition 1. *Let $n \geq 1$. An nth upwards d-dimensional Sierpiński gasket is a graph $G_n = G_n^d = (\Sigma^n, E_n)$ where*

$$E_n - \{\{x, y\} \mid \exists i, j \in \Sigma, i \neq j; \exists k \geq 0, w \in \Sigma^{\leq n}; x = i^k j w, y = j^k i w\}$$

An upwards d-dimensional Sierpiński gasket is an infinite graph $G_\omega = (\Sigma^\omega, E_\omega)$ where

$$E_\omega = \{\{\mathbf{x}, \mathbf{y}\} \mid \exists i, j \in \Sigma, i \neq j; \exists k \geq 0, \mathbf{w} \in \Sigma^\omega; \mathbf{x} = i^k j \mathbf{w}, \mathbf{y} = j^k i \mathbf{w}\}$$

Figure 2 describes the labeling of the edges. The structure of G_ω is discussed in the rest of the section. We define $G_0 = (\epsilon, \emptyset)$ to be a single vertex ϵ without edges. For a vertex $v = i^k j w$ where $i \neq j$ we say that v is of *rank* $k + 1$.

Notice that each string of length n in Σ^n
determines a particular vertex in G_n (Fig. 3). A
vertex $v = i^k w$ in G_n, where $w \in \Sigma^*$ does not
start with i, is said to be the *i-corner at level k*.
Similarly a vertex $\mathbf{v} = i^k \mathbf{w}$ of G_ω is the *i-corner
at level k* in G_ω. The *i*-corners at level n in G_n
are called the *corners* of G_n.

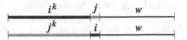

Fig. 2. A schematic description
of two adjacent vertices in G_n.

Let $w \in \Sigma^m$, $m \leq n$. A *w-induced subgraph* of G_n is the subgraph $G_n(w)$
with vertex set $V_n(w) = \{xw \mid x \in \Sigma^{n-m}\}$. For G_ω we extend the notion to
w-induced subgraph of size $n \geq 0$ to be the graph with vertices $\{x\mathbf{w} \mid x \in \Sigma^n\}$
denoted $G_\omega^n(\mathbf{w})$ where $\mathbf{w} \in \Sigma^\omega$. Directly from the definition it follows that
$G_\omega^n(\mathbf{w})$ is isomorphic to G_n by setting $x \mapsto x\mathbf{w}$.

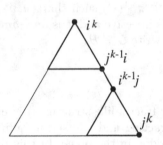
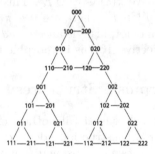

Fig. 3. Left, for $w \in \Sigma^{n-(k-1)}$, an *i*-corner of level k in $G_n(w)$ is adjacent to a *j*-corner
of level k. Right, G_3 with 0-induced subgraph $G_3(0)$ in color (purple, red, and orange),
with subgraph $G_3(10)$ in red and orange, and a vertex representing $G_3(210)$ in orange.
(Color figure online)

G_ω is a graph with the uncountable vertex set Σ^ω. As each vertex is of finite
degree, it has uncountably many components. This is discussed in Sect. 2.3.

We use the shift operator $\sigma : \Sigma^+ \cup \Sigma^\omega \to \Sigma^* \cup \Sigma^\omega$ to define homomorphisms
of these graphs. Recall that for a word $w = iu$ where $i \in \Sigma$ and $u \in \Sigma^* \cup \Sigma^\omega$,
we have $\sigma(w) = u$.

Definition 2. *For a fixed n, the graph shift is the map $\sigma_n : G_{n+1} \to G_n$ such
that for each vertex $v \in \Sigma^{n+1}$ in the graph G_{n+1}, $v \mapsto \sigma(v)$.*

Lemma 1. *For each n, σ_n is a strict homomorphism.*

Proof. The map σ_n is a homomorphism because σ maps an edge $\{i^k jw, j^k iw\} \in
E_{n+1}$ for $k > 0$ to $\{i^{k-1}jw, j^{k-1}iw\} \in E_n$. If $k = 0$, σ maps the edge $\{jw, iw\}$
to the vertex w. Note that σ is surjective on the set of vertices, and σ_n is strict:
if $\{i^k jw, j^k iw\}$ is E_n then $i^{k+1}jw \in \sigma^{-1}(i^k jw)$ and $j^{k+1}iw \in \sigma^{-1}(j^k iw)$. $\square$

We drop the subscript n in σ_n and write σ assuming that the domain of σ_n
fixes the index. One can view σ as a map that collapses the $(d+1)$-cliques into
vertices. The following lemma is also in [9, Theorem 4.3].

Lemma 2. *For $n \in \{1, 2, 3, \ldots\}$, $d+1$ vertices $\{v_0, \ldots, v_d\}$ form a clique in G_n if and only if there exists $w \in \Sigma^{n-1}$ such that $\{v_0, \ldots, v_d\} = \{0w, 1w, \ldots, dw\}$.*

Proof. Given a $(d+1)$-clique $v_0, \ldots, v_d$, color each vertex by the first symbol in its index sequence. No two adjacent vertices can share the same color, so each of the $d+1$ colors occurs once among these vertices, and without loss of generality we can assume that for each i, $v_i = iv_i'$ for some v_i'. We claim that all vertices have the same second symbol. If not, there exist two vertices (say v_0 and v_1) with different second symbols, $v_0 = 0iv_0''$ and $v_1 = 1jv_1''$ for $i \neq j$. Then as v_0 is adjacent to v_1, we must have for some $k > 1$, $v_0 = 0^k 1w$ and $v_1 = 1^k 0w$ for some w. But then $v_2 = 2w'$ for some w' would not be adjacent to neither v_0 nor v_1, which gives a contradiction. Therefore $i = j$. $\qquad\square$

It follows that each vertex $i^k \ell w$, $k > 0$, is the corner of a clique. By Definition 1, it is adjacent to d vertices $ji^{k-1}\ell w$, $j \neq i$, forming a $(d+1)$-clique, and is also adjacent to the vertex $\ell^k uw$ of the same rank, outside that clique.

2.2   Index Sequences and Isomorphism Types

In this section we show that the automorphisms of a Sierpiński gasket G_n, and also G_ω, correspond to the elements of the permutation group of Σ.

Proposition 1. *Let $0 \leq \ell < n \leq m$. Given an embedding π of G_n into G_m, there exists a unique automorphism τ on G_m such that $\tau \circ \sigma^\ell = \sigma^\ell \circ \pi$.*

$$
\begin{array}{ccc}
G_n & \xrightarrow{\;\pi\;} & G_m \\
\downarrow{\sigma^\ell} & & \downarrow{\sigma^\ell} \\
G_{n-\ell} & \xrightarrow{\;\exists! \tau\;} & G_{m-\ell}
\end{array}
$$

Proof. If $\ell = 0$ then σ^0 is the identity and $\tau = \pi$. For $\ell = 1$, define τ such that for each $i \in \Sigma$, $x \in \Sigma^{n-1}$, if $\pi(ix) = jy$ for $j \in \Sigma$ and $y \in \Sigma^{m-1}$, then $\tau(x) = y$. By definition we have $\tau \circ \sigma = \sigma \circ \pi$. Also, τ is unique because $\tau'(x) = \tau' \circ \sigma(ix) = \sigma \circ \pi(ix) = \sigma(jy) = y = \tau(x)$. We claim that τ is a well-defined embedding of G_{n-1} into G_{m-1}.

For any $x \in \Sigma^{n-1}$, by Lemma 2, $0x, \ldots, dx$ forms a (maximal) $(d+1)$-clique in G_n, which π maps to a $(d+1)$-clique in G_m, of vertices $0y, \ldots, dy$. There is a permutation γ of Σ such that $\pi(sx) = \gamma(s)y$ for each $s \in \Sigma$. So for any $s \in \Sigma$, $\tau(x) = \sigma(\pi(sx)) = \sigma(\gamma(s)y) = y$, hence τ is well defined. We see that τ is one-to-one: if $\tau(x_1) = \tau(x_2)$, then π maps both cliques $0x_1, \ldots, dx_1$ and $0x_2, \ldots, dx_2$ onto some clique $0y_1, \ldots, dy_1$ in G_m, therefore $x_1 = x_2$.

Now we claim that τ is a graph homomorphism, and hence an embedding. Suppose that $u = p^k qw$ and $v = q^k pw$ are adjacent in G_{n-1}. Then $pu \in \sigma^{-1}(u)$ and $qv \in \sigma^{-1}(v)$ are adjacent in G_n. They are mapped by π to some adjacent $i^s jz$ and $j^s iz$ in G_m. Then $\tau(u) = i^{s-1} jz$ is adjacent to $\tau(v) = j^{s-1} iz$. Note that $s > 0$ because τ is one-to-one.

For $\ell > 1$ inductively we have $\sigma^\ell \circ \pi = \sigma^{\ell-1} \circ \tau_1 \circ \sigma = \ldots = \tau_\ell \circ \sigma^\ell$ for some $\tau_1, \ldots, \tau_\ell$. Then we set $\tau = \tau_\ell$. □

Observe that π induces a canonical sequence of automorphisms τ_{n-k} from G_{n-k} to G_{n-k}. Given G_n and $r \leq n$, say that an *r-subgraph* of G_n is a pre-image of a vertex of G_{n-r} under σ^r. Notice that by an induction on r, an r-subgraph is isomorphic to G_r.

Corollary 1. *Fix an embedding π of G_n into G_m. For each $r \leq n$, π maps vertices of rank r to vertices of rank r, and r-subgraphs to r-subgraphs.*

Proof. Consider an edge $e = \{u, v\}$ and let r be the smallest such that $\sigma^r(u) = \sigma^r(v)$. By Proposition 1, $\pi(e)$ has the same property, that is, r is the smallest such that $\sigma^r(\pi(u)) = \sigma^r(\pi(v))$. Consequently, π maps vertices of rank r to vertices of rank r. Also by Proposition 1, π must map all the vertices of an r-subgraph to vertices of an r-subgraph, and no other vertices to that r-subgraph. □

Lemma 3. *For any $0 \leq n \leq m$, any embedding of G_n into G_m maps G_n into a w-induced subgraph of G_m for some $w \in \Sigma^{m-n}$.*

Proof. Let $\pi : \Sigma^n \to \Sigma^m$ be an embedding of G_n into G_m. By Proposition 1, there exists unique $\tau : \Sigma \mapsto \Sigma^{m-n+1}$ mapping the $(d+1)$-clique $\sigma^{n-1}(G_n) = G_1$ into a $(d+1)$-clique of $\sigma^{m-1}(G_m)$, and by Lemma 2, there exists a permutation γ of Σ and a string $w \in \Sigma^{m-n+1}$ such that for each $i \in \Sigma$, $\tau(i) = \gamma(i)w$. Therefore, for all vertices $x \in \Sigma^n$ we have $\sigma^n \circ \pi(x) = w$ and hence, $\pi(G_n)$ is isomorphic to a w-induced subgraph of G_m. □

For finite graphs, the following result is shown in [9].

Proposition 2. *For any n, the automorphism group of G_n is isomorphic to the permutation group of Σ.*

Proof. By Proposition 1, for an embedding π mapping G_n into G_n there is a unique $\tau_{n-\ell} : G_{n-\ell} \to G_{n-\ell}$ that commutes with the shift, i.e., $\tau_{n-\ell} \circ \sigma^\ell = \sigma^\ell \circ \pi$. For $\ell = n-1$ we have $\tau_1 : G_1 \to G_1$ such that $\tau_1 \circ \sigma^{n-1} = \sigma^{n-1} \circ \pi$. Since G_1 is a $(d+1)$-clique, τ_1 is a permutation $\gamma : \Sigma \to \Sigma$. We show that γ determines π.

Inductively, suppose $\tau_k : G_k \to G_k$ is an automorphism that is determined by γ such that $\tau_k(i_1 \cdots i_s) = \gamma(i_1) \cdots \gamma(i_s)$. We show that the same holds for τ_{k+1}. Consider a clique $\{0w, \ldots, dw\}$ in G_k. Each vertex iw is an image of a clique $\{0iw, \ldots, diw\}$ of G_{k+1} under σ. Choose i, j distinct from the first symbol of w and from each other. Because $\tau_k \sigma = \sigma \tau_{k+1}$, we have $\tau_{k+1}(jiw) = p\gamma(i)\gamma(w)$ and $\tau_{k+1}(ijw) = q\gamma(j)\gamma(w)$ for some $p, q \in \Sigma$. By Corollary 1, τ_{k+1} maps vertices of rank 2 to vertices of rank 2, so p and $\gamma(i)$ are distinct and similarly, q and $\gamma(j)$ are distinct. But there is an edge $\{jiw, ijw\}$ in G_{k+1}, so it must be that $\{p\gamma(i)\gamma(w), q\gamma(j)\gamma(w)\}$ is an edge in G_{k+1} as well, which implies that $p = \gamma(j)$ and $q = \gamma(i)$. Thus $\tau_{k+1}(ijw) = \gamma(i)\gamma(j)\gamma(w)$ as required. □

2.3   The Infinite Sierpiński Structures and Their Components

In this subsection, we show that the connected components of G_ω may be partitioned into uncountably many isomorphism classes, each with $(d+1)!$ components.

Definition 3. *For sequences* $\mathbf{u}, \mathbf{v} \in \Sigma^\omega$, *we say that* $\mathbf{u}$ *is equivalent to* $\mathbf{v}$ *if they differ at finitely many values.*

Observe that $\mathbf{u}$ is equivalent to $\mathbf{v}$ if and only if $\mathbf{u}$ and $\mathbf{v}$ are vertices on the same connected component of G_ω. If $\mathbf{u}$ is equivalent to $\mathbf{v}$, then $\mathbf{u} = x\mathbf{w}$ and $\mathbf{v} = y\mathbf{w}$ for some $x, y \in \Sigma^n$ and $\mathbf{w} \in \Sigma^\omega$. Hence, $\mathbf{u}$ and $\mathbf{v}$ are vertices of $G_\omega^n(\mathbf{w})$. On the other hand, if there is a path from $\mathbf{u}$ to $\mathbf{v}$ in G_ω, then that path is a finite sequence of edges, each joining vertices $i^k j\mathbf{w}'$ and $j^k i\mathbf{w}'$, and all these finitely many vertices must share a common infinite suffix.

We define $G_\omega[\mathbf{u}]$ to be the connected component of G_ω determined by the equivalence class of $\mathbf{u}$.

Definition 4. *We write* $\mathbf{u} \sim \mathbf{v}$ *if there exists a permutation* γ *of* Σ *such that* $\mathbf{v} = \gamma(\mathbf{u})$.

Directly from the definitions $\mathbf{u} \sim \mathbf{v}$ implies that $G_\omega[\mathbf{u}] \cong G_\omega[\mathbf{v}]$. We claim that the converse is true.

Theorem 1. *For any* $\mathbf{x}, \mathbf{y} \in \Sigma^\omega$, $G_\omega[\mathbf{x}] \cong G_\omega[\mathbf{y}]$ *if and only if* $\mathbf{x} \sim \mathbf{y}$.

Proof. If $\mathbf{x} \sim \mathbf{y}$, then there exists $\pi : \Sigma \to \Sigma$ such that $\mathbf{y} = \pi(\mathbf{x})$ and π is an isomorphism from $G_\omega[\mathbf{x}]$ onto $G_\omega[\mathbf{y}]$. Conversely, let π be an isomorphism from $G_\omega[\mathbf{x}]$ onto $G_\omega[\mathbf{y}]$. Without loss of generality we can assume that $\pi(\mathbf{x}) = \mathbf{y}$. For any $n < \infty$, let $\mathbf{x}_n = \sigma^n(\mathbf{x})$ and $\mathbf{y}_n = \sigma^n(\mathbf{y})$. Then π restricts to an isomorphism of $\mathbf{x}_n$-induced subgraph of $G_\omega[\mathbf{x}]$ to the $\mathbf{y}_n$-induced subgraph of $G_\omega[\mathbf{y}]$, $\pi : G_\omega^n(\mathbf{x}_n) \to G_\omega^n(\mathbf{y}_n)$ mapping $\mathbf{x}$ to $\mathbf{y}$. By Proposition 2, for each n, there is a permutation $\gamma = \tau_n$ of Σ such that for any $z \in \Sigma^n$, $\pi(z\sigma^n(\mathbf{x})) = \gamma(z)\sigma^n(\mathbf{y})$. Inductively, γ maps the nth symbol of $\mathbf{x}$ onto the nth symbol of $\mathbf{y}$ for all n, so $\mathbf{x} \sim \mathbf{y}$. $\square$

3   The Languages

We are interested in languages describing walks on the graphs. Each word in the language represents a label of a walk on the graph. The labeling is designed such that the label of the edge $\{x, y\}$ traversed from x to y uniquely determines the vertex y.

Given a graph $G = \langle V, E \rangle$, to each edge $e = \{x, y\}$ we associate a pair of arcs $\{(x, y), (y, x)\}$. Each arc indicates the direction of a walk traversing the edge e. We label the arcs with symbols from an alphabet Σ using a labeling function $\lambda : V \times V \to \Sigma$. Call the labeling λ *proper* if it is injective (deterministic) on the outgoing arcs and if $\lambda(x, y) \neq \lambda(y, x)$.

A *walk* in G from vertex x to vertex y is a sequence of successive arcs $p = (x, x_1)(x_1, x_2) \cdots (x_{n-1}, y)$ and its *length* is n. A walk is a *path* if no vertex occurs twice (except we permit $x = y$). If $x = y$, the walk is *cyclic*. The *distance between x and y* is the length of the shortest path from x to y, denoted $\text{dist}(x, y)$. The *diameter* of a finite graph is the maximal distance between any two vertices of the graph. The *label* of p is the sequence $\lambda(p) = \lambda(x, x_1)\lambda(x_1, x_2) \cdots \lambda(x_{n-1}, y)$. The *two-way label* of p is

$$\widehat{\lambda}(p) = [\lambda(x, x_1)\lambda(x_1, x)][\lambda(x_1, x_2)\lambda(x_2, x_1)] \cdots [\lambda(x_{n-1}, y)\lambda(y, x_{n-1})].$$

The set of labels of walks and the set of two-way labels of walks starting at a vertex x determine two languages, W_x and $\widehat{W}_x$, respectively. Proper labeling implies that for each vertex x in the graph there is at most one vertex y reached by a walk with label $w \in \Sigma^*$. So labels, and two-way labels of walks, define partial actions of Σ^* on the vertex set of G, and we write $xw = y$, and $x\widehat{w} = y$, respectively.

We note that for proper labeling the two-way labels of walks are restricted because they specify the return label of a traversed arc as well. For example, if $j \neq k$ then $[ik][ki][ij]$ cannot be a two-way label of a walk because λ is injective on the outgoing edges.

Consider the Sierpiński gaskets G_n and G_ω. We define λ for G_n, that can naturally extend to G_ω. The labeling alphabet is $\Sigma = \{0, \ldots, d\}$. For an edge $\{i^k jw, j^k iw\}$, $k \geq 0$ we label the corresponding arcs with

$$\lambda(i^k jw, j^k iw) = i \quad \text{and} \quad \lambda(j^k iw, i^k jw) = j.$$

These labels indicate direction: notice in Fig. 1 that "0" means move up, "1" means go left, and "2" means go right. Observe that this is a proper labeling of the arcs. By definition, the two arcs associated with an edge are labeled distinctly. Every vertex $i^k \ell w$ ($i \neq \ell$) can be written as $j^0 iw'$ where $w' = i^{k-1} \ell w$ and is in a $(d+1)$-clique, hence incident to $ji^{k-1} \ell w = i^0 jw'$ with outgoing arc labeled j for $j \neq i$. It is also incident to a vertex of the same rank $\ell^k iw$ with outgoing arc labeled i.

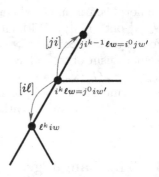

We claim that the isomorphism classes of G_ω can be captured by the two-way languages $\widehat{W}_\mathbf{u}$ for any $\mathbf{u}$ in its equivalence class. The Sierpiński structures have index sequences as vertices, so the address of a vertex is the vertex itself. Notice that if a vertex is a corner of G_n, then it is also a corner of each

Fig. 4. The arc labeled $[ji]$ is part of a clique while the arc labeled $[i\ell]$ connects two vertices of rank k.

copy of G_k, $k < n$, in which it occurs. We use the following result from [8] and include a proof for the convenience of the reader.

Lemma 4. *In G_n, if $i \neq j$, then $\text{dist}(i^n, j^n) = 2^n - 1$, which is the diameter of G_n.*

Proof. By construction, a side of G_{n+1} has twice as many vertices as a side of G_n. Hence, inductively $\text{dist}(i^n, j^n) = 2^n - 1$. This implies that the diameter of G_n is at least $2^n - 1$. We prove that the diameter is $2^n - 1$ by induction on n. The diameter of G_1, which is a clique, is $1 = 2^1 - 1$. For the inductive step, note that the copies of G_n within G_{n+1} are connected at their corners in G_{n+1} (Fig. 1(a)). If two vertices x, y in G_{n+1} are in the same subgraph isomorphic to G_n, then they are at most $2^n - 1$ apart, by the inductive hypothesis. If they are in distinct subgraphs isomorphic to G_n, say $G_{n+1}(i)$ and $G_{n+1}(j)$ resp., then there is a path from x to y through the edge $\{j^n i, i^n j\}$ which, by induction, is of length at most $2 \cdot (2^n - 1) + 1$.   □

Consider G_n and the w-induced subgraph $G_n(w)$ where $|w| < n$.

Lemma 5. *Given two vertices x and y in $G_n(w)$, the shortest path from x to y containing a vertex outside $G_n(w)$ is of length at least $2^{n+1} + 1$.*

Proof. Let p be a path connecting x and y, both of whom are in $G_n(w)$. Let $w = \ell u$ for $\ell \in \Sigma$. If p contains an edge outside $G_n(\ell u)$ (see Fig. 5), then two corners $c_1 = i^n \ell u$ and $c_2 = j^n \ell u$, for some $i \neq j$, occur in p. The path p also contains an edge from c_1 to a vertex $\ell^n iu \in G_n(iu)$, and similarly, c_2 is adjacent to $\ell^n ju$ in $G_n(ju)$. The subgraphs $G_n(iu)$ and $G_n(ju)$ are distinct, and as the corners $\ell^n iu$ and $\ell^n ju$ occur in p, p must have a subpath in $G_n(iu)$ from $\ell^n iu$ to another corner of $G_n(iu)$, as well as a subpath from a corner of $G_n(ju)$, distinct from $\ell^n ju$, to $\ell^n ju$. So p must have two subpaths each of length at least $2^n - 1$, and at least three additional edges (one from c_1 to $\ell^n iu$, one or more to connect the two far corners of $G_n(iu)$ and $G_n(ju)$, and one from $\ell^n ju$ to c_2. Hence p must be of length at least $2^{n+1} + 1$.   □

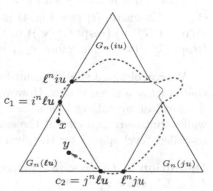

Fig. 5. A walk from x to y outside their shared subgraph.

Lemma 6. *For any vertex $x \in G_n$ there is a path in G_n from x to i^n with label i^k for some k.*

Proof. We note that for every vertex $x = i^s ju$ (for $s \geq 0$) there is an arc $(i^s ju, j^s iu)$ leading to $j^s iu$ with label i. The path visits vertices $x = i^s ju$, $j^s iu$, $ij^{s-1} iu$, $jij^{s-2} iu$, $i^2 j^{s-2} iu$, $j^2 ij^{s-2} iu$, $\ldots, i^n$, alternating between edges in a $(d+1)$-clique and edges between higher rank vertices, all with label i. The symbol i shifts to the right, so we observe that from vi^ℓ we eventually reach $v' i^{\ell+1}$.   □

We denote the path with label i^k from x to a corner $i^n u$ of a copy of G_n by $p_n(x, i)$, and similarly for G_ω the path from $x\mathbf{w}$ to $i^n \mathbf{w}$ with label i^k with $p_n(x\mathbf{w}, i)$.

Theorem 2. *For* $\mathbf{u}, \mathbf{v} \in \Sigma^\omega$ *in* G_ω, $\widehat{W}_\mathbf{u} = \widehat{W}_\mathbf{v}$ *if and only if* $\mathbf{u} = \mathbf{v}$.

Proof. Let $\mathbf{u} = u_1 u_2 u_3 \cdots$ and $\mathbf{v} = v_1 v_2 v_3 \cdots$; if $\mathbf{u} = \mathbf{v}$ then $\widehat{W}_\mathbf{u} = \widehat{W}_\mathbf{v}$. Conversely, given $\widehat{W}_\mathbf{u} = \widehat{W}_\mathbf{v}$, we prove that for each positive integer n, $u_n = v_n$, by induction on n. The set of two-way labels of walks of length 1 starting at $\mathbf{u}$ is $\{[iu_1] \mid i \neq u_1, i \in \Sigma\} \cup \{[u_1\ell]\}$ for some ℓ. Since $\widehat{W}_\mathbf{u} = \widehat{W}_\mathbf{v}$, it must be $u_1 = v_1$. The clique isomorphism from $G^1_\omega(\sigma(\mathbf{u}))$ to $G^1_\omega(\sigma(\mathbf{v}))$ that maps $i\sigma(\mathbf{u})$ into $i\sigma(\mathbf{v})$ preserves the labels on the arcs.

We claim that if $u_i = v_i$ for $i \leq n$ and $\widehat{W}_\mathbf{u} = \widehat{W}_\mathbf{v}$, then $u_{n+1} = v_{n+1}$. Let $x = u_1 \cdots u_n$ and $\mathbf{u} = x\mathbf{u}'$ and $\mathbf{v} = x\mathbf{v}'$. Let $G^n_\omega(\mathbf{u}')$ and $G^n_\omega(\mathbf{v}')$ be the $\mathbf{u}'$- (resp. $\mathbf{v}'$-) induced subgraph of size n containing $\mathbf{u}$ (resp. $\mathbf{v}$). Because $u_1 u_2 \cdots u_n = v_1 v_2 \cdots v_n = x$, choose the (restricted) isomorphism from $G^n_\omega(\mathbf{u}')$ onto $G^n_\omega(\mathbf{v}')$ that maps $y\mathbf{u}'$ to $y\mathbf{v}'$ for each $y \in \Sigma^n$. This isomorphism preserves the labels of the arcs. For an $i \in \Sigma$, choose k such that i^k is the label of a path from $x\mathbf{u}'$ to i^n. Because the restricted isomorphism preserves labels, $\widehat{\lambda}(p_n(x\mathbf{u}', i)) = \widehat{\lambda}(p_n(x\mathbf{v}', i)) = \widehat{w}_i$. For each $i \in \Sigma$, there exists exactly one ℓ such that $\widehat{w}_i[i\ell] \in \widehat{W}_\mathbf{u} = \widehat{W}_\mathbf{v}$ where $[i\ell]$ (see Fig. 4) is the label of the edge connecting the corner $i^n\ell\mathbf{u}''$ of $G^n_\omega(\mathbf{u}')$ (resp. $G^n_\omega(\mathbf{v}')$) to $\ell^n i\mathbf{u}''$ (resp. $\ell^n i\mathbf{v}''$) of $G^{n+1}_\omega(\mathbf{u}'')$ for some $\mathbf{u}''$ (resp. $G^{n+1}_\omega(\mathbf{v}'')$). Therefore $u_{n+1} = \ell = v_{n+1}$. $\square$

We can obtain a similar result for labels, rather that two-way labels, of walks that start at a given vertex. However, in order to identify the vertices, the information lost by taking labels instead of two-way labels is captured by taking walks that start and end at the same vertex. The labels of those paths form a so-called "cyclespace" for the given vertex.

Definition 5. *Given* $\mathbf{v}$ *in a Sierpiński gasket* G_ω, *the cyclespace of* $\mathbf{v}$ *is* $C_\mathbf{v} = \{w \in \Sigma^* \mid \mathbf{v}w = \mathbf{v}\}$.

Theorem 3. *Let* $\mathbf{u}, \mathbf{v} \in \Sigma^\omega$. *Then* $C_\mathbf{u} = C_\mathbf{v}$ *if and only if* $\mathbf{u} = \mathbf{v}$.

Proof. Clearly, $\mathbf{u} = \mathbf{v}$ implies $C_\mathbf{u} = C_\mathbf{v}$, so we prove the converse by induction on n for $\mathbf{u} = u_1 u_2 \cdots u_n \cdots$. Since there are no loops in G_ω the shortest cycles of positive length are of length 2 traversing oppositely oriented arcs of the same edge. Cycles of length 2 starting at $\mathbf{u}$ are $\{iu_1 \mid i \neq u_1, i \in \Sigma\}$. Since $C_\mathbf{u} = C_\mathbf{v}$ it must be $\{iu_1 \mid i \neq u_1, i \in \Sigma\} = \{iv_1 \mid i \neq v_1, i \in \Sigma\}$ and therefore $u_1 = v_1$. Suppose $x = u_1 \cdots u_n = v_1 \cdots v_n$, and $v_{n+1} \neq u_{n+1}$. Let $\mathbf{u}' = \sigma^{n+1}(\mathbf{u})$. For each $j \neq u_{n+1}$, let $c(n, j)$ be the label of a cyclic walk that starts at $\mathbf{u}$, follows $p_n(\mathbf{u}, j)$ to the corner $j^n u_{n+1}\mathbf{u}'$, then out to the adjacent vertex $u^n_{n+1}j\mathbf{u}$ in the neighboring subgraph $G^n_\omega(j\mathbf{u}')$ and back, traversing the edge $\{j^n u_{n+1}\mathbf{u}', u^n_{n+1}j\mathbf{u}'\}$ twice, and then down the side arcs of $G^n_\omega(u_{n+1}\mathbf{u}')$ with label u_{n+1} to the corner $u^n_{n+1}\mathbf{u}'$, and finally reversing the path $p_n(\mathbf{u}, u_{n+1})$ (Fig. 6(a)). Let w be the label of $p_n(\mathbf{u}, u_{n+1})^R$. Then $|w| \leq 2^n - 1$. The label of $c(n, j)$ is $j^k j u_{n+1} u^{2^n-1}_{n+1} w = j^{k+1} u^{2^n}_{n+1} w$.

As $u_i = v_i$, $i \leq n$, $\mathbf{u}$ and $\mathbf{v}$ are in corresponding positions in their n-subgraphs. The walk with the label $j^{k+1} u^{2^n}_{n+1} w$ from $\mathbf{v}$ starts with a path with label j^k and reaches a vertex $j^n v_{n+1}\mathbf{v}'$. From this vertex, an arc with label j

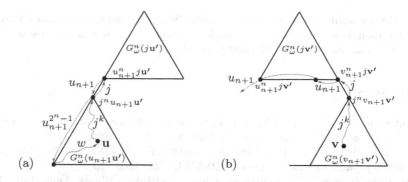

Fig. 6. The label of the cycle $c(n, j)$ at vertex **u**; (b) if $v_{n+1} \neq u_{n+1}$, the label of $c(n, j)$ is not a label of a cycle at **v**.

leads to $v_{n+1}^{n} j\mathbf{v}'$ in $G_{\omega}^{n}(j\mathbf{v}')$ where $\sigma^{n+1}(\mathbf{v}) = \mathbf{v}'$. But because $v_{n+1} \neq u_{n+1}$, an arc from $v_{n+1}^{n} j\mathbf{v}'$ with label u_{n+1} ends again in $G_{\omega}^{n}(j\mathbf{v}')$ and does not reach a vertex in $G_{\omega}^{n}(v_{n+1}\mathbf{v}')$ (Fig. 6(b)).

By Lemmas 4 and 6, as $u_{n+1} \neq v_{n+1}$, from $v_{n+1}^{n} j\mathbf{v}'$ following 2^{n} arcs labeled u_{n+1} leads to $u_{n+1}^{n} j\mathbf{v}'$, and then outward from $G_{\omega}^{n}(j\mathbf{v}')$. As w, the rest of the label of $c(n, j)$, is of length less than 2^{n}, one cannot return across $G_{\omega}^{n}(j\mathbf{v}')$ to **v** with a walk of label w. Because $ju_{n+1}^{2^{n}}w$ is of length at most 2^{n+1}, by Lemma 5, $ju_{n+1}^{2^{n}}w$ cannot be a label of a walk from $j^{n}v_{n+1}\mathbf{v}'$ out of $G_{\omega}^{n}(v_{n+1}\mathbf{v}')$ and back to **v**. Thus the label of $c(n, j)$ is not a label of a cycle from **v** back to itself, and that contradiction forces $v_{n+1} = u_{n+1}$. □

4   Concluding Remarks

The Sierpiński gaskets share many properties with other hierarchical structures, and we believe that this example initiates the development of a more general theory. In particular, a precise statement similar to Theorem 10.5.10 in [6], including necessary and sufficient hypotheses, would be of interest. That theorem was announced for tilings, but Sierpiński gaskets are not tilings, so a general statement covering hierarchical structures is desirable. In [12,13], we studied languages encoding traversals of periodic structures and found that they fell into an intersection hierarchy of context free languages. However, for Sierpiński gaskets, almost all traversal languages are not RE. We have found several "nice" examples that are not context free and we have found no examples that are context free, so we conjecture that no traversal languages are context free. If this is true, it would be interesting to know whether this result could be extended to recursive structures in general. In addition, we observe that the traversal languages capture the isomorphism types of the Sierpiński gaskets, and we ask what other structures have the same property.

Acknowledgement. We would like to thank Chaim Goodman-Strauss and Lorenzo Sadun for their kind assistance. This work has been supported in part by the NSF grants CCF-1526485 and the NIH grant GM109459.

References

1. Anderson, J.E., Putnam, I.F.: Topological invariants for substitution tilings and their associated C^*-algebras Erg. Th. Dyn. Syst. **18**(3), 509–537 (1998)
2. Goodman, R.P., et al.: Rapid chiral assembly of rigid DNA building blocks for molecular nanofabrication. Science **310**(5754), 166–1665 (2005)
3. Goodman-Strauss, C.: Matching rules and substitution tilings. Ann. Math. **147**, 181–223 (1998)
4. Goodman-Strauss, C.: Aperiodic hierarchical tilings. In: Sadoc, J.F., Rivier, N. (eds.) Foams and Emulsions. NATO ASI Series: Series E: Applied Sciences, vol. 354, pp. 481–496. Springer, Dordrecht (1999)
5. Grigorchuk, R., Šunić, Z.: Asymptotic aspects of Schreier graphs and Hanoi Towers groups. Proc. Symposia in Pure Mathematics **77**, 183–198 (2008)
6. Grünbaum, B., Shephard, G.C.: Tilings and Patterns. Freeman, New York (1987)
7. Han, D., Pal, S., Nangreave, J., Deng, Z., Liu, Y., Yan, H.: DNA origami with complex curvatures in 3-dimensional space. Science **332**, 342–346 (2011)
8. Klavžar, S., Milutinović, U.: Graphs $S(n, k)$ and a variant of the tower of Hanoi problem. Czechoslovak Math. J. **47**(1), 95–104 (1997)
9. Hinz, A.M., Klavžar, S., Milutinović, U., Petr, C.: The Tower of Hanoi — Myths and Maths. Springer, Basel (2013)
10. Jolivet, T., Kari, J.: Undecidable properties of self-affine sets and multi-tape automata. In: Csuhaj-Varjú, E., Dietzfelbinger, M., Ésik, Z. (eds.) MFCS 2014, Part I. LNCS, vol. 8634, pp. 352–364. Springer, Heidelberg (2014)
11. Jonoska, N., Karpenko, D.: Active tile self-assembly, part 2: recursion and self-similarity. Int. J. Found. Comp. Sci. **25**(2), 165–194 (2014)
12. Jonoska, N., Krajcevski, M., McColm, G.: Languages associated with crystallographic symmetry. In: Ibarra, O.H., Kari, L., Kopecki, S. (eds.) UCNC 2014. LNCS, vol. 8553, pp. 216–228. Springer, Heidelberg (2014)
13. Jonoska, N., Krajcevski, M., McColm, G.: Counter machines and crystallographic structures. Nat. Comput. **15**(1), 97–113 (2016)
14. Liu, D., Wang, M., Deng, Z., Walulu, R., Mao, C.: Tensegrity: construction of rigid DNA triangles with flexible four-arm DNA junctions. J. Am. Chem. Soc. **126**(8), 2324–2325 (2004)
15. Padilla, J.E., Sha, R., Chen, J., Jonoska, N., Seeman, N.C.: A signal-passing DNA-strand-exchange mechanism for active self-assembly of DNA nanostructures. Angew. Chem. Int. Ed. Engl. **54**(20), 5939–5942 (2015)
16. Rothemund, P.W.K.: Folding DNA to create nanoscale shapes and patterns. Nature **440**(7082), 297–302 (2006)
17. Sadun, L.: Personal communication (2016)
18. Šunić, Z.: Twin towers of Hanoi. Eur. J. Comb. **33**(7), 1691–1707 (2012)
19. Vecchia, G.D., Sanges, C.: A recursively scalable network VLSI implementation. Future Gener. Comput. Syst. **4**, 235–243 (1988)
20. Zhang, F., Jiang, S., Wu, S., Li, Y., Mao, C., Liu, Y., Yan, H.: Complex wireframe DNA origami nanostructures with multi-arm junction vertices. Nature Nanotechnol. **10**, 779–784 (2015)

21. Zhang, W., Oganov, A.R., Goncharov, A.F., Zhu, Q., Boulfelfel, S.E., Lyakhov, A.O., Stavrou, E., Somayazulu, M., Prakapenka, V.B., Konpkov, Z.: Unexpected stable stoichiometries of sodium chlorides. Science **342**(6165), 1502–1505 (2013)
22. Zheng, J., Birktoft, J.J., Chen, Y., Wang, T., Sha, R., Constantinou, P.E., Ginell, S.L., Mao, C., Seeman, N.C.: From molecular to macroscopic via the rational design of a self-assembled 3D DNA crystal. Nature **461**(7260), 74–77 (2009)

Discrete DNA Reaction-Diffusion Model for Implementing Simple Cellular Automaton

Ibuki Kawamata[1(✉)], Satoru Yoshizawa[1], Fumi Takabatake[1], Ken Sugawara[2], and Satoshi Murata[1]

[1] Department of Robotics, School of Engineering, Tohoku University, Sendai, Japan
kawamata@molbot.mech.tohoku.ac.jp
[2] Department of Information Science, Faculty of Liberal Arts,
Tohoku Gakuin University, Sendai, Japan

Abstract. We introduce a theoretical model of DNA chemical reaction-diffusion network capable of performing a simple cellular automaton. The model is based on well-characterized enzymatic bistable switch that was reported to work *in vitro*. Our main purpose is to propose an autonomous, feasible, and macro DNA system for experimental implementation.

As a demonstration, we choose a maze-solving cellular automaton. The key idea to emulate the automaton by chemical reactions is assuming a space discretized by hydrogel capsules which can be regarded as cells. The capsule is used both to keep the state uniform and control the communication between neighboring capsules.

Simulations under continuous and discrete space are successfully performed. The simulation results indicate that our model evolves as expected both in space and time from initial conditions. Further investigation also suggests that the ability of the model can be extended by changing parameters. Possible applications of this research include pattern formation and a simple computation. By overcoming some experimental difficulties, we expect that our framework can be a good candidate to program and implement a spatio-temporal chemical reaction system.

Keywords: DNA chemical reaction network · Cellular automaton · Spatio-temporal evolution · Pattern formation · Maze solving

1 Introduction

DNA is a suitable material to develop a system with desired structure and behavior because of its programmability. Elaborate systems from static structures to dynamic reactions have been reported [1–3]. For dynamic system that reacts in a single test tube, a variety of functionalities are demonstrated such as logic circuits, amplification, and oscillation [4–7]. Some DNA nano-structures can change their geometry in nano-scale precision [8].

Challenging topic of such dynamic systems is to increase the size to macro-scale [9,10]. One of the possible applications by scaling-up reactions is pattern

© Springer International Publishing Switzerland 2016
M. Amos and A. Condon (Eds.): UCNC 2016, LNCS 9726, pp. 168–181, 2016.
DOI: 10.1007/978-3-319-41312-9_14

formation. Common technique to achieve a pattern formation by chemical reaction is using a Turing pattern [11–13]. The technique is a good candidate to explain the patterns seen in nature [14], and worthy of future research.

Achieving simple patterns by DNA chemical reactions networks are demonstrated using UV stimulus or enzymatic reactions [15,16]. Since the reactions are limited in function, how to program a system with desired dynamics is of interest. For a well-mixed one-pot system, design principles have been addressed using abstractions and simulations of chemical reactions [8,17–19]. Recently, theoretical frameworks using both reaction and diffusion of DNA molecules for pattern formation and computation have also been reported [20–23].

To extend the programmability for one dimensional pattern formation, theoretical model that can emulate a cellular automaton by DNA was proposed [24]. Those theoretical models, however, consist of a huge chemical reaction network and seem to require large efforts of optimization when it comes to implement designed systems in real experiments. Furthermore, though the model of cellular automaton is well-designed and emulates an evolution of a specific cellular automaton, an external clock to control the phase of diffusion was assumed. A novel model that overcomes the problems and provides autonomous cellular automaton using simple and realistic chemical reactions may broaden the field of DNA computing.

In this paper, we propose a theoretical model of reaction diffusion system that implements a simple cellular automaton. The network employs an already well-characterized DNA bistable switch that is driven by enzyme reactions [25]. To discretize space, we assume a capsule of hydrogel that represents a single state of a cell [26,27]. While communication between capsules is done by slow diffusion, the concentration inside a capsule is ensured to be uniform by fast diffusion.

For the proof of concept, we formalize a concrete reaction-diffusion model and simulate the behavior of the model from some initial states. The introduced cellular automaton is capable of solving a maze. Inspired by a research using cellular automaton as a computation platform [28], we further discuss how to compute a simple deterministic finite automaton by our system.

2 Discrete Model

2.1 Transition Rules

We decide to emulate a simple cellular automaton that can solve a maze from specific initial state [29]. The automaton is related to a problem of routing and an example representation of the system was proposed [30]. First, we illustrate the discrete model of the cellular automaton.

Cells of the cellular automaton are arranged in a square lattice. Each cell has either state 'a' or state 'b', which represent wall and path, respectively. The transition rules are quite simple that only the state 'b' can switch to 'a' as shown in Fig. 1. A cell communicates only with four neighboring cells in north, south, east, and west.

A cell counts the number of neighboring cells in state 'a' and decides its transition. If the number is less than or equal to two, it keeps its state. Otherwise, the state changes from 'b' to 'a'.

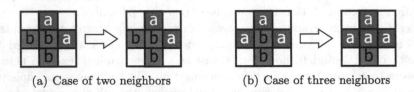

(a) Case of two neighbors   (b) Case of three neighbors

Fig. 1. The transition rules. A cell in state 'b' does not change its state if the number of neighboring cells in state 'a' is less than or equal to two. The cell switches to 'a', however, if there are 3 or more neighboring cells in state 'a'. Blue and red cells represents states 'a' and 'b', respectively. (Color figure online)

2.2   Example Simulation

As an example of the cellular automaton, we simulated a system from specific initial state using a software platform called "Ready" [31] (Fig. 2). Since the transition rules eliminate a path at a dead end, the route from the starting to the ending cells is preserved. Although the transition rules are very simple, the simulation result indicates that the cellular automaton is capable of computing a routing problem.

The model is still far from chemical reactions because all the state, space, and time are discrete in the model. In contrast, chemical reaction works under continuous concentration, space, and time. We have to link the gap between discrete and continuous systems.

3   Continuous Model

3.1   Bistable System

To discretize state, we make use of a bistable switch which is chemically implemented and verified by an *in vitro* experiment [25]. The switch is composed of signal DNA, template DNA, and enzymes (Fig. 3(a)). We illustrate single stranded DNA (ssDNA) as an arrow corresponding to the direction from 5' to 3' ends of phosphate backbone, which is a customary way of representing DNA.

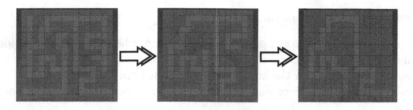

Fig. 2. The simulation of maze solving cellular automaton. Three frames of the simulation result are shown. Transition rules are adopted by a synchronized manner.

The signals are unmodified ssDNAs, which are named as 'a', 'b', 'inha', and 'inhb'. The templates are chemically modified ssDNAs that program the interactions between signals. The program is executed by collaborative reactions of polymerase and nickase. Since exonuclease decomposes signal strands, the state of the system is in a dynamic equilibration.

The switch has one of the two states, where either ssDNA 'a' or 'b' has higher concentration. If the concentration of 'a' is high, that of 'b' is very low, and vice versa. The dynamics are programmed by exclusive amplification reactions, whose topological interactions are explained in Fig. 3(b). The switch is capable of changing its state from one to the other by adding excess amount of the competitive strand.

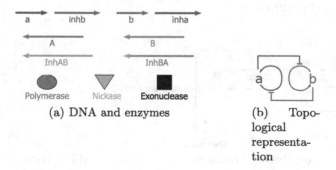

(a) DNA and enzymes   (b)   Topological representation

Fig. 3. Schematic of the bistable switch. (a) DNA strands and enzymes necessary for the bistable switch are summarized. Signal and templates strands are represented by right- and left- pointing arrows, respectively. We name each strand by the string below the strand. The reactions of the system are driven by three enzymes that are polymerase, nickase, and exonuclease. Using signal strands a and b as primers, templates A and B can produce DNA strands a and b in an autocatalytic manner, respectively. Templates InhAB and InhBA can also produce signal strands inhb and inha using a and b as primers, respectively. Produced inha and inhb hybridize to templates A and B, which will prevent the autocatalytic production of a and b, respectively. (b) Topological representation of the system. Though the signal 'a' and 'b' produces themselves by auto-catalytic reactions, they inhibit the production of one another (Color figure online).

We list some features of the switch as below.

- We can discretize a state of the solution even when the concentration of molecules is continuous.
- It is possible to switch the state of the solution from 'b' to 'a'.
- Detailed ordinary differential equations (ODEs) and a parameter set are given.
- The system is experimentally simple and reliable.

3.2   Capsule of Hydrogel

To discretize space, we think of encapsulating the switch in a hydrogel capsule. The capsule has a shell of hydrogel and core of solution (Fig. 4(a)). Since the hydrogel is a buffer fixed by a polymer network, small molecules can diffuse slowly. A molecule that is larger than the pore size of the network, however, cannot pass through the hydrogel. Of course, all the molecules diffuse relatively fast in a solution and the concentration of molecules inside a capsule becomes uniform.

An idea to prevent the template strands, which encode the state of the switch, from diffusing is necessary. We propose to attach molecules such as large DNA structure or other polymer [32] to the 5' ends of the templates strands. Those assumptions guarantee that one cell has only one state, while signal strands can diffuse to neighboring cells. The space is made by arranging such capsules in a square lattice (Fig. 4(b)).

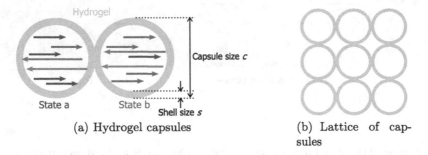

(a) Hydrogel capsules

(b) Lattice of capsules

Fig. 4. Concept of hydrogel capsules. (a) Hydrogel capsules contain DNA strands for the switch. Enzymes are assumed to be distributed in all the area, though they are not shown. The left and right capsules are in state 'a' and 'b', respectively. The size of the capsule is represented by two length parameters c and s. (b) The capsules are arranged in square lattice, where capsules are contacting by the hydrogel shell. One capsule has four neighboring capsules to match the model of the cellular automaton (Color figure online).

4   Reaction Diffusion Model

We formalized reaction diffusion equations with 26 variables and 19 parameters summarized in the Appendix A. The ODEs and kinetic parameters were taken from the detailed model of the original bistable switch [25,33]. The only difference is the terms of diffusion for diffusing molecular species.

Following the names of each structure of the original article, the variables were assigned to all the signal strands, templates strands, and possible intermediate structures. The parameters include rate constant, Michaelis-Menten constants, and diffusion coefficients. Note that state 'a' is more favorable than state 'b' due to the difference of the kinetic constants such as denaturation of DNA.

Since the speed of diffusion is different between gel and solution, the term of diffusion is formalized by an inner product of the differential operator ∇. We roughly estimated the diffusion coefficients of DNA in solution and hydrogel from experimental data [34,35].

To be a concrete model, we assumed that the capsule is made of liquid-core and a 1.5 % alginate hydrogel shell [36]. We fixed the ratio between capsule size c and the thickness of the shell s to be $c = 8s$. We used $s = 200\,\mu m$ as a default value unless otherwise specified.

5   Simulation Results

5.1   Continuous Space

First we simulated the system under continuous space to prove that the transition rules are possible to achieve. All the results were obtained by coding the system for the reaction-diffusion simulator "Ready" [31]. In practice, the space was represented by a square lattice with total 1872 grids.

By numerically solving the equations from defined initial states with nine cells, we observed expected transitions of the states of the cells (Fig. 5(a),(b)). We further changed the parameter of shell thickness s and the initial concentrations of template strands and checked if the desired state transitions happened. As shown in the phase diagram (Fig. 5(d)), those conditions crucially affected the result of transition.

5.2   Discrete Space

Since the continuous space simulation was computationally expensive, we discretize the space to simulate a larger space. In the modified model for the discrete space, we ignored the diffusion coefficients in solution and only took into account those in hydrogel shell. As a result, we have successfully simulated the spatio-temporal evolution of the maze problem (Fig. 6) using "Ready" [31] again. Although the space was discrete, the concentrations of each molecule were simulated by continuous ODEs. The result strongly indicates that the DNA system with our assumptions can perform a simple computation written in a cellular automaton.

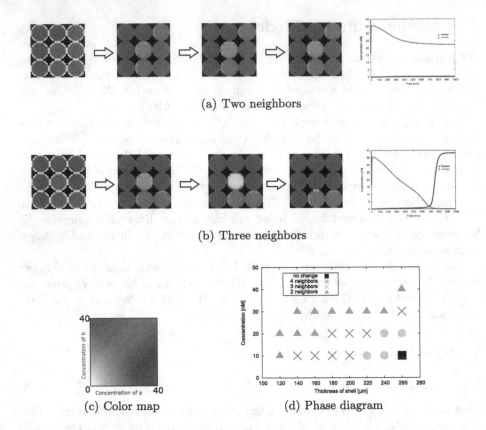

(a) Two neighbors

(b) Three neighbors

(c) Color map

(d) Phase diagram

Fig. 5. Simulation results under continuous space. If the initial state of a cell was 'a' and 'b', concentration of the corresponding signal strands of the core was set to 40 nM, respectively. One capsule was represented by a circle with 16 grids in diameter. Initial concentrations of the template strands were 20 nM in every place. Other signal strands and intermediate structures had 0 nM as an initial condition. As shown in (c), blue and red channels correspond to the concentrations of strand 'a' and 'b', respectively. (a) When a cell had two neighbors that were in state 'a', the state did not change. Time evolutions of the concentrations of signal strands in the center cell are shown in the right graph. X and y axes are time in minutes and concentration in nM. (b) The same simulation result for the three neighbors. In this case, the state changed from 'b' to 'a'. (d) Phase diagram of transitions condition. The result is a summary of simulations (for 1000 min) by varying the shell size and initial concentrations of templates strands. The desired transition occurred only when the conditions of cross mark were satisfied. The legend of the diagram indicates the minimum number of neighbors for the state transition. (Color figure online)

After some simulations, we found that the rule is not limited to solve mazes. It was possible to carry other types of simulations (Fig. 7). Specifically, we performed the simulations of forming unique pattern, starting from a random initial

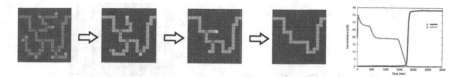

Fig. 6. Simulation result of the maze problem under discrete space. Distance between cells was changed to 650 μm. We used 20 nM as initial concentrations of signal and templates strands. Similar to the continuous simulation, time evolutions of the concentrations are shown. For the time evolution, we selected the cell that changed the number of neighbors in state 'a' for three times.

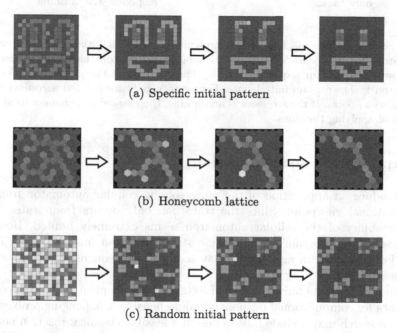

(a) Specific initial pattern

(b) Honeycomb lattice

(c) Random initial pattern

Fig. 7. Other simulation results (a) As a first demonstrations, we simulated a smile face from a specific initial pattern. (b) By changing the cell distance to 900 μm in a honeycomb lattice, the transition rules slightly changed. The state 'b' changed to 'a' when there are 5 or more neighboring cells in state 'a'. (c) In the case of random initial pattern.

pattern, and assuming a hexagonal lattice. The first simulation result suggests the application of our framework for other pattern formation problem.

The second and third simulations were carried in consideration of experimental implementation. It may be difficult to arrange the capsules in a square lattice nor write a complex initial pattern. Those results suggest that our framework can be easily extended depending on the experimental demands.

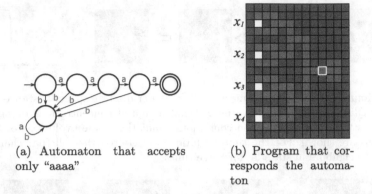

(a) Automaton that accepts only "aaaa"

(b) Program that corresponds the automaton

Fig. 8. State transition machine and its implementation as an initial state of the cellular automaton. (a) A schematic representation of an automaton that reads sequence of letters and accepts four sequential 'a'. (b) The program of the maze solving cellular automaton is shown as an initial state. Four empty cells are painted according to the four letters $x_1 \cdots x_4$. If the sequence is acceptable, the marked cell changes its state as a result of applying the rules.

6   Application and Discussion

We introduce an application of the maze solving cellular automaton from the computational viewpoint. Since the transition only occurs from states 'b' to 'a', the ability of the cellular automaton seems extremely limited. However, it is possible to program a very simple state transition machine as an initial state. For example, an automaton that accepts four sequential 'a' can be programmed (Fig. 8).

Although it treats finite number of letters, the concept of using such cellular automata for computational purpose is comprehensive. Challenging problems for further research may include how to design a feasible chemical reaction network that can emulate a Turing universal cellular automaton like the game of life [37]. Candidates to extend the ability of our framework is to adopt the techniques to design DNA chemical reaction networks described in Sect. 1. From the results of our and other theoretical models [24], it looks still difficult to overcome the trade-off between the ability of computation and the network complexity in terms of the number of molecular species.

Finally, we point out some technical difficulties we are aware of when implementing our system in real experiments. The alginate hydrogel contains calcium as a cross-linker, which may affect the kinetics of enzymes used in the system. If we have to avoid the alginate hydrogel, other polymer that has the same ratio between the scale of the capsule and diffusion coefficients must substitute the shell. Formation of uniform hydrogel capsules and arranging them in a desired lattice is also of problem. Writing the initial pattern may be achieved by modifying DNA with a photo-responsive molecule [38].

The energy source to drive the reactions is important. We assumed that sufficient substrates such as dNTPs are provided at the initial state. If the reaction time becomes long, it may be necessary to supply them from external bath.

In this paper, we propose a theoretical reaction-diffusion model that is based on well-characterized DNA and enzyme reactions. We numerically simulate the model and show the capability to emulate a maze-solving cellular automaton. The important idea is to encapsulate molecules in hydrogel capsules that is arranged in a lattice. Unlike the conventional theoretical model capable of emulating a cellular automaton by DNA chemical reaction network, our model does not require external clock and evolves autonomously. Our framework contributes to aid the experimental implementation of feasible DNA chemical reaction-diffusion network for pattern formation and computation.

Acknowledgement. We appreciate Masami Hagiya to motivate this research. Helpful advice from the experimental viewpoints were given by Hiroyuki Asanuma, Takashi Arimura, Yusuke Hara, and Nobuyoshi Miyamoto. We thank Teijiro Isokawa and Ferdinand Peper for discussion including the suggestion to simulate a normal automaton by a cellular automaton. This research was supported by Grant-in-Aid for Scientific Research on Innovative Areas "Molecular Robotics" (No. 24104005) and Grant-in-Aid for Young Scientists (Start-up, 26880002).

A   Reaction diffusion model

The equations of our model are shown below. Terms for diffusion, which we added to the original equations, are highlighted by red color.

$$\frac{\partial}{\partial t}[\text{a}] = \nabla \cdot (D_{\text{fast}} \nabla [\text{a}]) + k_{\text{d}}^{\text{a}} \times ([\text{aA}] + [\text{Aa}] + 2 \times [\text{aAa}] + [\text{aInhAB}] + [\text{aInhABinhb}]) + k_{\text{h}} \times [\text{inha}] \times ([\text{aA}] + [\text{Aa}])$$
$$- k_{\text{h}} \times [\text{a}] \times (2 \times [\text{A}] + [\text{aA}] + [\text{Aa}] + 2 \times toe \times [\text{Ainh}] + [\text{InhAB}] + [\text{InhABinhb}])$$
$$+ k_{\text{pol,sd}} \times [\text{aAa}]/K_{\text{m,sd}}/C_{\text{pol}} - k_{\text{exo}} \times [\text{a}]/K_{\text{m,input}}/C_{\text{exo}}$$

$$\frac{\partial}{\partial t}[\text{b}] = \nabla \cdot (D_{\text{fast}} \nabla [\text{b}]) + k_{\text{d}}^{\text{b}} \times ([\text{bB}] + [\text{Bb}] + 2 \times [\text{bBb}] + [\text{bInhBA}] + [\text{bInhBAinha}]) + k_{\text{h}} \times [\text{inhb}] \times ([\text{bB}] + [\text{Bb}])$$
$$- k_{\text{h}} \times [\text{b}] \times (2 \times [\text{B}] + [\text{bB}] + [\text{Bb}] + 2 \times toe \times [\text{Binh}] + [\text{InhBA}] + [\text{InhBAinha}])$$
$$+ k_{\text{pol,sd}} \times [\text{bBb}]/K_{\text{m,sd}}/C_{\text{pol}} - k_{\text{exo}} \times [\text{b}]/K_{\text{m,input}}/C_{\text{exo}}$$

$$\frac{\partial}{\partial t}[\text{A}] = \nabla \cdot (D_{\text{slow}} \nabla [\text{A}]) + k_{\text{d}}^{\text{a}} \times ([\text{aA}] + [\text{Aa}]) + k_{\text{d}}^{\text{inha}} \times [\text{Ainh}] - k_{\text{h}} \times [\text{A}] \times (2 \times [\text{a}] + [\text{inha}])$$

$$\frac{\partial}{\partial t}[\text{B}] = \nabla \cdot (D_{\text{slow}} \nabla [\text{B}]) + k_{\text{d}}^{\text{b}} \times ([\text{bB}] + [\text{Bb}]) + k_{\text{d}}^{\text{inhb}} \times [\text{Binh}] - k_{\text{h}} \times [\text{B}] \times (2 \times [\text{b}] + [\text{inhb}])$$

$$\frac{\partial}{\partial t}[\text{aA}] = \nabla \cdot (D_{\text{slow}} \nabla [\text{aA}]) + k_{\text{h}} \times [\text{a}] \times ([\text{A}] - [\text{aA}]) + k_{\text{h}} \times toe \times [\text{a}] \times [\text{Ainh}] + k_{\text{d}}^{\text{a}} \times [\text{aAa}]$$
$$- k_{\text{h}} \times [\text{inha}] \times [\text{aA}] - k_{\text{d}}^{\text{a}} \times [\text{aA}] - k_{\text{pol}} \times [\text{aA}]/K_{\text{m}}/C_{\text{pol}}$$

$$\frac{\partial}{\partial t}[\text{bB}] = \nabla \cdot (D_{\text{slow}} \nabla [\text{bB}]) + k_{\text{h}} \times [\text{b}] \times ([\text{B}] - [\text{bB}]) + k_{\text{h}} \times toe \times [\text{b}] \times [\text{Binh}] + k_{\text{d}}^{\text{b}} \times [\text{bBb}]$$
$$- k_{\text{h}} \times [\text{inhb}] \times [\text{bB}] - k_{\text{d}}^{\text{b}} \times [\text{bB}] - k_{\text{pol}} \times [\text{bB}]/K_{\text{m}}/C_{\text{pol}}$$

$$\frac{\partial}{\partial t}[\text{Aa}] = \nabla \cdot (D_{\text{slow}} \nabla [\text{Aa}]) + k_{\text{h}} \times [\text{a}] \times ([\text{A}] - [\text{Aa}]) + k_{\text{h}} \times toe \times [\text{a}] \times [\text{Ainh}] + k_{\text{d}}^{\text{a}} \times [\text{aAa}]$$
$$- k_{\text{h}} \times [\text{inha}] \times [\text{Aa}] - k_{\text{d}}^{\text{a}} \times [\text{Aa}]$$

$$\frac{\partial}{\partial t}[\text{Bb}] = \nabla \cdot (D_{\text{slow}} \nabla [\text{Bb}]) + k_{\text{h}} \times [\text{b}] \times ([\text{B}] - [\text{Bb}]) + k_{\text{h}} \times toe \times [\text{b}] \times [\text{Binh}] + k_{\text{d}}^{\text{b}} \times [\text{bBb}]$$
$$- k_{\text{h}} \times [\text{inhb}] \times [\text{Bb}] - k_{\text{d}}^{\text{b}} \times [\text{Bb}]$$

$$\frac{\partial}{\partial t}[\text{aAa}] = \nabla \cdot (D_{\text{slow}} \nabla [\text{aAa}]) + k_{\text{h}} \times [\text{a}] \times ([\text{aA}] + [\text{Aa}]) - 2 \times k_{\text{d}}^{\text{a}} \times [\text{aAa}]$$
$$+ k_{\text{nick}} \times [\text{Aaa}]/K_{\text{nick}} - k_{\text{pol,sd}} \times [\text{aAa}]/K_{\text{m,sd}}/C_{\text{pol}}$$

$$\frac{\partial}{\partial t}[\text{bBb}] = \nabla \cdot (D_{\text{slow}} \nabla [\text{bBb}]) + k_{\text{h}} \times [\text{b}] \times ([\text{bB}] + [\text{Bb}]) - 2 \times k_{\text{d}}^{\text{b}} \times [\text{bBb}]$$
$$+ k_{\text{nick}} \times [\text{Bbb}]/K_{\text{nick}} - k_{\text{pol,sd}} \times [\text{bBb}]/K_{\text{m,sd}}/C_{\text{pol}}$$

$$\frac{\partial}{\partial t}[\text{Aaa}] = \nabla \cdot (D_{\text{slow}} \nabla [\text{Aaa}]) + k_{\text{pol}} \times [\text{aA}]/K_{\text{m}}/C_{\text{pol}} + k_{\text{pol,sd}}$$
$$\times [\text{aAa}]/K_{\text{m,sd}}/C_{\text{pol}} - k_{\text{nick}} \times [\text{Aaa}]/K_{\text{nick}}$$

$$\frac{\partial}{\partial t}[\text{Bbb}] = \nabla \cdot (D_{\text{slow}} \nabla [\text{Bbb}]) + k_{\text{pol}}$$
$$\times [\text{bB}]/K_{\text{m}}/C_{\text{pol}} + k_{\text{pol,sd}} \times [\text{bBb}]/K_{\text{m,sd}}/C_{\text{pol}} - k_{\text{nick}} \times [\text{Bbb}]/K_{\text{nick}}$$

$$\frac{\partial}{\partial t}[\text{inha}] = \nabla \cdot (D_{\text{fast}} \nabla [\text{inha}]) + k_{\text{d}}^{\text{inha}} \times ([\text{Ainh}] + [\text{InhBAinha}] + [\text{bInhBAinha}])$$
$$- k_{\text{h}} \times [\text{inha}] \times ([\text{InhBA}] + [\text{bInhBA}] + [\text{A}] + [\text{aA}] + [\text{Aa}])$$
$$+ k_{\text{pol,sd}} \times [\text{bInhBAinha}]/K_{\text{m,sd}}/C_{\text{pol}} - k_{\text{exo}} \times [\text{inha}]/K_{\text{m,inh}}/C_{\text{exo}}$$

$$\frac{\partial}{\partial t}[\text{inhb}] = \nabla \cdot (D_{\text{fast}} \nabla [\text{inhb}]) + k_{\text{d}}^{\text{inhb}} \times ([\text{Binh}] + [\text{InhABinhb}] + [\text{aInhABinhb}])$$
$$- k_{\text{h}} \times [\text{inhb}] \times ([\text{InhAB}] + [\text{aInhAB}] + [\text{B}] + [\text{bB}] + [\text{Bb}])$$
$$+ k_{\text{pol,sd}} \times [\text{aInhABinhb}]/K_{\text{m,sd}}/C_{\text{pol}} - k_{\text{exo}} \times [\text{inhb}]/K_{\text{m,inh}}/C_{\text{exo}}$$

$$\frac{\partial}{\partial t}[\text{Ainh}] = \nabla \cdot (D_{\text{slow}} \nabla [\text{Ainh}]) + k_{\text{h}} \times [\text{inha}] \times ([\text{A}] + [\text{aA}] + [\text{Aa}]) - 2$$
$$\times k_{\text{h}} \times toe \times [\text{a}] \times [\text{Ainh}] - k_{\text{d}}^{\text{inha}} \times [\text{Ainh}]$$

$$\frac{\partial}{\partial t}[\text{Binh}] = \nabla \cdot (D_{\text{slow}} \nabla [\text{Binh}]) + k_{\text{h}} \times [\text{inhb}] \times ([\text{B}] + [\text{bB}] + [\text{Bb}]) - 2$$
$$\times k_{\text{h}} \times toe \times [\text{b}] \times [\text{Binh}] - k_{\text{d}}^{\text{inhb}} \times [\text{Binh}]$$

$$\frac{\partial}{\partial t}[\text{InhAB}] = \nabla \cdot (D_{\text{slow}} \nabla [\text{InhAB}]) + k_{\text{d}}^{\text{a}} \times [\text{aInhAB}] + k_{\text{d}}^{\text{inhb}} \times [\text{InhABinhb}] - k_{\text{h}} \times [\text{InhAB}] \times ([\text{a}] + [\text{inhb}])$$

$$\frac{\partial}{\partial t}[\text{InhBA}] = \nabla \cdot (D_{\text{slow}} \nabla [\text{InhBA}]) + k_{\text{d}}^{\text{b}} \times [\text{bInhBA}] + k_{\text{d}}^{\text{inha}} \times [\text{InhBAinha}] - k_{\text{h}} \times [\text{InhBA}] \times ([\text{b}] + [\text{inha}])$$

$$\frac{\partial}{\partial t}[\text{aInhAB}] = \nabla \cdot (D_{\text{slow}} \nabla [\text{aInhAB}]) + k_{\text{h}} \times [\text{a}] \times [\text{InhAB}] - k_{\text{h}} \times [\text{aInhAB}] \times [\text{inhb}] + k_{\text{d}}^{\text{inhb}} \times [\text{aInhABinhb}]$$
$$- k_{\text{d}}^{\text{a}} \times [\text{aInhAB}] - k_{\text{pol}} \times [\text{aInhAB}]/K_{\text{m}}/C_{\text{pol}}$$

$$\frac{\partial}{\partial t}[\text{bInhBA}] = \nabla \cdot (D_{\text{slow}} \nabla [\text{bInhBA}]) + k_{\text{h}} \times [\text{b}] \times [\text{InhBA}] - k_{\text{h}} \times [\text{bInhBA}] \times [\text{inha}] + k_{\text{d}}^{\text{inha}} \times [\text{bInhBAinha}]$$
$$- k_{\text{d}}^{\text{b}} \times [\text{bInhBA}] - k_{\text{pol}} \times [\text{bInhBA}]/K_{\text{m}}/C_{\text{pol}}$$

$$\frac{\partial}{\partial t}[\text{InhABinhb}] = \nabla \cdot (D_{\text{slow}} \nabla [\text{InhABinhb}]) + k_{\text{h}} \times [\text{inhb}] \times [\text{InhAB}] - k_{\text{h}} \times [\text{InhABinhb}] \times [\text{a}]$$
$$+ k_{\text{d}}^{\text{a}} \times [\text{aInhABinhb}] - k_{\text{d}}^{\text{inhb}} \times [\text{InhABinhb}]$$

$$\frac{\partial}{\partial t}[\text{InhBAinha}] = \nabla \cdot (D_{\text{slow}} \nabla [\text{InhBAinha}]) + k_{\text{h}} \times [\text{inha}] \times [\text{InhBA}] - k_{\text{h}} \times [\text{InhBAinha}] \times [\text{b}]$$
$$+ k_{\text{d}}^{\text{b}} \times [\text{bInhBAinha}] - k_{\text{d}}^{\text{inha}} \times [\text{InhBAinha}]$$

$$\frac{\partial}{\partial t}[\text{aInhABinhb}] = \nabla \cdot (D_{\text{slow}} \nabla[\text{aInhABinhb}]) + k_{\text{h}} \times [\text{a}] \times [\text{InhABinhb}] + k_{\text{h}} \times [\text{aInhAB}] \times [\text{inhb}] - k_{\text{d}}^{\text{a}} \times [\text{aInhABinhb}]$$

$$- k_{\text{d}}^{\text{inhb}} \times [\text{aInhABinhb}] + k_{\text{nick}} \times [\text{InhABainhb}]/K_{\text{nick}} - k_{\text{pol,sd}} \times [\text{aInhABinhb}]/K_{\text{m,sd}}/C_{\text{pol}}$$

$$\frac{\partial}{\partial t}[\text{bInhBAinha}] = \nabla \cdot (D_{\text{slow}} \nabla[\text{bInhBAinha}]) + k_{\text{h}} \times [\text{b}] \times [\text{InhBAinha}] + k_{\text{h}} \times [\text{bInhBA}] \times [\text{inha}] - k_{\text{d}}^{\text{b}} \times [\text{bInhBAinha}]$$

$$- k_{\text{d}}^{\text{inha}} \times [\text{bInhBAinha}] + k_{\text{nick}} \times [\text{InhBAbinha}]/K_{\text{nick}} - k_{\text{pol,sd}} \times [\text{bInhBAinha}]/K_{\text{m,sd}}/C_{\text{pol}}$$

$$\frac{\partial}{\partial t}[\text{InhABainhb}] = \nabla \cdot (D_{\text{slow}} \nabla[\text{InhABainhb}]) + k_{\text{pol}} \times [\text{aInhAB}]/K_{\text{m}}/C_{\text{pol}} + k_{\text{pol,sd}} \times [\text{aInhABinhb}]/K_{\text{m,sd}}/C_{\text{pol}}$$

$$- k_{\text{nick}} \times [\text{InhABainhb}]/K_{\text{nick}}$$

$$\frac{\partial}{\partial t}[\text{InhBAbinha}] = \nabla \cdot (D_{\text{slow}} \nabla[\text{InhBAbinha}]) + k_{\text{pol}} \times [\text{bInhBA}]/K_{\text{m}}/C_{\text{pol}} + k_{\text{pol,sd}} \times [\text{bInhBAinha}]/K_{\text{m,sd}}/C_{\text{pol}}$$

$$- k_{\text{nick}} \times [\text{InhBAbinha}]/K_{\text{nick}},$$

where

$$C_{\text{pol}} = 1 + [\text{aA}]/K_{\text{m}} + [\text{bB}]/K_{\text{m}} + [\text{aAa}]/K_{\text{m,sd}} + [\text{bBb}]/K_{\text{m,sd}}$$
$$+ [\text{aInhAB}]/K_{\text{m}} + [\text{bInhBA}]/K_{\text{m}} + [\text{aInhABinhb}]/K_{\text{m,sd}} + [\text{bInhBAinha}]/K_{\text{m,sd}}$$

$$C_{\text{exo}} = 1 + [\text{a}]/K_{\text{m,input}} + [\text{b}]/K_{\text{m,input}} + [\text{inhb}]/K_{\text{m,inh}} + [\text{inha}]/K_{\text{m,inh}}$$

$$K_{\text{nick}} = K_{\text{mn}} + [\text{Aaa}] + [\text{Bbb}] + [\text{InhABainhb}] + [\text{InhBAbinha}].$$

As kinetic parameters, we used the fitted values of the original article [25]. Diffusion coefficient of DNA in solution was roughly estimated from experimental values [34, 35].

$$k_{\text{h}} = 0.06[\text{nM}^{-1} \cdot \text{min}^{-1}], \quad k_{\text{d}}^{\text{a}} = k_{\text{h}}/0.013[\text{min}^{-1}], \quad k_{\text{d}}^{\text{b}} = k_{\text{h}}/0.0045[\text{min}^{-1}],$$

$$k_{\text{d}}^{\text{inha}} = k_{\text{h}}/5.3[\text{min}^{-1}], \quad k_{\text{d}}^{\text{inhb}} = k_{\text{h}}/1.3[\text{min}^{-1}], \quad toe = 0.01,$$

$$k_{\text{pol}} = 2100[\text{nM} \cdot \text{min}^{-1}], \quad k_{\text{pol,sd}} = 420[\text{nM} \cdot \text{min}^{-1}], \quad k_{\text{nick}} = 80[\text{nM} \cdot \text{min}^{-1}], \quad k_{\text{exo}} = 300[\text{nM} \cdot \text{min}^{-1}],$$

$$K_{\text{m}} = 80[\text{nM}], \quad K_{\text{m,sd}} = 5.5[\text{nM}], \quad K_{\text{mn}} = 30[\text{nM}], \quad K_{\text{m,input}} = 440[\text{nM}], \quad K_{\text{m,inh}} = 150[\text{nM}].$$

$$D_{\text{fast}} = \begin{cases} 1.2 \times 10^{-8} & [\text{m}^2 \cdot \text{min}^{-1}] \text{ (in solution)} \\ 6.0 \times 10^{-10} & [\text{m}^2 \cdot \text{min}^{-1}] \text{ (in hydrogel)} \end{cases}, \quad D_{\text{slow}} = \begin{cases} 1.2 \times 10^{-8} & [\text{m}^2 \cdot \text{min}^{-1}] \text{ (in solution)} \\ 3.0 \times 10^{-12} & [\text{m}^2 \cdot \text{min}^{-1}] \text{ (in hydrogel)} \end{cases}$$

References

1. Rangnekar, A., LaBean, T.H.: Building DNA nanostructures for molecular computation, templated assembly, and biological applications. Acc. Chem. Res. **47**(6), 1778–1788 (2014)
2. Zhang, F., Nangreave, J., Liu, Y., Yan, H.: Structural DNA nanotechnology: state of the art and future perspective. J. Am. Chem. Soc. **136**(32), 11198–11211 (2014)
3. Zhang, D.Y., Seelig, G.: Dynamic DNA nanotechnology using strand-displacement reactions. Nat. Chem. **3**(2), 103–113 (2011)
4. Seelig, G., Soloveichik, D., Zhang, D.Y., Winfree, E.: Enzyme-free nucleic acid logic circuits. Science **314**(5805), 1585–1588 (2006)
5. Qian, L., Winfree, E.: Scaling up digital circuit computation with DNA strand displacement cascades. Science **332**(6034), 1196–1201 (2011)
6. Turberfield, A.J., Yurke, B.: Engineering entropy-driven reactions and networks catalyzed by DNA. Science **318**(5853), 1121–1125 (2007)
7. Fujii, T., Rondelez, Y.: Predator-prey molecular ecosystems. ACS Nano **7**(1), 27–34 (2013)

8. Kuzuya, A., Ohya, Y.: Nanomechanical molecular devices made of DNA origami. Acc. Chem. Res. **47**(6), 1742–1749 (2014)

9. Murata, S., Konagaya, A., Kobayashi, S., Saito, H., Hagiya, M.: Molecular robotics: a new paradigm for artifacts. New Gener. Comput. **31**, 27–45 (2013)

10. Hagiya, M., Konagaya, A., Kobayashi, S., Saito, H., Murata, S.: Molecular robots with sensors and intelligence. Acc. Chem. Res. **47**(6), 1681–1690 (2014)

11. Turing, A.M.: The chemical basis of morphogenesis. Philos. Trans. R. Soc. B Biol. Sci. **237**(641), 37–72 (1952)

12. Lee, K.-J., McCormick, W.D., Pearson, J.E., Swinney, H.L.: Experimental observation of self-replicating spots in a reaction-diffusion system. Nature **369**(6477), 215–218 (1994)

13. Vanag, V.K., Epstein, I.R.: Tomography of reaction-diffusion microemulsions reveals three-dimensional turing patterns. Science **331**(1309), 1309–1312 (2011)

14. Kondo, S., Miura, T.: Reaction-diffusion model as a framework for understanding biological pattern formation. Science **329**(5999), 1616–1620 (2010)

15. Chirieleison, S.M., Allen, P.B., Simpson, Z.B., Ellington, A.D., Chen, X.: Pattern transformation with DNA circuits. Nat. Chem. **5**(12), 1000–1005 (2013)

16. Padirac, A., Fujii, T., Estévez-Torres, A., Rondelez, Y.: Spatial waves in synthetic biochemical networks. J. Am. Chem. Soc. **135**(39), 14586–14592 (2013)

17. Soloveichik, D., Seelig, G., Winfree, E.: DNA as a universal substrate for chemical kinetics. Proc. Nat. Acad. Sci. **107**(12), 5393–5398 (2010)

18. Phillips, A., Cardelli, L.: A programming language for composable DNA circuits. J. R. Soc. Interface **6**(Suppl 4), S419–S436 (2009)

19. Aubert, N., Mosca, C., Fujii, T., Hagiya, M., Rondelez, Y.: Computer-assisted design for scaling up systems based on DNA reaction networks. J. R. Soc. Interface **11**(93), 20131167 (2014)

20. Allen, P.B., Chen, X., Simpson, Z.B., Ellington, A.D.: Modeling scalable pattern generation in DNA reaction networks. Artif. Life **13**, 441–448 (2012). http://dx.doi.org/10.7551/978-0-262-31050-5-ch058

21. Scalise, D., Schulman, R.: Designing modular reaction-diffusion programs for complex pattern formation. Technology **02**(01), 55–66 (2014)

22. Dalchau, N., Seelig, G., Phillips, A.: Computational design of reaction-diffusion patterns using DNA-based chemical reaction networks. In: Murata, S., Kobayashi, S. (eds.) DNA 2014. LNCS, vol. 8727, pp. 84–99. Springer, Heidelberg (2014)

23. Hagiya, M., Wang, S., Kawamata, I., Murata, S., Isokawa, T., Peper, F., Imai, K.: On DNA-based gellular automata. In: Ibarra, O.H., Kari, L., Kopecki, S. (eds.) UCNC 2014. LNCS, vol. 8553, pp. 177–189. Springer, Heidelberg (2014)

24. Scalise, D., Schulman, R.: Emulating cellular automata in chemical reaction-diffusion networks. In: Murata, S., Kobayashi, S. (eds.) DNA 2014. LNCS, vol. 8727, pp. 67–83. Springer, Heidelberg (2014)

25. Padirac, A., Fujii, T., Rondelez, Y.: Bottom-up construction of in vitro switchable memories. Proc. Nat. Acad. Sci. **109**(47), E3212–E3220 (2012)

26. Fischlechner, M., Schaerli, Y., Mohamed, M.F., Patil, S., Abell, C., Hollfelder, F.: Evolution of enzyme catalysts caged in biomimetic gel-shell beads. Nat. Chem. **6**(9), 791–796 (2014)

27. Machado, A.H., Lundberg, D., Ribeiro, A.J., Veiga, F.J., Miguel, M.G., Lindman, B., Olsson, U.: Encapsulation of DNA in macroscopic and nanosized calcium alginate gel particles. Langmuir. **29**(51), 15926–15935 (2013)

28. Cook, M.: Universality in elementary cellular automata. Complex Syst. **15**, 1–40 (2004)

29. Nayfeh, B.A.: Cellular automata for solving mazes. Dr. Dobb's J. **18**(2), 32–38 (1993)
30. Saber, M.A., Mirenkov, N.: A visual representation of cellular automata-like systems. J. Visual Lang. Comput. **15**(6), 409–438 (2004)
31. Hutton, T., Munafo, R., Trevorrow, A., Rokicki, T., Wills, D.: Ready, a cross-platform implementation of various reaction-diffusion systems. https://github.com/GollyGang/ready
32. Allen, P., Chen, X., Ellington, A.: Spatial control of DNA reaction networks by DNA sequence. Molecules **17**(12), 13390–13402 (2012)
33. Zhang, D.Y., Winfree, E.: Control of DNA strand displacement kinetics using toehold exchange. J. Am. Chem. Soc. **131**(47), 17303–17314 (2009)
34. Stellwagen, E., Yongjun, L., Stellwagen, N.C.: Unified description of electrophoresis and diffusion for DNA and other polyions. Biochemistry **42**(40), 11745–11750 (2003)
35. Pluen, A., Netti, P.A., Jain, R.K., Berk, D.A.: Diffusion of macromolecules in agarose gels: comparison of linear and globular configurations. Biophys. J. **77**(1), 542–552 (1999)
36. Bremond, N., Santanach-Carreras, E., Chu, L.-Y., Bibette, J.: Formation of liquid-core capsules having a thin hydrogel membrane: liquid pearls. Soft Matter **6**(11), 2484–2488 (2010)
37. Rendell, P.: Turing universality of the game of life. In: Adamatzky, A. (ed.) Collision-Based Computing, pp. 513–539. Springer, London (2002)
38. Feng, L., Romulus, J., Li, M., Sha, R., Royer, J., Kun-Ta, W., Qin, X., Seeman, N.C., Weck, M., Chaikin, P.: Cinnamate-based DNA photolithography. Nat. Mater. **12**, 747–753 (2013)

Universal Totalistic Asynchonous Cellular Automaton and Its Possible Implementation by DNA

Teijiro Isokawa[1](✉), Ferdinand Peper[2], Ibuki Kawamata[3], Nobuyuki Matsui[1], Satoshi Murata[3], and Masami Hagiya[4]

[1] University of Hyogo, Himeji, Japan
isokawa@eng.u-hyogo.ac.jp
[2] Center for Information and Neural Networks,
National Institute of Information and Communications Technology,
Osaka University, Osaka, Japan
[3] Tohoku University, Sendai, Japan
[4] The University of Tokyo, Tokyo, Japan

Abstract. This paper presents a Cellular Automaton (CA) model designed for possible implementation by the reaction and diffusion of DNA strands. The proposed CA works asynchronously, whereby each cell undergoes its transitions independently from other cells and at random times. The state of a cell changes in a cyclic manner, rather than according to an any-to-any mapping. The transition rules are designed as totalistic, i.e., the next state of a cell is determined only by the number of states in the neighborhood of the cell, not by their relative positions. Universal circuit elements are designed for the CA as well as wires and crossings to connect them, which implies that the CA is Turing-complete.

1   Introduction

Since their introduction by von Neumann in the 1950's *Cellular Automata* (CAs) have attracted extensive research interest, varying from computation to the simulation of phenomena in nature. Studies on computation usually evolve around the question how closely a CA is able to emulate a Turing-universal model, or around the implementation of a computing problem on a CA, like the firing squad problem [7] or the majority problem [4]. Surprisingly, there have been relatively few efforts to physically implement computation on CAs, and the attempts to do so have mostly focused on the realm of silicon [14], but with little follow-up. The success of VLSI in the last 50 years has been strongly credited to the ongoing use of the von Neumann architecture, at the cost of neglecting CAs for this purpose. CAs, however, have some strong arguments speaking for them. Their regularity has the potential for bottom-up manufacturing [3], like molecular self-assembly. Biological implementations of CAs have attracted even less efforts, even though CAs have features, such as their modular structure, that make them suitable for such a framework. The efforts in this direction have aimed to implement

© Springer International Publishing Switzerland 2016
M. Amos and A. Condon (Eds.): UCNC 2016, LNCS 9726, pp. 182–195, 2016.
DOI: 10.1007/978-3-319-41312-9_15

the enclosures surrounding each cell compartment by gels, that are dissolved or reestablished depending on control asserted from a supervising mechanism [5].

Even less tried is the use of DNA to assert control over the behavior of cells in CAs, even though DNA has a significant history in being used for computation, like in the Hamiltonian Path Problem (HPP) [2]. This type of computation relies on a loose control, in which DNA molecules encoding an instance of HPP interact with each other in a solvent, organizing themselves into molecules that represent a solution of the problem. More microscale control of computation by DNA, however, has only been touched upon recently [8,10,12], but one of the problems it faces is the lack of a well-defined chemical environment in which operations are enclosed. Such control is important, because it is a precursor to the successful realization of molecular robots [9], which to date remains a futuristic, though exciting, goal. The few attempts to realize CAs by DNA [6,13] have adopted outside control in which an external clock signal, which may be optical, chemical, etc., regulates interactions between cells as well as the timing of the interactions, but these models cannot operate autonomously.

This paper lines out the conditions a CA model should satisfy in order to be suitable for implementing DNA-based computation. It does so by focusing on the particulars of DNA, and investigating how they are best represented in a CA framework. As an illustration, a CA satisfying the conditions is proposed. The CA is asynchronously timed, i.e., there is no central clock according to which all cells update their states in lock-step. The CA will also satisfy the requirement that no states of cells next to each other are the same, except for two common states that carry little information, i.e., the resting state and the state indicating an empty wire. This makes it easier for the CA to distinguish between the DNA in a cell and that in its neighbors. Rules in the CA are designed such that states are updated in a cyclic way. This facilitates implementation by DNA because it decreases the number of possible reactions. We also discuss totalistic CAs, which express their transition rules in terms of the *number* of neighboring cells in certain states rather than the specific *locations* of those cells. This makes them very suitable for a DNA-based framework, apart from the fact that totalistic CA are also inherently rotation- and reflection-symmetric. The initial design of transition rules will be in a non-totalistic form, but we will convert them to two types of totalistic rules. We introduce an additional condition on transition rules, which, when satisfied, will be called *Boolean totalistic*. The state transition of a cell satisfying this condition is determined by the mere presence of certain states in the cell's neighborhood, rather than by the number of those states. Boolean totalistic CAs are more amenable to implementation by DNA, because they do not require counting of the number of states in cell neighborhoods.

This paper is organized as follows. Section 2 describes preliminaries on the CA and the circuit elements we will emulate on it. Section 3 shows the design of the CA. We finish with the conclusions and a discussion in Sect. 4.

2   Preliminaries

2.1   Possible DNA Implementation of Model

Our proposal for the implementation of a CA by DNA revolves around the switching element presented and analyzed in [10, 12], which is based on six kinds of chemicals: two DNAs for representing the state of a switch, called α and β, and four template DNAs $p\alpha$, $p\beta$, $i\alpha$, and $i\beta$ promoting or inhibiting the production of α and β. The catalytic reactions between these chemicals lead to a bistable system that can be in state α or state β, depending on the proportion of their corresponding promoters and inhibitors.

This bistable system can be extended to an n-state system ($n > 2$), but it requires constraints on the transitions that are allowed to keep physical implementations practical. Any-to-any state transitions would require $O(n^2)$ promoters and inhibitors, but this number can be reduced to $O(n)$ by designing transitions to occur in a cyclic fashion.

2.2   Cellular Automaton Model

The cellular automaton (CA) in this paper is a two-dimensional CA of identical cells. A cell has a state that is an element of a finite set of states, and it is connected to four cells that share its edges (von Neumann neighborhood). The cellular space of this CA is shown in Fig. 1, where the state of a cell is shown by a symbol in the cell. The state of a cell changes according to the states of the cell itself and its neighboring cells. In our initial design we use transition rules describing state changes that have the form illustrated in Fig. 2. The transition rules of this type are defined as a function $(s_c, s_n, s_e, s_s, s_w) \to s'_c$, where s_c denotes the state of the cell itself, and s_n, s_e, s_s, and s_w denote the states of its northern, eastern, southern, and western neighboring cell, respectively. The state of the cell after update is denoted by s'_c. These transition rules will be transformed into another type of transition rules, called *totalistic*, which are described as $s_1(n_1)\ s_2\ (n_2)\ s_3\ (n_3) \cdots \to s'_c$ where s_i and n_i ($i \leq 5$) denote the states of cells and their numbers in this state in a cell's neighborhood, respectively. This rule means that the state of the cell is changed to s'_c if the number of the neighboring cells in state s_1 is n_1, in state s_2 is n_2, and so on. This type of rule is called *inner totalistic*, because in the count of the number of states in a cell's neighborhood, the state of the cell itself is included. The rules are *outer totalistic* otherwise. In case of outer totalistic rules, if the cell's state is additionally defined in the left hand side of transition rules, the CA is called *inner dependent* and a transition rule takes the form $s_c\ s_1(n_1)\ s_2\ (n_2)\ s_3\ (n_3) \cdots \to s'_c$. If the cell's state is not defined in the left hand side, the rule is called *inner independent*. For a CA based on DNA this is the ideal situation, because the influence of DNA in the cell itself can be completely shut out. However, it is difficult to achieve Turing universality in a CA model with outer totalistic inner independent rules, and it tends to require a larger neighborhood of a cell [1].

The state of a cell in the presented CA changes in a cyclic manner, according to a cycle $s_1 \rightarrow s_2 \rightarrow \cdots \rightarrow s_n \rightarrow s_1 \rightarrow \cdots$ consisting of n states. Each of the cells in this paper undergoes its transitions asynchronously, unlike the typical synchronous CA models in which all cells are updated at once each time.

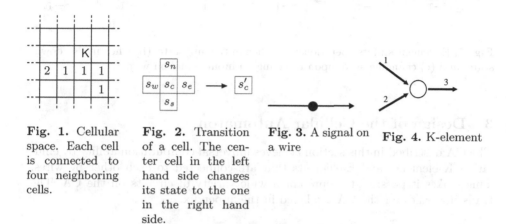

Fig. 1. Cellular space. Each cell is connected to four neighboring cells.

Fig. 2. Transition of a cell. The center cell in the left hand side changes its state to the one in the right hand side.

Fig. 3. A signal on a wire

Fig. 4. K-element

2.3   Circuit Elements

One scheme for computation on CAs is based on the emulation of circuit elements and their signals. A NAND gate can be used to compute any Boolean function, but this is rather complex for asynchronous CA and requires timing conditions for ensuring its correct operation. So, we choose another set of circuit elements that are more suitable for asynchronous operation. These elements form the basis of so-called *delay-insensitive circuits*, which allow any delay in signals without this affecting the correctness of the outcome of a computation.

A few decades ago Priese [11] proposed circuit elements from which arbitrary delay-insensitive circuits can be constructed. His circuit elements consist of two logic elements, signals, and wires, whereby a signal flows along a wire in a certain direction (Fig. 3) and is operated upon by the logic elements. Priese's logic elements, called E-element and K-element [11], are schematically shown in Figs. 4 and 5. The circuits constructed from E-elements and K-elements have in common that they employ only one signal at a time. Though inefficient, this is sufficient to guarantee universality.

The K-element has two input wires (1 and 2 in Fig. 4) and one output wire (3 in Fig. 4), and it accepts a signal coming from either input wire and outputs it to the output wire.

The E-element has two input wires (S and T) and three output wires (S', T_u, and T_d), as well as two internal states ('up' or 'down'). Input from wire T will be redirected to either of the output wires T_u or T_d, depending on the internal state of the element: when this state is 'up' (resp. 'down'), a signal on the input wire T flows to the output wire T_u (resp. T_d) as in Fig. 5(a) (resp. Fig. 5(b)). When accepting a signal from input wire S, an E-element flips its internal state, after which it outputs an acknowledge signal to output wire S′, as shown in Fig. 5(c).

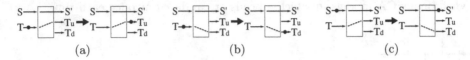

(a)   (b)   (c)

Fig. 5. E-element and its operations: (a) when in the 'up' state, (b) when in the 'down' state, and (c) changing state upon receiving an input signal on wire S.

3   Design of the Cellular Automaton

The CA described in this section achieves universal computation ability by emulating K-elements and E-elements that are connected to each other by wires. This makes it possible to represent a wide variety of circuits on the CA. The transition rules for the CA are listed in the appendix.

| 1 | 1 | 3 | 2 | 1 | 1 | 1 | $\xrightarrow{1}$ | 1 | 1 | 3 | 2 | Z | 1 | 1 | $\xrightarrow{2}$ | 1 | 1 | 3 | Y | Z | 1 | 1 | 3

(a)   (b)   (c)

| 1 | 1 | 1 | Y | Z | 1 | 1 | $\xrightarrow{4}$ | 1 | 1 | 1 | 3 | Z | 1 | 1 | $\xrightarrow{5}$ | 1 | 1 | 1 | 3 | 2 | 1 | 1 |

(d)   (e)   (f)

Fig. 6. A signal propagating to the right on a wire. The cell state 1 is used for wires, and the head and tail of a signal are represented by the states 2 and 3, respectively.

3.1   Signal and Wire

Figure 6(a) shows a configuration consisting of a linear array of state 1 cells, which constitutes a wire, with a state 2 cell on it, which represents the head of a signal, next to a state 3 cell, which is the tail. We refer to a cell on a wire as a *general wire cell* (*Gwc*). There are five transition rules driving the signal to the right, which are described as (see Appendix A):

Rule #1 : $(1, 0, 1, 0, 2) \to Z$ Rule #4 : $(Y, 0, Z, 0, 1) \to 3$

Rule #2 : $(2, 0, Z, 0, 3) \to Y$ Rule #5 : $(Z, 0, 1, 0, 3) \to 2$

Rule #3 : $(3, 0, Y, 0, 1) \to 1$

The propagation of a signal on a wire is shown in Fig. 6(b)–(f), where the numbers attached to the arrows between configurations denote the applied transition rules. A Gwc through which a signal passes goes through the cycle of states $1 \to Z \to 2 \to Y \to 3 \to 1 \to \cdots$, triggered by the state 2 in a neighboring cell. The design of the CA is such that the cells carrying a signal all have different states from their neighbors. This makes it easier to distinguish between DNA representing the states in neighboring cells.

3.2   Crossing of Wires

In order to pass a crossing of wires, a signal has to choose an appropriate output terminal from three terminals. To this end, a crossing recognizes the direction a signal comes from and outputs it to the terminal at the opposite side. In the configuration of the wire crossing in Fig. 7(a) the cell states C_0 and C_1 are used to mark whether the terminals should be used as output or not. These marker cells are called *corner cells* (Cc), and the cell on a wire between two corner cells is a *crossing terminal* (Ct). Figure 7(b)–(h) show a signal proceeding through the *crossing point* (Cp) in the center. The signal, which is about to enter the crossing in Fig. 7(b), has to wait for the neighboring corner cells to change their states from C_0 to C_1 (Fig. 7(c)), before it can proceed to Cp (Fig. 7(d)). Two C_1 corner cells at both sides of a wire thus indicate that a signal is about to pass or is in the process of passing. The transition rules are designed such that the corner cells at the input side of a signal on a crossing will never be in state C_1 at the same time as the corner cells at the opposite side of the crossing, unless the signal is already halfway through (Fig. 7(f)). Accordingly, the signal cannot turn left or right at the crossing, because when its head is at Cp, the corresponding corner cells for output terminals to the crossing wire have the different states C_0

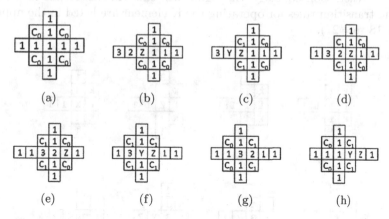

(a)   (b)   (c)   (d)

(e)   (f)   (g)   (h)

Fig. 7. (a) Configuration for the crossing of wires. (b) Signal entering from the left waits at the terminal, which has the corner cells with state C_0 at both sides. (c),(d) Signal proceeds to the crossing point after the state of the corner cells have changed to C_1. (e) The signal recognizes the terminal to which it should be output (at the right), because it is the only side at which the two corner cells are in state C_0. (f) The corner cells at the output side with state C_0 change their states to C_1 to process the incoming signal for output. At this stage the signal is already halfway through, so it cannot exit via a side wire, even if the corresponding terminals both have corner cells in state C_1. (g) The corner cells in state C_1 at the input side revert to state C_0 after the signal has passed them. (h) The signal has almost passed the crossing, and after it has exited the corner cells at the output side will revert to state C_0, allowing the crossing to accept the next signal.

and C_1 (Fig. 7(e)). The transition rules for driving a signal through a crossing are listed in the appendix (rules #6 to #17).

3.3   K-element

For the construction of the K-element, it is again necessary to distinguish between input and output terminals through the use of marker cells adjacent to the wires. Unlike in the crossing, however, a *marker cell* (Km) in a K-element can stay in a stationary state K, which marks the two input wires. Next to the marker cells are the *input terminals* (Ki). The *K-element's center cell* (Kc), i.e., the cell marked by $*$ in Fig. 8(a), has a cycle of states that is slightly different from the cycle of a Gwc. This cycle $1 \rightarrow Z \rightarrow X \rightarrow Y \rightarrow 3 \rightarrow 1 \rightarrow \cdots$ uses state X instead of state 2 to prevent a signal from erroneously exiting via an input wire. We employ a marker cell (Kl) with stationary state L left of the center cell to avoid ambiguities when transforming the transition rules into inner-totalistic form (see Sect. 3.5). A signal entering the K-element from the top and exiting from the output terminal at its right is shown in Fig. 8. The transition rules are designed such that the wire cell directly right of the center cell reacts to the center cell being in state X, whereas a wire cell with a state K cell adjacent to it will not react. Consequently, the signal will exit via the output in a correct way. The transition rules for operating the K-element are listed in the appendix (rules #18 to #27).

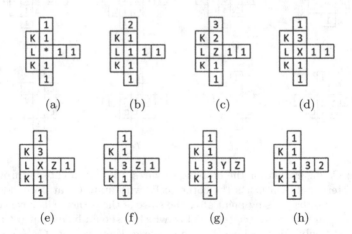

(a)   (b)   (c)   (d)

(e)   (f)   (g)   (h)

Fig. 8. (a) Configuration for the K-element, which accepts signals from the northern and southern input wires and outputs them on the eastern wire. (b) Signal coming from the north of the K-element, (c) after which it proceeds to the center of the K-element. (d) Due to the special cycle (X instead of 2 in a wire cell) in the center cell, (e) only the eastern wire cell next to it is activated for propagating the signal. (f),(g) The signal proceeds to the east, (h) and the state of the center cell is restored to its initial state 1.

3.4   E-element

Figure 9(a) shows the construction of the E-element, whereby the arrows with the symbols correspond to the terminals of the E-element in Fig. 5. The state U or D of the E-element is stored by the cell in the center, which we denote by Es. For technical reasons, the center cell can also assume the temporary states U' and D', so its cycle is $U' \to U \to D' \to D \to U' \to \cdots$. The cell left of the center cell, the *E-element's state read out (Esro)* cell, is used to read out the state when a signal is input to terminal T. Depending on the state of the E-element, this cell has two cycles it can go through, i.e., $1 \to Z \to u \to Y \to 3$ for state U and $1 \to Z \to d \to Y \to 3$ for state D. This is the only cell for which the cycle is not unique. The cell in the static state E at the bottom of the E-element is a *marker (Em)* used for discriminating between the terminals T_u or T_d, so that the corresponding output cells $ETuo$ and $ETdo$ react appropriately to the state of Esro.

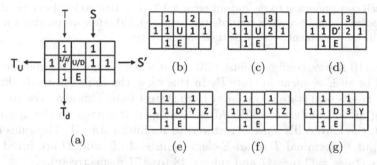

Fig. 9. (a) Configuration of the E-element. The cell labeled U/D stores the state. (b) E-element in state U accepting a signal from input terminal S. (c) Signal arriving at the center cell that encodes the state of the E-element. (d) The state of the center cell starts to change from state D to U through an intermediate state D'. (e) After the signal passes through, (f) this state finally settles to D. (g) The signal exits from the output terminal S'.

There are four different situations in which an E-element processes an input signal. The first two situations concern a signal input to the S terminal, whereby the E-element is in state U or D. The third and fourth situation concerns input to the T terminal, again with the E-element in state U or D, respectively. Due to space limitations, we only show the two most representative situations.

Figure 9(b)–(g) show a series of configurations occurring when an E-element in state U receives an input at the S terminal. The cell in state U changes its state to D via an intermediate state D' through the interaction of the cell with its right neighbor, which is called the *E-element state switch trigger (Esst)*. After this operation, terminal S' outputs an acknowledge signal. The rules in case of an input to terminal S of an E-element in state U and D are listed in the appendix (rules #28 to #34 and rules #35 to #41 respectively).

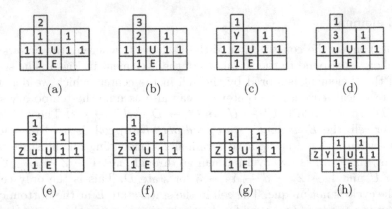

Fig. 10. Operations of an E-element in the state U after accepting a signal from terminal T. (a) A signal is input at terminal T, and (b), (c) proceeds to the cell left of the state-encoding cell (the center cell). (d) The cell left of the center cell changes its state to u, according to the state of the neighboring cell (which is in the state U here). (e) The cell corresponding to the output terminal T_u is activated by the cell state u, (f) and the output signal proceeds towards the west. (g), (h) After outputting the signal, the cells in the E-element recover to their initial states.

Figure 10 shows configurations that arise when a signal is input to the T terminal of an E-element in state U. In this case, the Esro cell reads this state and changes its own state accordingly from state 1 to u. This gives rise to a signal emerging at output terminal T_u. After the signal is output to the appropriate terminal, the Esro cell's state is restored to its initial state 1. The rules in case of an input to terminal T of an E-element in state U and D are listed in the appendix (rules #42 to #47 and rules #48 to #57 respectively).

3.5   Rule Representations by Totalistic Rules

This section describes how the non-totalistic transition rules in the previous sections are transformed into totalistic rules. The original rules and their totalistic equivalents are listed in the Appendix. Though the transformation is straightforward, since it only involves counting of states in the neighborhood of a cell, we will also consider equivalence of rules. Obviously, when two totalistic transition rules have the same left hand sides and right hand sides they are equivalent, even though the original non-totalistic rules may not, but we go further than that. Rather than counting the number of cells in certain states in a neighborhood, we will merely take into account the presence of certain states in a cell's neighborhood (Boolean totalistic). As argued in the introduction, the reason for this is that it is difficult to distinguish between different amounts of DNA. We have confirmed that our outer-totalistic inner-dependent rules and inner-totalistic rules are all Boolean totalistic. Unfortunately, the outer-totalistic inner-independent equivalents of the rules, which are not listed in the Appendix, turn out to be ambiguous, so the left-hand side of such a rule does not uniquely define the right-hand side. When considered as Boolean totalistic rules, there are even

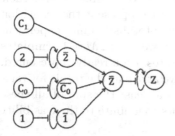

Fig. 11. DNA circuit for rule #6 used by the crossing terminal cell (Ct).

Table 1. Number of DNA templates required for all cell types

Cell type	#. templates
Gwc	48
Cc	15
Ct	60
Cp	50
Ki	58
Kc	50
Kl	1
Km	1
Esst	58
Es	46
Em	1
ETuo	48
Esro	109
ETdo	53

more ambiguities. Outer-totalistic inner-independent rules would be ideal for DNA implementations, since the state of a cell itself would be completely irrelevant for a transition. However, state-flipping rules, like rules #33, #34, #40, and #41, cannot work without information on the state of the cell itself, so they cannot be represented by outer-totalistic inner-independent rules. Outer-totalistic inner-dependent rules are the least likely to suffer from ambiguity problems in the current CA, but their implementation in terms of DNA is the most complicated of all types of totalistic rules, since the state of a cell itself needs to be considered separately in a transition. Inner-totalistic rules lie somewhere in between in terms of the complexity for implementations by DNA.

4   Discussion and Conclusions

This paper presents a CA that is designed with implementations by DNA in mind. Figure 11 gives an example of a DNA circuit generated from transition rule #6: $(1, C_0, 1, C_0, 2) \rightarrow Z$ in the spirit of [12]. Arrowheads indicate promotors and flat heads indicate inhibitors. DNA strings with self-arrows are autonomously generated as long as they are not inhibited. Typically a state in the left hand side of a transition rule is among the DNA strings that inhibit the DNA strings labeled by symbols with a bar on top, and they in turn generate a DNA string that inhibits the generation of output. Rule #6 is a bit special, because it requires a DNA string C_1 even though C_1 is not in the left hand side of rule #6. Accordingly, the inhibition by DNA string C_1 ensures that the combination of states C_0 and C_1 will not generate output to side wires of the crossing.

To calculate the number of DNA templates that produce DNA signals for each type of cell, we first consider the number of states the cell can be in. If this number is N, then there are N templates required to represent the states. Additionally, $C(N, 2)$ (number of combinations when selecting 2 out of N) templates are required to represent the processes of duplication of templates and their mutual inhibition. Each cell also requires templates to represent the transition rules that can be applied to it. Typically, for an outer-totalistic inner-dependent rule with M different symbols in the left hand side, we need $2M + 1$ templates per rule in addition to the templates by which states are already represented. Adding up all the templates for each type of cell, we arrive at the totals for templates in Table 1. To realize the CA we would need at least the sum of all these table entries, which totals 598. The following factors contribute to the feasibility of implementations of the CA by DNA.

First, neighboring cells have different states except when they are in state 0 (background state) and state 1 (wire state). Since the impact of a certain DNA string on a reaction is much higher in a cell undergoing a transition than when the same DNA string is in a neighboring cell, the latter will be drowned out by the former, so it will become difficult to detect the DNA string in the neighboring cell. When neighboring cells have different states this situation will not occur.

Second, state changes of cells follow cyclic patterns. This will not only reduce the number of interactions to be described—a number linear in the number of states in a cycle, rather than quadratic if transitions between any pair of states are possible—it is also conductive to an easier implementation by DNA strings, allowing constructions described in [8,10].

Third, the transition rules are totalistic. This facilitates rotation-symmetry and reflection-symmetry of the rules, thereby greatly reducing their required number. It is also more in the spirit of DNA computing, since it allows to formulate transitions in terms of quantities or the presence of DNA, rather than the relative positions of the DNA.

Fourth, the outer-totalistic inner-dependent and the inner-totalistic versions of the transition rules are unambiguous. Even better, these rules are also Boolean totalistic, as discussed in Sect. 3.5. This allows us to focus on the presence or absence of particular DNA strings, rather than on their amount, and it makes the rules more robust.

Though the CA was designed for implementation by DNA, there are still obstacles towards this end. Foremost among them is that the number of required DNA strings (598) is far above what is currently technically feasible by experiment, which is around 30. Second, while states of cells usually revert back to their original states after a signal has passed, this tends to be difficult to implement in terms of DNA. However, cyclic reactions are known to exist in biochemistry [8], so this may not be an impossible obstacle to overcome.

Universal computation is a relatively simple functionality to implement on CAs, but it is already a very powerful capability to have in a system. As such, computability should be considered an important yardstick in a system as to its ability to carry out a wide variety of other operations that may be useful for the implementation of molecular robotics. This paper hopefully provides insight in the conditions a system should satisfy to this end.

Acknowledgment. This work was supported by a Grant-in-Aid for Scientific Research on Innovative Areas "Molecular Robotics" (No. 15H00825) of The Ministry of Education, Culture, Sports, Science, and Technology, Japan.

A   Transition Rules Used in this Paper

Three forms for each of rules used in this paper are shown, non-totalistic (NT), outer totalistic and inner-dependent (OT&ID), and inner totalistic (IT).

Rule No	NT form	OT&ID form		IT form
1	$(1,0,1,0,2) \to Z$	1	$0(2)\ 1(1)\ 2(1) \to Z$	$0(2)\ 1(2)\ 2(1) \to Z$
2	$(2,0,Z,0,3) \to Y$	2	$0(2)\ 3(1)\ Z(1) \to Y$	$0(2)\ 2(1)\ 3(1)\ Z(1) \to Y$
3	$(3,0,Y,0,1) \to 1$	3	$0(2)\ 1(1)\ Y(1) \to 1$	$0(2)\ 1(1)\ 3(1)\ Y(1) \to 1$
4	$(Y,0,Z,0,1) \to 3$	Y	$0(2)\ 1(1)\ Z(1) \to 3$	$0(2)\ 1(1)\ Y(1)\ Z(1) \to 3$
5	$(Z,0,1,0,3) \to 2$	Z	$0(2)\ 1(1)\ 3(1) \to 2$	$0(2)\ 1(1)\ 3(1)\ Z(1) \to 2$
6	$(1,C_0,1,C_0,2) \to Z$	1	$1(1)\ 2(1)\ C_0(2) \to Z$	$1(2)\ 2(1)\ C_0(2) \to Z$
7	$(2,C_1,Z,C_1,3) \to Y$	2	$3(1)\ Z(1)\ C_1(2) \to Y$	$2(1)\ 3(1)\ Z(1)\ C_1(2) \to Y$
8	$(3,C_1,Y,C_1,1) \to 1$	3	$1(1)\ Y(1)\ C_1(2) \to 1$	$1(1)\ 3(1)\ Y(1)\ C_1(2) \to 1$
9	$(Y,C_1,Z,C_1,1) \to 3$	Y	$1(1)\ Z(1)\ C_1(2) \to 3$	$1(1)\ Y(1)\ Z(1)\ C_1(2) \to 3$
10	$(Z,C_1,1,C_1,3) \to 2$	Z	$1(1)\ 3(1)\ C_1(2) \to 2$	$1(1)\ 3(1)\ Z(1)\ C_1(2) \to 2$
11	$(1,1,1,1,2) \to Z$	1	$1(3)\ 2(1) \to Z$	$1(4)\ 2(1) \to Z$
12	$(2,1,Z,1,3) \to Y$	2	$1(2)\ 3(1)\ Z(1) \to Y$	$1(2)\ 2(1)\ 3(1)\ Z(1) \to Y$
13	$(3,1,Y,1,1) \to 1$	3	$1(3)\ Y(1) \to 1$	$1(3)\ 3(1)\ Y(1) \to 1$
14	$(Y,1,Z,1,1) \to 3$	Y	$1(3)\ Z(1) \to 3$	$1(3)\ Y(1)\ Z(1) \to 3$
15	$(Z,1,1,1,3) \to 2$	Z	$1(3)\ 3(1) \to 2$	$1(3)\ 3(1)\ Z(1) \to 2$
16	$(C_0,0,1,Z,0) \to C_1$	C_0	$0(2)\ 1(1)\ Z(1) \to C_1$	$0(2)\ 1(1)\ Z(1)\ C_0(1) \to C_1$
17	$(C_1,0,1,1,0) \to C_0$	C_1	$0(2)\ 1(2) \to C_0$	$0(2)\ 1(2)\ C_1(1) \to C_0$
18	$(1,2,0,1,K) \to Z$	1	$0(1)\ 1(1)\ 2(1)\ K(1) \to Z$	$0(1)\ 1(2)\ 2(1)\ K(1) \to Z$
19	$(Z,3,0,1,K) \to 2$	Z	$0(1)\ 1(1)\ 3(1)\ K(1) \to 2$	$0(1)\ 1(1)\ 3(1)\ Z(1)\ K(1) \to 2$
20	$(2,3,0,Z,K) \to Y$	2	$0(1)\ 3(1)\ Z(1)\ K(1) \to Y$	$0(1)\ 2(1)\ 3(1)\ Z(1)\ K(1) \to Y$
21	$(Y,1,0,Z,K) \to 3$	Y	$0(1)\ 1(1)\ Z(1)\ K(1) \to 3$	$0(1)\ 1(1)\ Y(1)\ Z(1)\ K(1) \to 3$
22	$(3,1,0,Y,K) \to 1$	3	$0(1)\ 1(1)\ Y(1)\ K(1) \to 1$	$0(1)\ 1(1)\ 3(1)\ Y(1)\ K(1) \to 1$
23	$(1,2,1,1,L) \to Z$	1	$L(1)\ 1(2)\ 2(1) \to Z$	$L(1)\ 1(3)\ 2(1) \to Z$
24	$(Z,3,1,1,L) \to X$	Z	$L(1)\ 1(2)\ 3(1) \to X$	$L(1)\ 1(2)\ 3(1)\ Z(1) \to X$
25	$(X,3,Z,1,L) \to Y$	X	$L(1)\ 1(1)\ 3(1)\ Z(1) \to Y$	$L(1)\ 1(1)\ 3(1)\ X(1)\ Z(1) \to Y$
26	$(Y,1,Z,1,L) \to 3$	Y	$L(1)\ 1(2)\ Z(1) \to 3$	$L(1)\ 1(2)\ Y(1)\ Z(1) \to 3$
27	$(3,1,Y,1,L) \to 1$	3	$L(1)\ 1(2)\ Y(1) \to 1$	$L(1)\ 1(2)\ 3(1)\ Y(1) \to 1$
28	$(1,2,1,0,U) \to Z$	1	$0(1)\ 1(1)\ 2(1)\ U(1) \to Z$	$0(1)\ 1(2)\ 2(1)\ U(1) \to Z$
29	$(Z,3,1,0,U) \to 2$	Z	$0(1)\ 1(1)\ 3(1)\ U(1) \to 2$	$0(1)\ 1(1)\ 3(1)\ Z(1)\ U(1) \to 2$
30	$(2,3,Z,0,D') \to Y$	2	$0(1)\ 3(1)\ Z(1)\ D'(1) \to Y$	$0(1)\ 2(1)\ 3(1)\ Z(1)\ D'(1) \to Y$
31	$(Y,1,Z,0,D) \to 3$	Y	$0(1)\ 1(1)\ Z(1)\ D(1) \to 3$	$0(1)\ 1(1)\ Y(1)\ Z(1)\ D(1) \to 3$
32	$(3,1,Y,0,D) \to 1$	3	$0(1)\ 1(1)\ Y(1)\ D(1) \to 1$	$0(1)\ 1(1)\ 3(1)\ Y(1)\ D(1) \to 1$
33	$(U,0,2,E,1) \to D'$	U	$0(1)\ 1(1)\ 2(1)\ E(1) \to D'$	$0(1)\ 1(1)\ 2(1)\ E(1)\ U(1) \to D'$
34	$(D',0,Y,E,1) \to D$	D'	$0(1)\ 1(1)\ Y(1)\ E(1) \to D$	$0(1)\ 1(1)\ Y(1)\ E(1)\ D'(1) \to D$

(*continued*)

(continued)

Rule No	NT form	OT&ID form		IT form
35	$(1,2,1,0,D) \to Z$	1	$0(1)\ 1(1)\ 2(1)\ D(1) \to Z$	$0(1)\ 1(2)\ 2(1)\ D(1) \to Z$
36	$(Z,3,1,0,D) \to 2$	Z	$0(1)\ 1(1)\ 3(1)\ D(1) \to 2$	$0(1)\ 1(1)\ 3(1)\ Z(1)\ D(1) \to 2$
37	$(2,3,Z,0,U') \to Y$	2	$0(1)\ 3(1)\ Z(1)\ U'(1) \to Y$	$0(1)\ 2(1)\ 3(1)\ Z(1)\ U'(1) \to Y$
38	$(Y,1,Z,0,U) \to 3$	Y	$0(1)\ 1(1)\ Z(1)\ U(1) \to 3$	$0(1)\ 1(1)\ Y(1)\ Z(1)\ U(1) \to 3$
39	$(3,1,Y,0,U) \to 1$	3	$0(1)\ 1(1)\ Y(1)\ U(1) \to 1$	$0(1)\ 1(1)\ 3(1)\ Y(1)\ U(1) \to 1$
40	$(D,0,2,E,1) \to U'$	D	$0(1)\ 1(1)\ 2(1)\ E(1) \to U'$	$0(1)\ 1(1)\ 2(1)\ E(1)\ D(1) \to U'$
41	$(U',0,Y,E,1) \to U$	U'	$0(1)\ 1(1)\ Y(1)\ E(1) \to U$	$0(1)\ 1(1)\ Y(1)\ E(1)\ U'(1) \to U$
42	$(1,2,U,1,1) \to Z$	1	$1(2)\ 2(1)\ U(1) \to Z$	$1(3)\ 2(1)\ U(1) \to Z$
43	$(Z,3,U,1,1) \to u$	Z	$1(2)\ 3(1)\ U(1) \to u$	$1(2)\ 3(1)\ Z(1)\ U(1) \to u$
44	$(u,3,U,1,Z) \to Y$	u	$1(1)\ 3(1)\ Z(1)\ U(1) \to Y$	$1(1)\ 3(1)\ Z(1)\ U(1)\ u(1) \to Y$
45	$(Y,1,U,1,Z) \to 3$	Y	$1(2)\ Z(1)\ U(1) \to 3$	$1(2)\ Y(1)\ Z(1)\ U(1) \to 3$
46	$(3,1,U,1,Y) \to 1$	3	$1(2)\ Y(1)\ U(1) \to 1$	$1(2)\ 3(1)\ Y(1)\ U(1) \to 1$
47	$(1,0,u,0,1) \to Z$	1	$0(2)\ 1(1)\ u(1) \to Z$	$0(2)\ 1(2)\ u(1) \to Z$
48	$(1,2,D,1,1) \to Z$	1	$1(2)\ 2(1)\ D(1) \to Z$	$1(3)\ 2(1)\ D(1) \to Z$
49	$(Z,3,D,1,1) \to d$	Z	$1(2)\ 3(1)\ D(1) \to d$	$1(2)\ 3(1)\ Z(1)\ D(1) \to d$
50	$(d,3,D,Z,1) \to Y$	d	$1(1)\ 3(1)\ Z(1)\ D(1) \to Y$	$1(1)\ 3(1)\ Z(1)\ D(1)\ d(1) \to Y$
51	$(Y,1,D,Z,1) \to 3$	Y	$1(2)\ Z(1)\ D(1) \to 3$	$1(2)\ Y(1)\ Z(1)\ D(1) \to 3$
52	$(3,1,D,Y,1) \to 1$	3	$1(2)\ Y(1)\ D(1) \to 1$	$1(2)\ 3(1)\ Y(1)\ D(1) \to 1$
53	$(1,d,E,1,0) \to Z$	1	$0(1)\ 1(1)\ E(1)\ d(1) \to Z$	$0(1)\ 1(2)\ E(1)\ d(1) \to Z$
54	$(Z,3,E,1,0) \to 2$	Z	$0(1)\ 1(1)\ 3(1)\ E(1) \to 2$	$0(1)\ 1(1)\ 3(1)\ Z(1)\ E(1) \to 2$
55	$(2,3,E,Z,0) \to Y$	2	$0(1)\ 3(1)\ Z(1)\ E(1) \to Y$	$0(1)\ 2(1)\ 3(1)\ Z(1)\ E(1) \to Y$
56	$(Y,1,E,Z,0) \to 3$	Y	$0(1)\ 1(1)\ Z(1)\ E(1) \to 3$	$0(1)\ 1(1)\ Y(1)\ Z(1)\ E(1) \to 3$
57	$(3,1,E,Y,0) \to 1$	3	$0(1)\ 1(1)\ Y(1)\ E(1) \to 1$	$0(1)\ 1(1)\ 3(1)\ Y(1)\ E(1) \to 1$

References

1. Adachi, S., Lee, J., Peper, F., Umeo, H.: Kaleidoscope of life: a 24-neighbourhood outer-totalistic cellular automaton. Phys. D **237**(6), 800–817 (2008)
2. Adleman, L.M.: Molecular computation of solutions to combinatorial problems. Science **266**, 1021–1024 (1994)
3. Biafore, M.: Cellular automata for nanometer-scale computation. Phys. D **70**, 415–433 (1994)
4. Capcarrere, M.S., Sipper, M., Tomassini, M.: Two-state, $r = 1$ cellular automaton that classifies density. Phys. Rev. Lett. **77**, 4969–4971 (1996)
5. Hagiya, M., Wang, S., Kawamata, I., Murata, S., Isokawa, T., Peper, F., Imai, K.: On DNA-based gellular automata. In: Ibarra, O.H., Kari, L., Kopecki, S. (eds.) UCNC 2014. LNCS, vol. 8553, pp. 177–189. Springer, Heidelberg (2014)
6. Jonoska, N., Seeman, N.C.: Molecular ping-pong game of life on a two-dimensional dna origami array. Philos. Trans. R. Soc. Lond. A: Math. Phys. Eng. Sci. **373**(2046) (2015). (Article Number 20140215)
7. Minsky, M.: Computation: Finite and Infinite Machines. Prentice-Hall, Englewood Cliffs (1967)
8. Montagne, K., Plasson, R., Sakai, Y., Fujii, T., Rondelez, Y.: Programming an in vitro DNA oscillator using a molecular networking strategy. Mol. Syst. Biol. **7**(1), 476–485 (2011)
9. Murata, S., Konagaya, A., Kobayashi, S., Hagiya, M.: Molecular robotics: a new paradigm for artifacts. New Gener. Comput. **31**(1), 27–45 (2013)
10. Padirac, A., Fujii, T., Rondelez, Y.: Bottom-up construction of in vitro switchable memories. Proc. Natl Acad. Sci. U.S.A. **109**(47), E3212–E3220 (2012)

11. Priese, L.: Automata and concurrency. Theor. Comput. Sci. **25**(3), 221–265 (1983)
12. Rondelez, Y.: Competition for catalytic resources alters biological network dynamics. Phys. Rev. Lett. **108**(1), 018102 (2012)
13. Scalise, D., Schulman, R.: Emulating cellular automata in chemical reaction-diffusion networks. In: Murata, S., Kobayashi, S. (eds.) DNA 2014. LNCS, vol. 8727, pp. 67–83. Springer, Heidelberg (2014)
14. Toffoli, T.: CAM: a high-performance cellular-automaton machine. Phys. D **10**, 195–204 (1984)

Author Index

Printed in the United States
By Bookmasters

Printed in the United States
By Bookmasters